I0886367

Robert Pęczkowski

Colour profiles
Artur Juszczak

North American Aviation P-51B/C & F-6C Mustang

STRATUS

Published in Poland in 2019
by Wydawnictwo
STRATUS sp.j.
Skr. Poczt. 123,
27-600 Sandomierz 1
E-mail: office@mmpbooks.biz
www.stratusbooks.pl

as
MMPBooks,
E-mail: office@mmpbooks.biz

http://www.mmpbooks.biz

ISBN
978-83-65958-39-6

Editor in chief
Roger Wallsgrove

Editorial Team
Bartłomiej Belcarz
Robert Pęczkowski
Artur Juszczak

Scale Plans
Dariusz Karnas

Colour Plates
Artur Juszczak

DTP
Stratus sp. j.

Printed by
Wydawnictwo
Diecezjalne i Drukarnia
w Sandomierzu
www.wds.pl

PRINTED IN POLAND

Table of contents

Photos ©

- **Persons:** Robert Bourlier, Jack Canary Chris Davis, Dariusz Karnas, James Kightly, Randy Malmstrom, Wojtek Matusiak, family of Wallace Moyle, Robert Panek, Bogdan Rogoziński, Roger Wallsgrove, Mirosław Wasielewski, courtesy of Col. A. W. Traylor's family.
- **Companies and institutions:** US National Archives, NAA, The Polish Institute and Sikorski Museum

Acknowledgements

I would love to express my sincere thanks to all people and organisations who supported this book (in alphabetical order): Robert Bourlier, Chris Davis, Dariusz Karnas, Zbigniew Kolacha, Randy Malmstrom, Wojtek Matusiak, Robert Panek, Bogdan Rogoziński, Roger Wallsgrove, Mirosław Wasielewski

Cover photo: P-51C restored as "Lope's Hope 3rd", the airplane of Donald Lopez of the 75th FS, 23rd FG, 14th AF, China. (Aircorp Aviation in Bemidji, MN and John LaTourelle Photography via R. Bourlier)

Introduction

The history of the design and development of the iconic P-51 Mustang is so well known that it is superfluous to repeat much of the story here. To summarise, the British Purchasing commission approached North American Aviation (NAA) early in 1940 to build Curtiss P-40s under licence for the RAF, as Curtiss had insufficient capacity to meet the urgent British requirements. NAA made a counter proposal, to design and build a better fighter using the same Allison engine, in much the same time as would be needed to tool up for P-40 production. There had already been preliminary design work on such a fighter, making use of some data from Curtiss relating to their projected P-46 design. In the event, the ensuing NA-73 design owed little to the P-46, apart from the ventral radiator which was carefully designed to minimize drag (and ultimately proved capable of delivering some net thrust). One novel feature of the NA-73 was the use of a laminar-flow wing section, as designed by NACA. The overall design was a model of aerodynamic cleanliness, for the time, and the prototype proved significantly faster than the P-40 using an identical engine. In addition, the aircraft had an excellent range (the perennial weakness of British fighters, from the '30s to the '60s!).

The RAF happily ordered the new design, named "Mustang", and these Allison-powered aircraft served very effectively in the army cooperation, reconnaissance and ground attack roles from 1942 onwards. They were not used much by Fighter Command, as the Mustang had poor performance at medium to high altitudes compared to the Spitfire and opposing German fighters. The USAAF belatedly realised the potential of the design, and ordered some as the P-51 and A-36, the latter a dive-bomber variant.

NAA XP-51 s/n 41-038 at NACA Langley Memorial Aeronautical Laboroatory. (NAA)

Mustang X

In April 1942, the Royal Air Force's Air Fighting Development Unit (AFDU) tested the Allison V-1710-engined Mustang at higher altitudes and found it wanting, but their commanding officer, Wing Commander Ian Campbell-Orde, was so impressed with its manoeuvrability and low-altitude speed that he invited Ronald W. Harker from Rolls-Royce's Flight Test establishment at Hucknall to fly it.

On 30 April 1942, Ronald W. Harker took a brief hop in a RAF Mustang I, AG422, at the airbase at Duxford. Like many other pilots, he was highly impressed with the Mustang, but it was quickly evident that performance, although exceptional up to 15,000 ft (4,572 m), was inadequate at higher altitudes. It was due largely to the single-stage supercharged Allison engine, which lacked power at higher altitudes. He wrote in the report that the airplane would be perfect for the new Merlin 60 engines that Rolls-Royce was just beginning to produce. The Merlin 60 engine had originally been intended for the pressurized high-altitude aircraft. Rolls-Royce management was intrigued by the idea and stepped into action.

Engineers rapidly concluded that the Mustang powered by a two-stage Merlin 61 would have a significant improvement in performance, and started converting a Mustang to Merlin engine.

The theoretical performance of the Mustang with the Merlin 61 and Merlin XX, calculated in a Rolls-Royce report dated 8 June 1942, was that a speed of 441 mph (710 km/h) could be achieved at 25,500 ft (7,770 m) with a Merlin 61 and 400 mph (644 km/h) at 18,600 ft (5,670 m) with a Merlin XX. The calculation were mostly done by a Polish engineer, Witold Challier, who worked as a performance engineer.

With a minimum of modification to the engine bay, the Merlin 61 engine fitted into the adapted engine formers. A smooth engine cowling with an additional "chin" radiator was tried out in various configurations, as the two-stage Merlin required a greater cooling capacity than could be obtained with the standard Mustang radiator. The Merlin 65 series engine was utilized in all the prototypes as it was identical to the Merlin 66 powering the Spitfire IX, allowing for a closer comparison.

The first step to incorporate a Merlin into the Mustang was made in May 1942, when a standard Allison-engined Mustang I was delivered to the Rolls-Royce facility at Hucknall for evaluation. It was planned to convert two more aircraft.

The first aircraft, Mustang I with serial AG518, was in fact not modified and was replaced by Mustang I AM121 and later supplemented with another two Mustang Is – AL963 and AL975.

US Forces in Britain were also looking for a suitable long-range escort fighter and requested conversion of two aircraft – AM203 and AM208 – and sent them to Hucknall. This made a total of five Mustangs to be converted with the Merlin engine, such conversion being designated Mustang Mk X.

The first aircraft, fitted with a Merlin 65 and Rotol four blade prop (from a Spitfire IX), was AL975/G. The aircraft flew on 13th October 1942, piloted by Captain R. T. "Ronnie" Shepherd, Rolls-Royce's chief test pilot. The new chin intake under the nose combined both the carburettor

Mustang X serial AL975/G. (via W. Matusiak)

Front view of the Mustang X, serial AL975/G. (via W. Matusiak)

air intake and the intercooler radiator. There was a noticeable difference in profile, as small beard radiator ducts of varying shapes were fitted in addition to the standard ventral duct.

This aircraft achieved a top speed of 425 mph (684 km/h) at 21,000 ft (6,401 m).

When the second conversion, AM208, flew on 13th November, its main radiator front flap was permanently fixed and sealed. Such modification gave a 6–7 mph (10–11 km/h) boost in speed. AM208 reached 433 mph (697 km/h) at 22,000 ft (6,506 m).

AM203 flew for the first time as a Mk X on 13th December, also piloted by Ronnie Shepherd. It had a 11' 4" wooden propeller. Later the aircraft was tested with a high-speed gloss finish to compare the results against the standard matt scheme. There was no significant variation in performance.

AL963 flew into Hucknall on 26th June 1942 for performance and handling trials before conversion.

Its nose contours had a much "sleeker" appearance, due to the intercooler radiator being relocated to the main radiator duct. Other changes included a small fin extension and the "blanking" of cowling louvres. This example was able to reach 422 mph (679 km/h) at 22,400 ft (6,828 m).

It was sent to the USAAF Air Technical Section at Bovingdon for evaluation. Later the aircraft went to the AFDU on service trails, then returned to Hucknall. Then the aircraft received a dorsal fin. In the next stage, the aircraft was tested with an SU fuel injection pump.

Side view of the Mustang X, serial AL975/G. (via W. Matusiak)

Mustang X serial AL975/G after a few modifications. (via W. Matusiak)

Starboard side of the Mustang X serial AL975/G with Merlin engine. (via W. Matusiak)

***Below:** Starboard side of the Mustang X serial AL975/G. Aircraft during test. (via W. Matusiak)*

Posrt side of the Mustang X, serial AM208. (via W. Matusiak)

Mustang X, serial AM208 in flight. (via W. Matusiak)

Below: *Another shot of the Mustang X, serial AM208 in flight. (via W. Matusiak)*

Starboard side of the Mustang X serial AL9963. (Author's coll.)

AM121 was the fifth aircraft converted. It was decided to retain the original configuration and study drag problems with the cooling system. A broader chord fin was installed. Eventually it was fitted with a Merlin 65, but with no actual development flying planned. It also went to the AFDU for service trials. Then the aircraft was loaned to the USAAF 8th Fighter Command at Bovingdon. The aircraft was returned to Hucknall to have a broad-chord fin incorporated and then flew to Rotol, Staverton, to evaluate a Rotoloid coating for the propeller blades.

The performance of these re-engined aircraft was excellent, with maximum speed obtained at Boscombe Down being 433 mph at 22,000 feet. However, the yaw stability was degraded by the increased side area of the nose. The success of these tests led Rolls-Royce to propose the production of 500 Merlin 65 engines to re-engine most of the RAF's Mustang fleet to Mark X standard. This idea was soon abandoned, as the Rolls-Royce production was needed for other purposes and the Mustang with Merlin engine had been adopted for production in the USA.

At the same time Rolls-Royce took steps to interest both the USAAF and North American Aviation in the project. The main role in this was played by the US military attache in London, Major Thomas Hitchcock. He became enthusiastic over the prospect of the Mustang with a Merlin engine. Production of the Merlin Mk XX (by Packard under licence) began about a year earlier to provide engines for Canadian production of Lancasters and other aircraft. The USAAF was able to accept the idea of the Mustang with a Merlin engine only without misgivings over the engine supply situation. Also NAA was close to the end of the its contracts for Allison Mustangs, so it was a good time to obtain a good new fighter. On 25 July 1942 the USAAF contracted NAA for installation of Packard-built Merlins in two P-51s from the Lend-lease production batch. As NA-101, these aircraft were initially designated XP-78 and later became XP-51Bs. Packard-built V-1650-3 engines were used.

Port side of the Mustang X serial AM121. (Author's coll.)

Mustang X, serial AM203 on the ground. (Author's coll.)

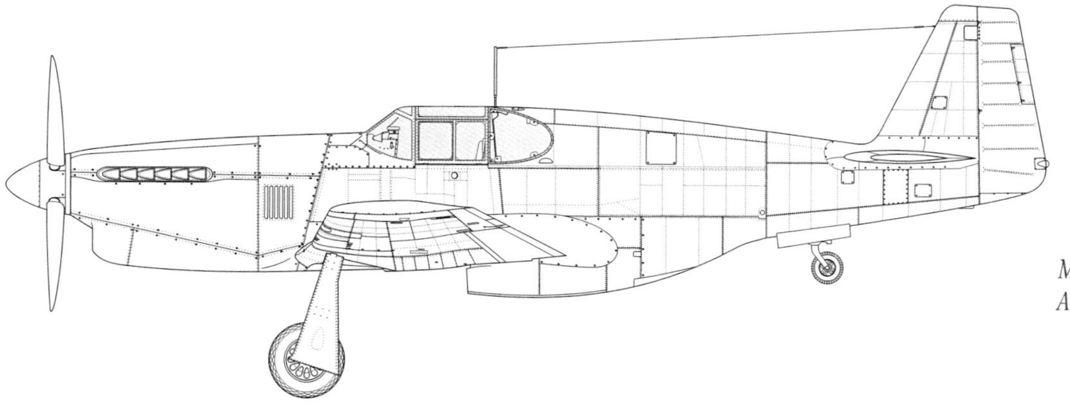

Mustang X, serial AL975/G. 1/72 scale.

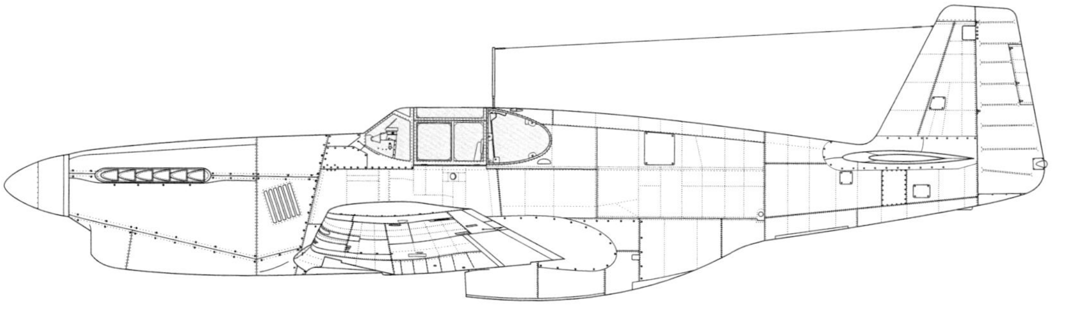

Mustang X, serial AL121. 1/72 scale.

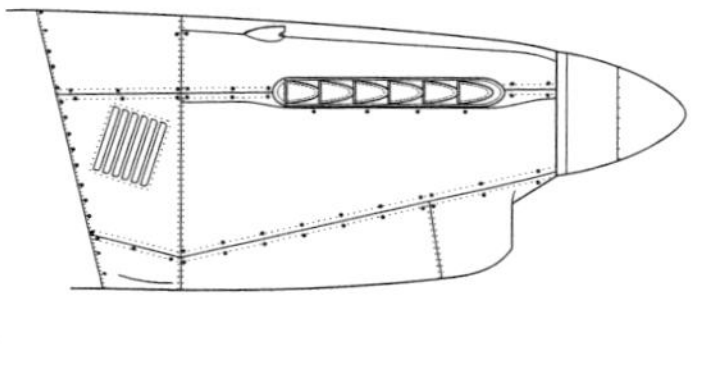

Mustang X, serial AL203 nose. 1/72 scale.

XP-51B (NA-101)

NAA selected two P-51s for the conversion. Aircraft were from the batch of Mustang IAs that had been repossessed from the RAF by the USAAF. Their serial numbers were 41-37352 (RAF Serial FD450) and 41-37421 (RAF serial FD519). Because these aircraft were different from the earlier Mustangs that they were given a new designation – XP-78. The designation of these two aircraft was later changed to XP-51B. .

North American completed two XP-51Bs at the end of the November 1942.

With the V-1650-3 engine the carburettor air intake was moved under the nose, similar to the Mustang X, but NA decided to locate the supercharger intercooler within the ventral radiator, which was enlarged (deepened) for this. The next version of the radiator had a sharply-angled inlet standing more than two inches away from the underside of the fuselage. The new radiator inlet was designed by Irving Ashkenas, eliminated the boundary layer effect. This resulted in less drag than in the Mustang X.

NAA reported that the conversion needed about 223,000 man-hours to get the configuration right.

The airframe was strengthened to make full use of the increased power available. It was fitted with a four-bladed propeller of 11' 2" (3.4 m). Also for production aircraft, the position of the wing was lowered by 3 in (7.6 cm) and altered relative to earlier Mustangs. Fuselage of the P-51B was different to the earlier P-51 in many respects.

The first flight was taken on 30 November with Bob Chilton at the controls. It was initially flown without armament. The performance improvement was noticeable. The XP-51B achieved a level speed of 441 mph at 29,800 feet, over 100 mph faster than the Allison-engined P-51 at that altitude. At all heights, the rate of climb was almost doubled. Air tests confirmed the predictions made for the Merlin-Mustang.

XP-51B with early version of the radiator and no carburettor air intake under the nose. 1/72 scale

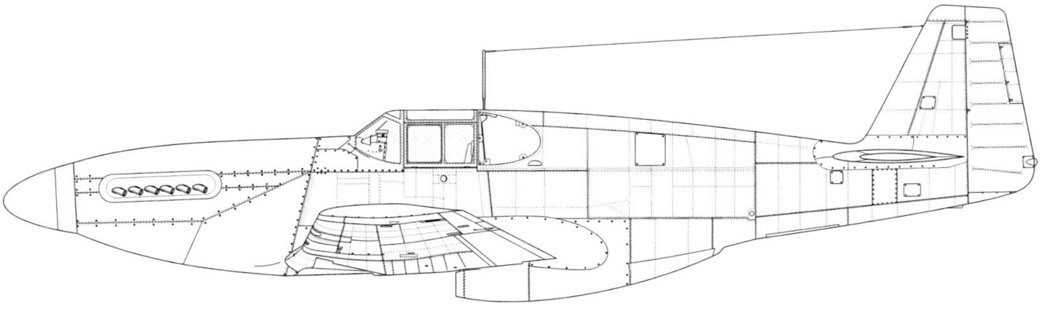

XP-51B with early version of the radiator and no carburettor air intake under the nose. (NAA)

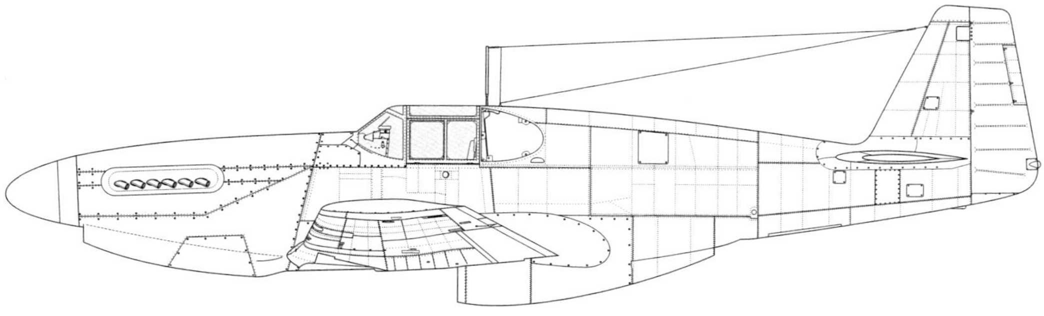

***Left:** XP-51B with different engine cowling and early version of the radiator. 1/72 scale.*

Two photos of XP-51B, s/n 41-37421 with early verson of the radiator. (US National Archives)

Above: XP-51B, s/n 41-37421 (ex RAF serial FD519) with new version of the radiator. (US National Archives)
Right: XP-51B, s/n 41-37352 with the final version of the radiator. 1/72 scale.

Bottom: XP-51B, (ex RAF FD450), s/n 41-37352. (US National Archives)

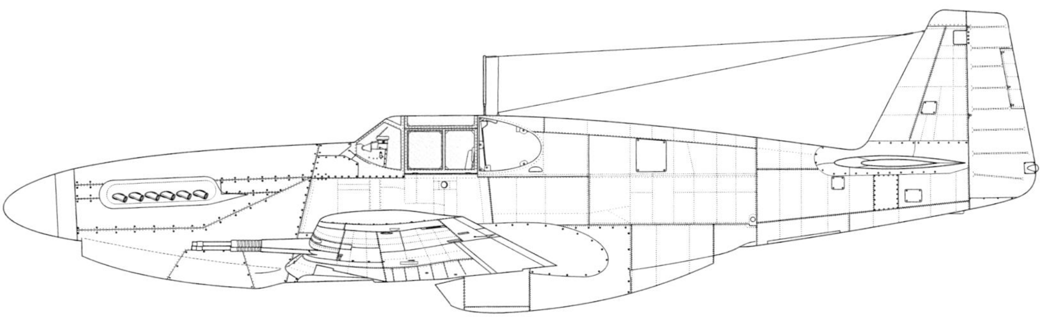

Series production

By the end of January 1943 the production standard for the P-51B/C had been decided.

With the beginning of 1943, the Merlin-Mustang program suddenly expanded. Massive production of Merlin engines was to take place at both the Packard factory at Detroit and at the Continental factory at Muskegon. The Inglewood, California factory was greatly expanded and moved solely to Mustang production, the B-25 Mitchell program being transferred to Kansas City. Production of the AT-6 series aircraft had been transferred from Inglewood to a new plant built in great haste at Dallas, Texas, even earlier. The USAAF instructed NAA to expand the Dallas plant even further as a second source for Mustangs. Inglewood-built Mustangs were designated P-51B, Dallas-built Mustangs were designated P-51C.

The first production P-51B flew on 5 May, 1943, and the first P-51C flew on 5 August 1943. The P-51Cs on the 1942 and 1943 budgets were given the company designation NA-103. 1,350 NA-103s were built. Texas-built aircraft in the 1944 budget were designated NA-111.

Initially, the P-51B and C had the Packard V-1560-3 engine (based on the Merlin 68) rated at 1,400 hp for take-off and 1,450 hp at 19,800 feet, and carried four 0.50-inch machine guns with a total of 1,260 rounds. There were 400 P-51B-1-NAs and 250 P-51C-1-NTs (similar to P-51B-5) built.

P-51B-1-NA, s/n 43-12300 of the 75th Tactical Reconnaissance Group at Meridian, MS., November, 1943 where the 118th TRS pilots trained before deploying to the CBI. On 28 November 1944 this airplane belly-landed 12-miles east-northeast of Hammond, Louisiana, after the Merlin engine failed. (via R. Bourlier)

Bottom: *P-51B-1-NA, s/n 43-12093. The first produced P-51B. Aircraft sill with markings used till 28 June 1943. (NAA)*

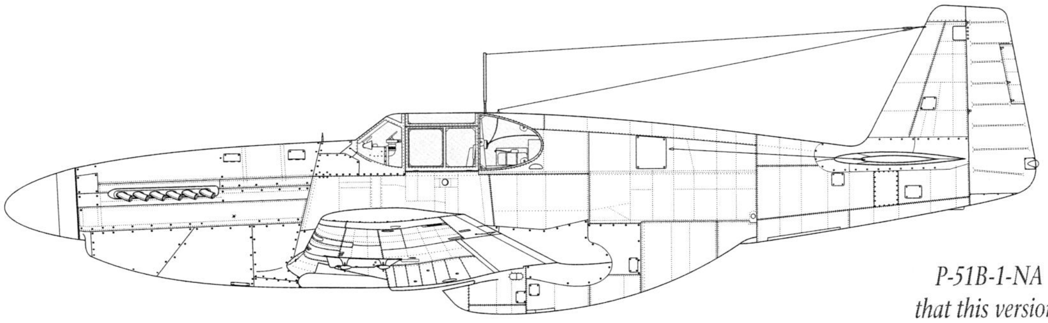

P-51B-1-NA side view. Note that this version have different carrburetor air intake without side sand filters. 1/72 scale.

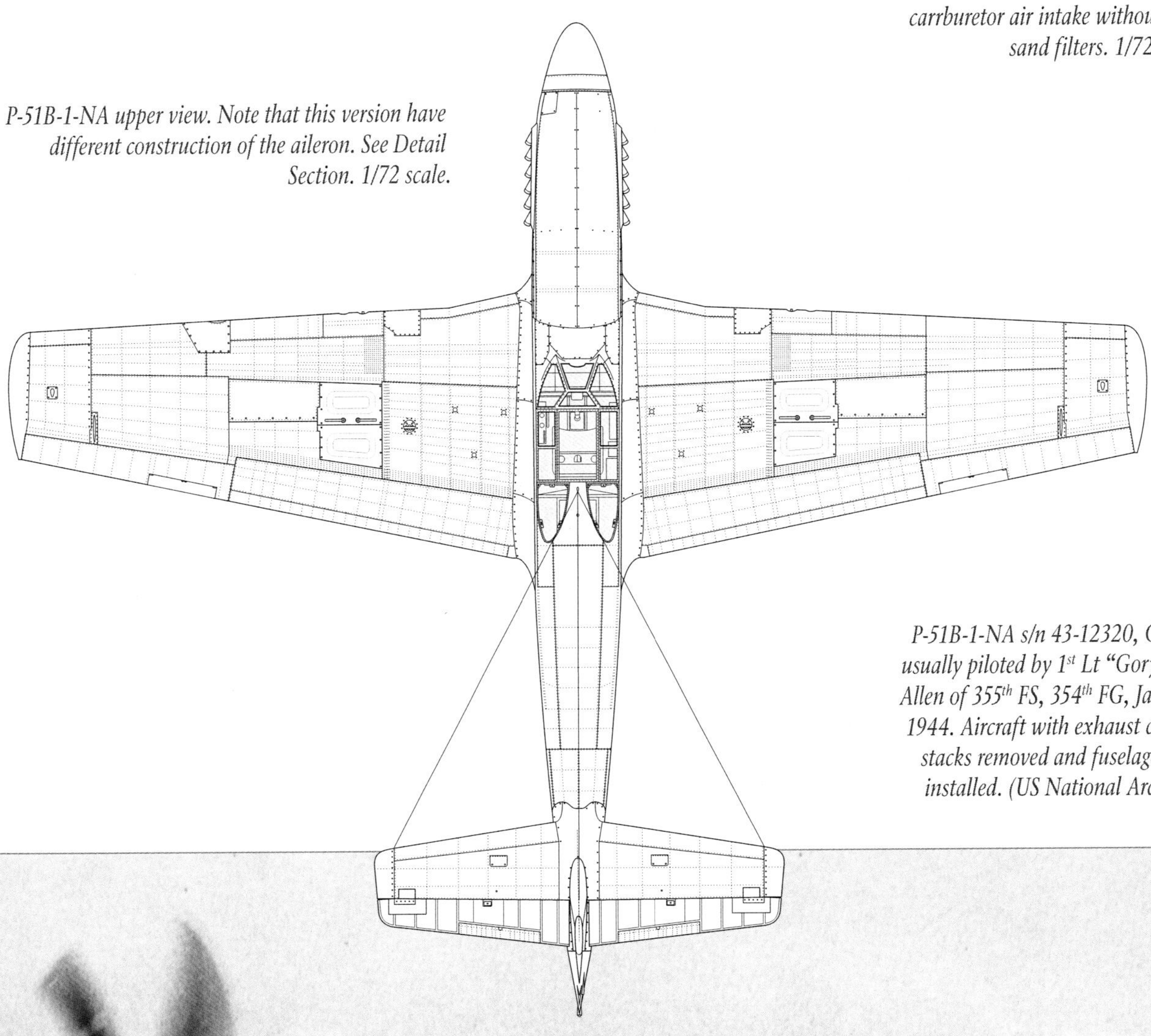

P-51B-1-NA upper view. Note that this version have different construction of the aileron. See Detail Section. 1/72 scale.

P-51B-1-NA s/n 43-12320, GQ+G usually piloted by 1st Lt "Gory Gus" Allen of 355th FS, 354th FG, January 1944. Aircraft with exhaust covers/ stacks removed and fuselage tank installed. (US National Archives)

P-51B-1-NA s/n 43-12366. Lt Charles H. Clark climbing into the cockpit. Aircraft probably of "Pioneer Mustang Group," the 354th FG. Note details of the undercariage wheel well. (US National Archives)

P-51B-1-NA s/n 43-12172, FT-T of 356th FS, 354th FG, December 1943. Pitot tube and IFF under the starboard wing are well visible. (US National Archives)

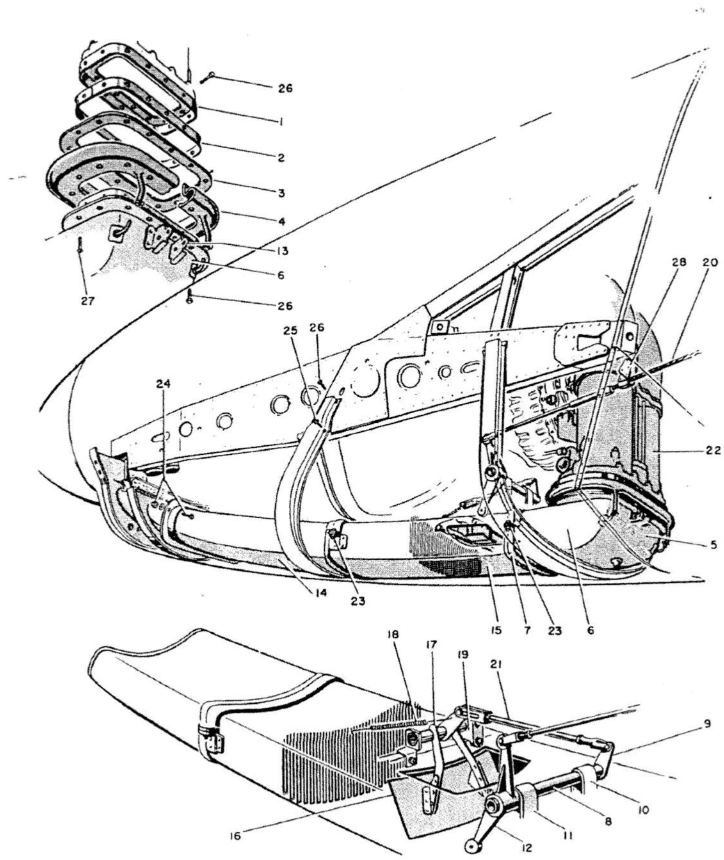

CARBURETOR AIR INDUCTION SCOOP (102A)

Above: Nose details of P-51B-1-NA s/n 43-12172, FT-T Note the lack of the dust filter on the engine cowling. (US National Archives)
Right: *Details of the early version of the carburetor air intake of the P-51B-1-NA (Model 102A) without sand filters. (Airplane Spare Parts)*

Nose of P-51B-1-NA. (US National Archives)

There are several versions and many production batches of the P-51B/C.

USAAF contractor's Block	NA Model Code		USAAF Serial numbers
P-51B-l-NA (26.08.1942)	**102A** Contract No. AC-33923		AAP 43-12093 to 12492
		102AA	AAF 43-12093 to 12108
		102AB	AAF 43-12109 to 12132
		102AC	AAF 43-12133 to 12159
		102AD	AAF 43-12160
		102AE	AAF 43-12161 to 12166
		102AF	AAF 43-12167 to 12202
		102AG	AAF 43-12203 to 12212
		102AH	AAF 43-12213 to 12221
		J02AJ	AAF 43-12222
		102AK	AAF 43-12223 to 12292
		102AL	AAF 43-12293 to 12297
		102AM	AAF 43-12298 to 12316
		102AN	AAF 43-12317 to 12379
		l02AP	AAF 43-l2380
		102AQ	AAF 43-12381 to 12426
		l02AR	AAF 43-12427 to 12446
		102AS	AAF 43-12447 to 12492
P-51C-1-NT, C-5, C-10 (08.10.1942)	**103** Contract No. AC-33940		AC 42-102979 to 103978
			AAF 43-24902 to 25251
P-51C-l-NT	103A		AC 42-102979 to 103328
		103AA	AC 42-102979 to 102988
		103AB	AC 42-102989 to 103018
		103AC	AC 42-1030l9 to 103028
		103AD	AC 42-103029 to 103038
		103AE	AC 42-103039 to 103078
		103AF	AC 42-103079 to 103178
		103AG	AC 42-103179 to 103278
		103AH	AC 42-103279 to 103328
P·51C-5-NT	l03B		AC 42-103329 to 103778
		103BA	AC 42-103329 to 103378
		103BB	AC 42-103379 to 103478
		103BC	AC 42-103479 to 103578
		l03BD	AC 42-103579 to 103778
P-51C-10-NT	103C		AC 42-103779 to 103978
			AAF 43-24902 to 25251
		103CA	AC 42-l03779 to 103978
		103CB	AAF 43-24902 to 25001
		103CC	AAF 43-25002 to 25251
P-51B-5-NA; – 10; – l5 (20.10.1942)	**104** Contract No. AC-30479		AAF 43-6313 to 7202
			AC 42-106429 to 106978
			AAF 43-24752 to 24901
P-518-5-NA	104A		AAF 43-6313 to 7112
		104AA	AAF 43-6313
		104AB	AAF 43-6314 to 6316
		104AC	AAF 43-6317 to 6337
		104AD	AAF 43-6338 to 6343
		104AE	AAF 43-6341 to 6412
		l04AF	AAF 43-6413 to 6420
		104AG	AAF 43-6421 to 6462
		104AH	AAF 43-6463 to 6464
		104AJ	AAF 43-6465
		l04AK	AAF 43-61166 to 6512
		104AL	AAF 43-6513
		104AM	AAF 43-6514 to 6588
		104AN	AAF 43-6589 to 6612
		104AP	AAF 43-661) to 6637
		114AQ	AAF 43-6638 to 6712
		104AR	AAF 43-6713 to 6812
		104AS	AAF 43-6813 to 6837
		104AT	AAF 43-6838 to 6852
		104AU	AAF 43-6853 to 6912
		104AV	AAF 43-69l3 to 6987
		104AW	AAF 43-6988 To 7112
P51-B-10-NA	104B		AAF 43-7113 to 7202
			AC 42-106429 to 106738
		104BA	AAF 43-7113 to 7202
		104BB	AC 42-1061429 to 106538
		104BC	AC 42-106541 to 106638
		104BD	AC 42-106639 To 106738
P-5lB-l5-NA	l04C		AC 42-106741 to 106978
			AAF 43-24752 To 24901
P-51C-10-NT; – 11-NT (03.05.1943)	**111** Contract No. AC-40063		AAF 44-10753 to 11152
P-51C-10-NT			AAF 44-10753 to 10782
P-51C-11-NT			AAF 44-10783 to 10817
P-51C-10-NT			AAF 44-10818 to 10852
P-51C-11-NT			AAF 44-10853 to 10858
P-51C-10-NT			AAF 44-10859 to 11036
P-51C-11-NT			AAF 44-11037 to 11122
P-51C-10-NT			AAF 44-11123 to 11152

During production airframe and other components were improved and changed.

The first changes were introduced with **P-51B-5-NA** and **P-51C-1-NT** versions.

A new cockpit layout was introduced with rearranged instrument panels and other improvements, including electrical equipment. New pilot's seat was also introduced.

Additional wing reinforcements were fitted, and the aileron construction was redesigned.

New carburettor air induction scoop was introduced.

Oil tank was improved.

Tail wheel modifications were performed.

New N-3B gun sight was also introduced (from models 104 and 103AF).

New camera gun mount was introduced from models 104AF and 103BB (**P-51C-5-NT**)

Also there were many other improvements in the internal construction to strengthen it.

P-51B-5-NA, some of **P-51B-10-NA** and some of **P-51C-1-NA** (models 104A, 104BA to 104BB and 103AE to 103AF) had an additional carburettor hot air duct inlet cover – see scale plans.

Redesigned tank coolant header was introduced from model 104AR and 103BD.

Right: P-51B-5-NA, s/n 43-7107 awaiting a delivery to the combat unit. Note fuselage tank installed. (US National Archives)

Below: P-51B-7-NA (B-5 with fuselage tank installed after production). Aircraft s/n 43-7060, "Tommy's Dad" of 74th FS, 23rd FG, 14th AF, usually flown by John C. "Pappy" Herbst. Liuchow, China, 1944. Note hot air duct inlet cover seen only on the some P-51B-5. (US National Archives)

P-51C-1-NT, s/n 42-103314, "Whistler's Wing's of 339th FG 505th FS. (US National Archives)

P-51B-5-NA side view. Aircraft shown with fuselage fuel tank. Also hot air duct inlet cover is shown. 1/72 scale.

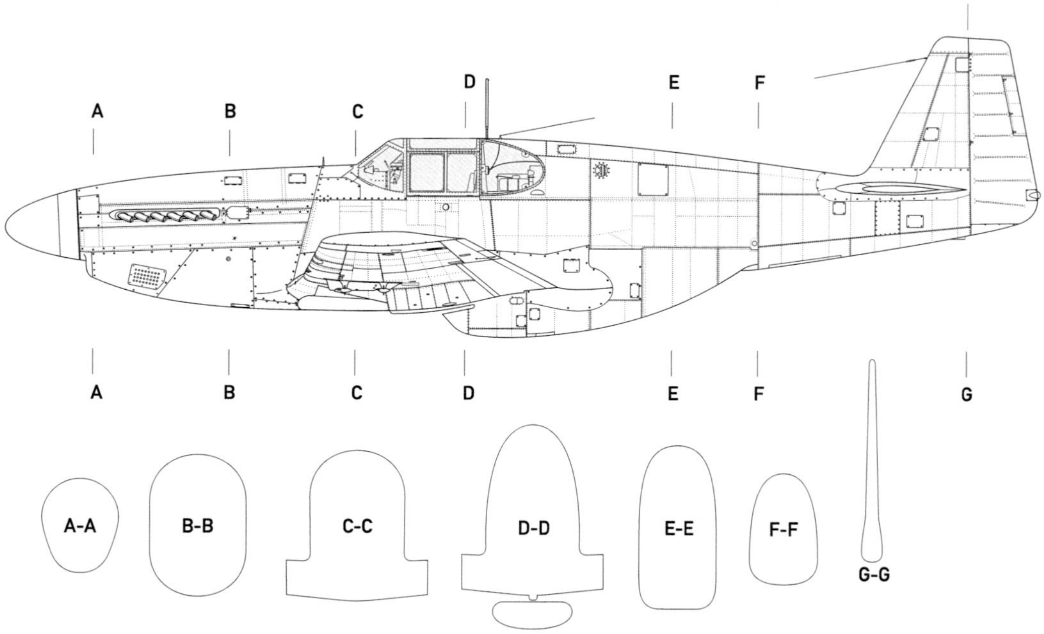

Below: *P-51B-5-NA, s/n 43-6877), "The Stars Look Down" of the 355th FS, 354th FG at Criqueville airfield (A-2), France, 1944. The Mustang was modified by the 461st Air Service Squadron with a "rumble seat. On 4 July 1944 MGen Quesada, Co 9th AF IX Fighter Command flew Gen. Eisenhower over the St. Lo combat sector. (US National Archives)*

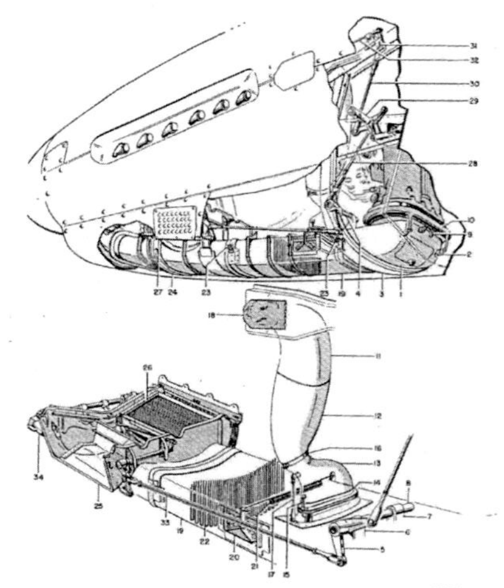

Drawing of the carburetor air scoop used on the models 104, 104 and 111. No. 18 is the hot air scoop used only on the some P-51B-5 series. (Airplane Parts Catalog)

P-51B-10-NA and P-51C-10-NT

Fuselage 85 gal tank was introduced. About 500 modification kits were also produced to be retrofitted in older aircraft. (More info see Post-production Modification chapter.)

Fuselage 85 gal tank was probably introduced on P-51C model 103BB.

Addition of this tank produced unexpected results. When the tank was fully fuelled it moved the centre of gravity beyond the point of danger. Special orders were introduced to control use of this tank in flight.

Installation of a new antenna mast, AN-104A type.

Coolant and oil cooler exit flap actuators modification (from models 104BB, P-51B only).

Non-magnetic counterbalance mounted in the left wing aileron (P-51C model 103AG).

New exhaust stacks, made of .50 inch material

P-51B-10-NA, s/n 42-106485 "Maggie's Drawers", A9-V of the 380th FS, 363rd FG, was lost during an escort mission to Berlin on 29 April 1944. 2nd Lt Albert G. Johnson (US National Archives)

P-51C-10-NT, s/n 42-103798, "Julienne Hi!", coded FT-X of the 353rd FS, 354th FG. June 1944. (US National Archives)

P-51C-10-NT, s/n 42-103960, "Skipper's Darlin' III". Capt. Andrew D. Turner, commander of the 100th FS, 332nd FG, 15th AF, 8 August 1944. (US National Archives)

P-51C-10-NT, s/n 43-25066, N2-Y of the 383rd FS, 364th FG. Aircraft was forced to belly-land at Honington on 22 April 1945 when, when was in the hands of 2nd Lt Dean L. Jessen. Note tail fillet installed. (US National Archives)

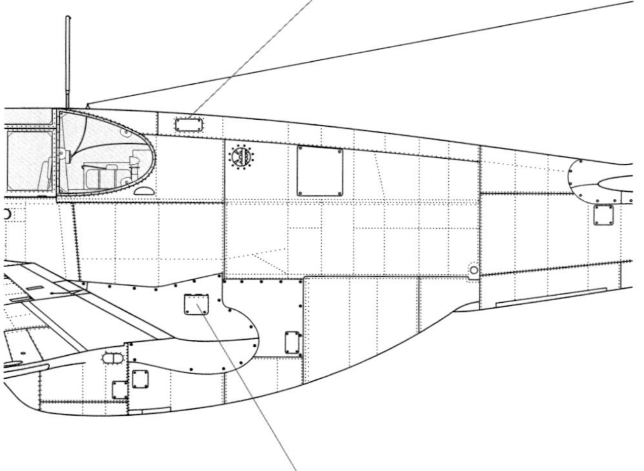

Battery Access Door and Fuselage Fuel Tank Vent Line Access Door were introduced when fuselage fuel tank was added.

P-51B-15-NA (model 104C) and P-51C-5-NT (model 103B)
Packard V-1650-7 engine was installed.

P-51C-10-NT and P-51B-15NA (only last model 104BD)
Fuselage tank grounding jack was introduced.

P-51C-11-NT.
The last production section with most of the post production changes introduced at the production line.

Many of the model differences are shown in the Detail Photos section.

Inglewood built 1,988 P-51Bs and Dallas built 1,750 P-51Cs in total.

P-51B-15-NA s/n 43-24806 was originally assigned to the 376th FS (as E9-H), 361st FG. Later declared 'war weary' and reassigned to the 384th FSq, 364th FG, 19 July 1945. (US National Archives)

P-51B-15-NA 42-106933 of 504th FS, 339th FG. Capt. Lee D. "Dutch" Eisenhart on the wing of his Mustang. (US National Archives)

P-51B-15-NA 43-24804 "Miss Priss", 5Q-P. Personal aircraft of Capt. James M. McLure of the 504th FS, 339th FG. (US National Archives)

P-51B-15-NA, s/n 42-106783, "Flying Panther", coded B6-L of 363rd FS, 357th FG at Leiston, assigned to Capt.Edward K. Simpson, Jr (officially credited with 4.25 confirmed aerial victories). (US National Archives)

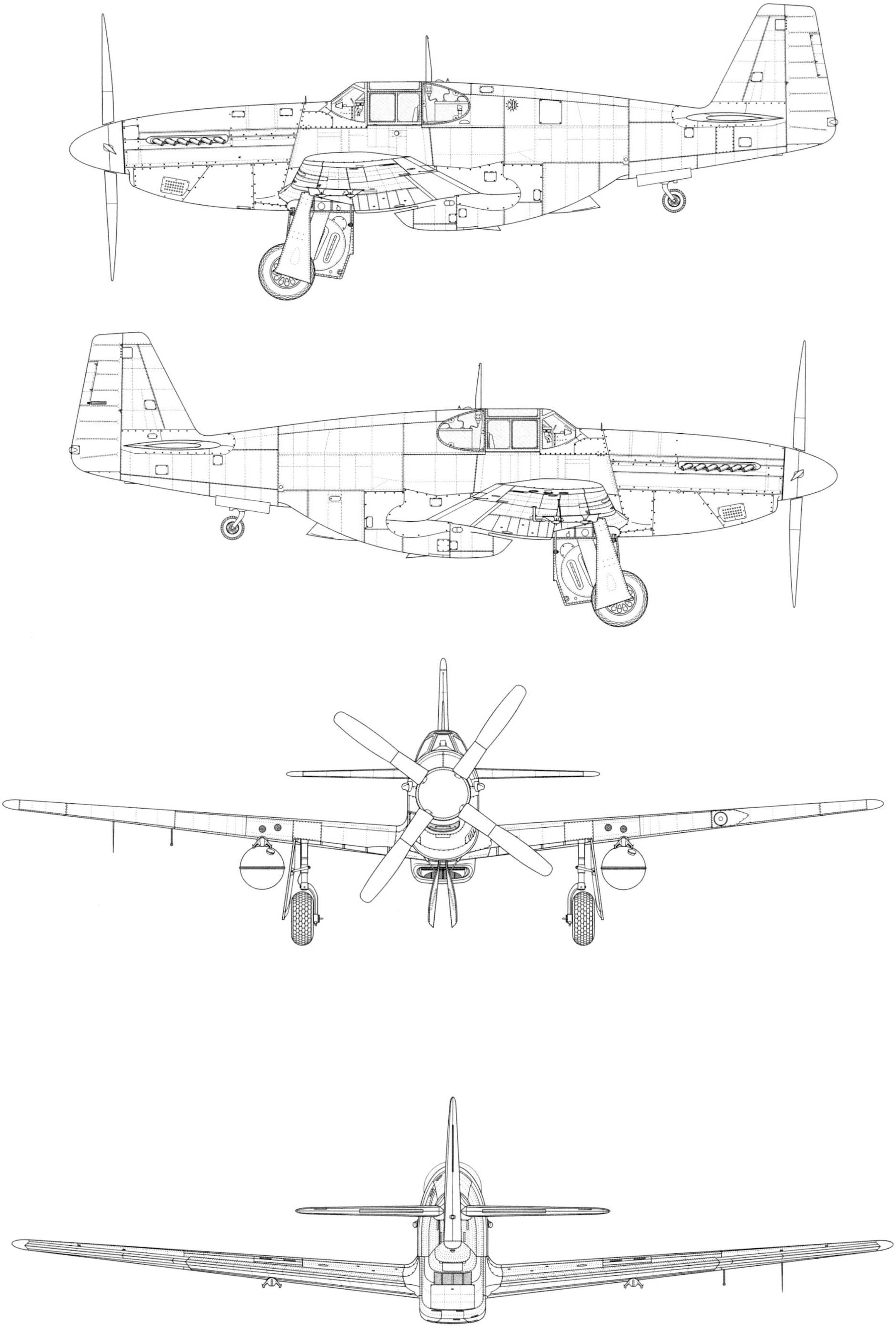

P-51B-15-NA scale plans.
1/72 scale.

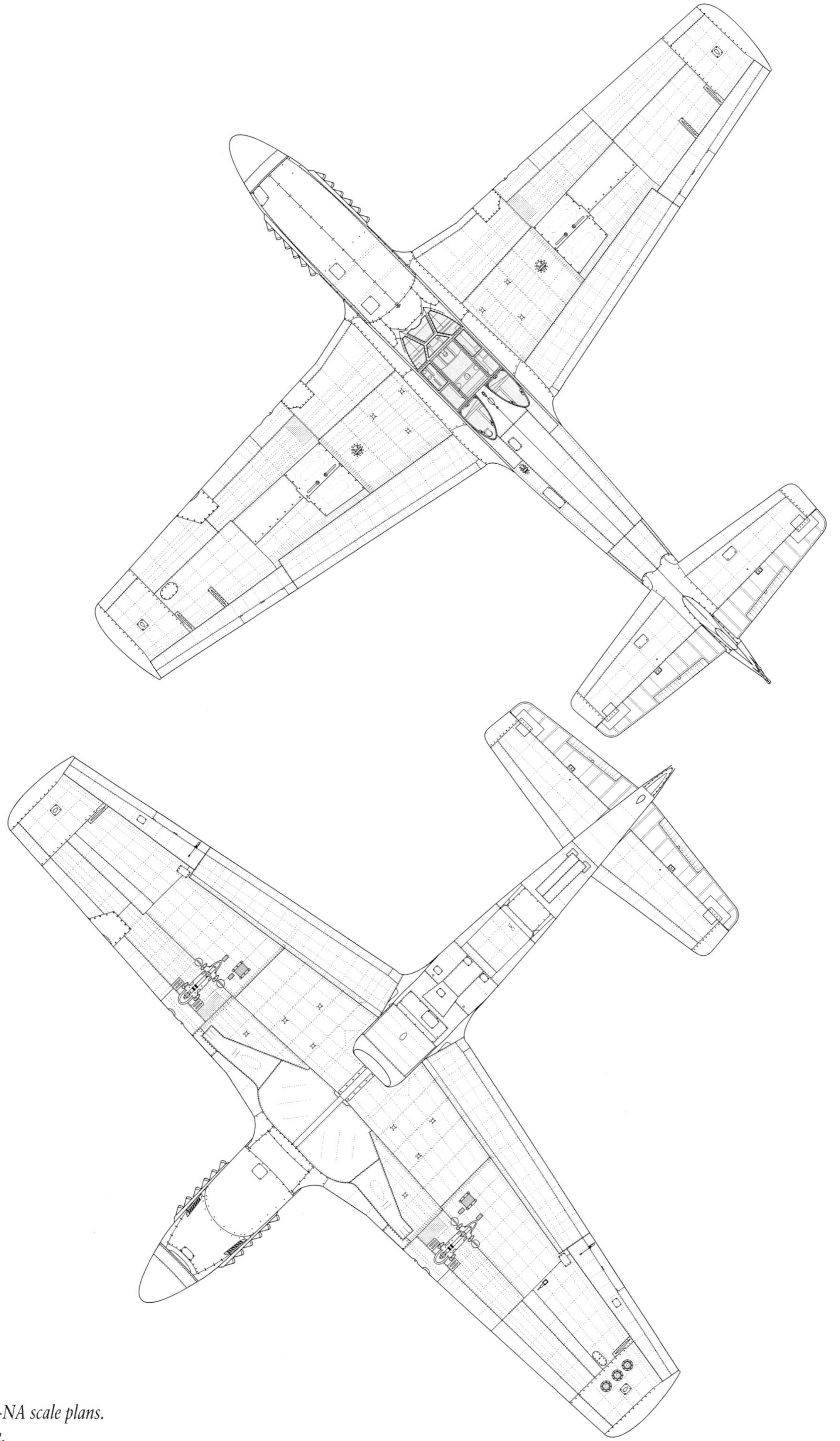

P-51B-15-NA scale plans.
1/72 scale.

Mustangs of the 376th FS, 361st FG, 8th AF.
P-51B-5-NA, s/n 43-7040. Later was sent to 479th FG as 'War Weary'.
P-51B-10-NA, s/n 42-106944, "Flying Jeanie III" E9-A.
P-51B-10-NA, s/n 42-106945, "Smokey", lost in taxi accident on 11 May 1944, with Lt.Col. Freedman.
P-51B-15-NA, s/n 42-106707 "Sleepy Time Gal", E9-S.
(US National Archives)

***Above:** P-51C-10-NT, s/n 43-25235, "Mugs" of 118th TRS. Mustang flown by 1st Lt. Lynn Decker.*

***Left:** 1st Lt Lynn E. Decker. (Both photos via R. Bourlier)*

Above: P-51C-10-NT, s/n 44-11112, Suichuan – 118th TRS Mustang severely damaged from a forced belly-landing.

Below: 1st Lt. Ray Crowell, Flying the "Hump", 29 July, 1944. The photo was taken from the B-25 pathfinder airplane, Lt. Crowell leads a flight of 8 Mustangs and 8 P-40s over the "Hump" from Chabua, India to Kunming, China. Mustang s/n 43-24956 would become 118th TRS "Battling Betty" assigned to 2nd Lt. Robert Murray. (Both photos R. Bourlier coll.)

Post-production modifications

All Mustang versions were improved and modified not only during production, but also when in service. Such modifications were called Technical Orders and were performed in Field Depots or even in units. Technical Orders were not only structural modifications, but also recommendations for the pilots how to fly and mechanics how to check airframes.

Many of the modifications were the same as modifications made during production and retrofitted to older aircraft.

Modification of Coolant Header Tank Relief Valve Locking Collar P-51B
(Technical Order No. 01-60JD-5, 9 September 1943.)
To prevent loosening of locking collar, the collar will be inspected and reworked if necessary.
P-51B – 102A model.

Replacement of Propeller Governor Control Bracket – P-51B
(Technical Order No. 01-60JD-7, 27 December 1943.)
To eliminate propeller pitch vibration caused by vibration of the propeller governor bracket.
P-51B – 102A model.

Instillation of Additional Oxygen Cylinders – P-51B
(Technical Order No. 01-60JD-8, 11 November 1943.)
To provide a sufficient oxygen supply for long-distance flights, two additional oxygen cylinders, type D-2, will be installed.
P-51B – up to model 102AB inclusive.

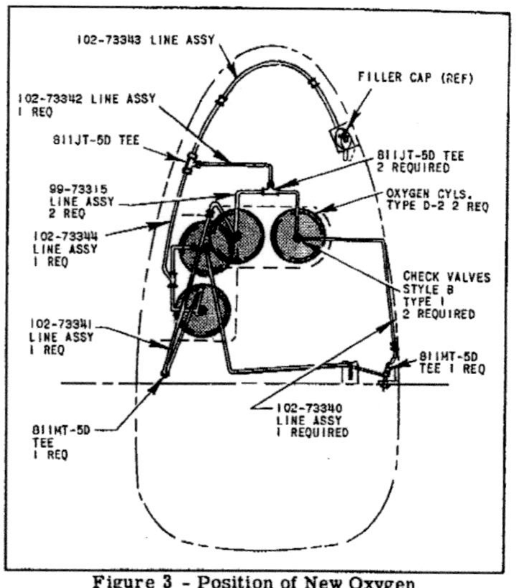

Figure 3 - Position of New Oxygen Equipment (Looking Aft)

Position of the new oxygen bottles. (Technical Order drawing)

Provisions for access to Cuno Oil Filter Drain Plug – P-51B
(Technical Order No. 01-60JD-18, 28 November 1943)
To provide sufficient clearance between the engine mount canted frame and the Cuno oil filter.
All produced P-51B aircraft.

Reworking of Propeller Spinner Assembly – P-51B
(Technical Order No. 01-60JD-1, 18 November 1943.)
To prevent the failure of the propeller spinner. All spinners will be inspected and reworked.
P-51B – up to model 104AE inclusive.

Rework of Tail Wheel Idler Camshaft Declutching Cable – P-51A and P-51C,
(Technical Order No. 01-60JD-12, 12 February 1944.)
To prevent the possibility of the elevator controls becoming jammed due to the elevator horn assembly slipping off the declutching camshaft assembly.
P-51C – 103AA model inclusive.

Installation of Coolant Radiator Inlet Support Bracket and Strap P-51B
(Technical Order No. 01-60JD-13, 14 February 1944.)
To eliminate the possibility of the elevator cables rubbing against the coolant radiator inlet line.
P-51B – up to model 102AB inclusive.

Installation of a Screen for the Carburettor Hot-Air Door – P-51B
(Technical Order No. 01-60JD-16, 15 June 1944.)
To eliminate possible damage to engine caused by bolts, nuts and other objects dropping into the intake system, a carburettor hot-air door screen will be installed in P-51B airplanes.
P-51B – up to 102A model inclusive.

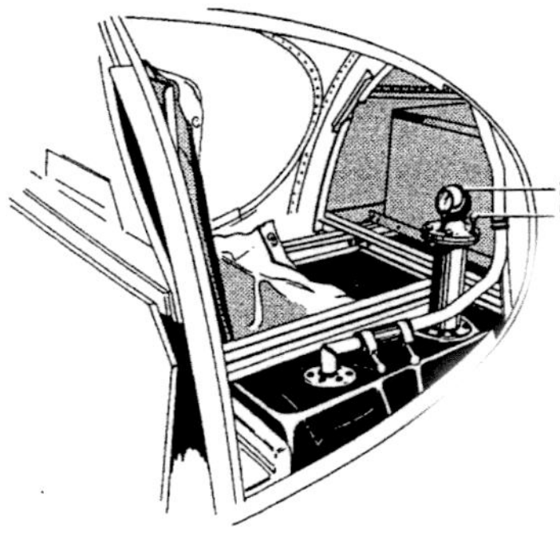

P-51B/C 85 gallon Fuselage Fuel Tank Modification Technical Order was introduced around October 1943.

Installation of the 85 gallon tank for P-51B-1, P-51B-5 and P-51C-1.

There were three places to install the 85 gallon tank – at the factories (Inglewood and Dallas), US Field Depots like Buffalo and Niagara and ETO Depots (BAD2 Warton primarily). The US Depots got NAA Modification Kits starting in the last week of October, 1943. The UK BAD2 received them starting in December 1943.

Many of the Depot modifications (both UK and US) led to re-marking the Mustangs as P-51B-7 and P-51C-3, but not all. Most ETO P-51B-1s also received the 85 gallon tank modification but with no other marking except a "white cross" near the data plate – different in dimension and location.

Battery access door and fuselage fuel tank vent line access door were introduced when fuselage fuel tank was added. About 550 modification kits were produced by NAA.

The tank modification required from 300–450 man hours to install in the P-51B/C – 1/-5.

Drawings from Airplane Parts Catalog with details of the fuselage fuel tank.

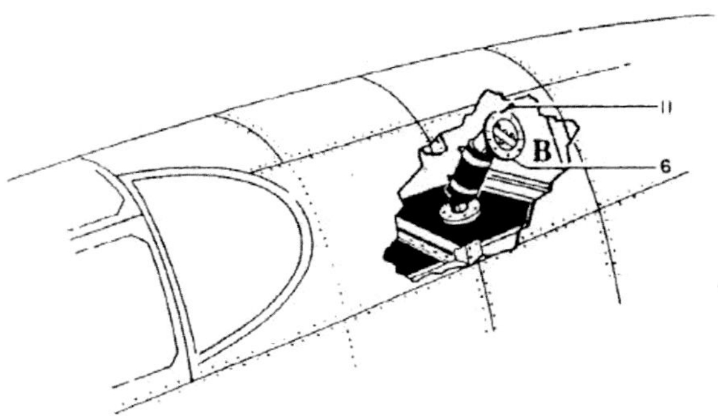

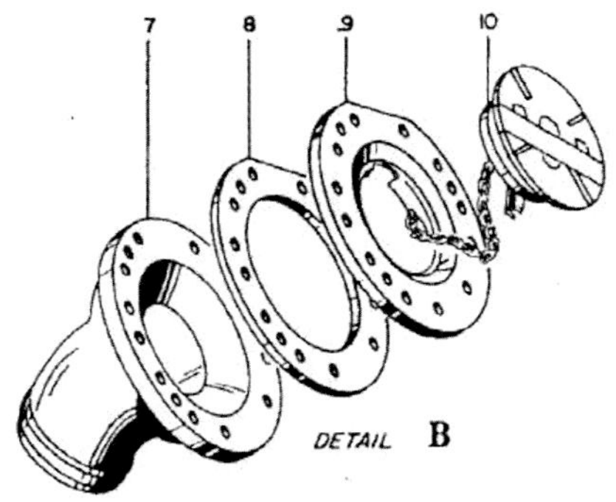

P-51B-1-NA, s/n 43-12175 with fuselage tank installed, see small white cross indicated such installation. Aircraft belonged to 353rd FS, 354th FG, 8th AF. (US National Archives)

P-51 aircraft flight restrictions
(Technical Order No. IF-57A-6, 25 January 1943)
Spin restriction.

1. Pending further investigation and completion of spin tests, P-51 series aircraft will not be intentionally spun.
2. Fast spins of unusual characteristics with the airplane's nose 30 degrees above the horizon have been encountered in P-51 series and recovery from a spin of this type is extremely difficult.
3. In the event of spin of this nature occurs, recovery should be accomplished by the intermittent use of maximum power on and off.

P-51 aircraft flight restrictions (
Technical Order No. 01-60J-6, 31 August 1943)

1. "As a result of recent extensive spin tests, P-51 series airplanes will not be intentionally spun except under the following condition:
   a. Intentional "power-off" spins will be permitted provided such spins are started above 12,000 feet.
2. Intentional "power-off" spins and snap rolls are prohibited.
   a. It is impossible to do a good snap roll in the subject airplanes and most attempts usually end up in a power spin.
   b. In the event of a power spin being entered inadvertently, the throttle should be closed immediately and normal recovery methods used. Recovery from a two to five turns power spin may require up to six turns with a loss in altitude of as much as 9,000 feet."

High speed rolls.
(Technical Order No. 01-60J-6A, 19 January 1944)
"Due to recent horizontal stabilizer failures which are believed to have resulted from high speed rolls, all P-51B and subsequent model aircraft will not perform slow rolls while travelling in excess of 300 mph indicated air speed."
Above was replaced by Technical Order No. 01-60J-6B dated 27 January 1944 with almost the same restriction.
Technical Order No. 01-60J-6c from 6 June 1944 replaced above and stated:
"Due to recent horizontal stabilizer failures which are believed to have resulted from high speed rolls, all P-51B, P-51C and P-51D airplanes will not perform slow rolls pending the installation of the dorsal fin and rudder reverse trim tab in compliance with Technical Order No. 01-60J-18"

Rework of Fuel Gauge and addition of Fuel Vent System – P-51B and P-51C
(Technical Order No. 01-60JD-25, 12 February 1944)
To eliminate the collapsing of the fuel tanks in flight, causing inaccurate reading of the fuel gauge, aircraft should be reworked.
P-51B – up to model 102AP inclusive.
P-51C – model 103AA.

Relocation of Battery Sump – P-51B and P-51C
(Technical Order No. 01-60JD-27, 4 February 1944)
To enable maintenance to be performed on the battery sump when the 85-gallon fuselage tank is installed. The battery sump will be relocated.
P-51B – up to model 104AW inclusive.
P-51C – up to model 103BA.

Replacement of propeller Control Front Bell Crank – P-51B and P-51C (Technical Order No. 01-60J-17)
To avoid elongation and failure of the propeller control front bell crank at the control rod attaching hole, it will be replaced with the new item.
P-51B – model 104AW inclusive.
P-51C – model 103AF inclusive.

Removal of Carburettor Cold Air Door Controls – P51B (Technical Order No. 01-60JD-28, 30 May 1944)

To eliminate confusion, the unused part of the carburettor cold air door control system will be removed.

P-51B – up to model 103AS.

Rework of Gun Camera Mount and Adjacent Nose Rib – P-51A, P-51B and P-51C. (Technical Order No. 01-60J-9, 12 July 1944)

To strengthen the gun camera mount and to prevent excessive vibration of the gun camera. Will be applied to the following aircraft:

P-51B – models 102A, 104AA to 104AE.

P-51C – models 103A to 103BB.

Later this technical order was replace by a Technical Order from 11 October 1944 with almost the same information.

Photo from Technical Order, showing installation of AN-95A IFF aerial.

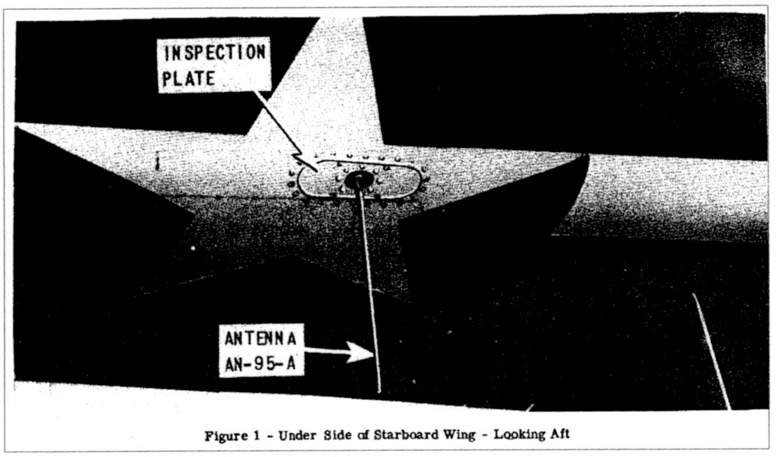

Figure 1 - Under Side of Starboard Wing - Looking Aft

Modification of installation of Antenna AN-95A, part of radio set SCR-695A – P-51B-1 (Technical Order No. 01-60J-11)

All P-51B-1 aircraft.

Rework of Tail Wheel Idler Camshaft Declutching Cable Guide P-51C (Technical Order No. 01-60J-12, 12 February 1944)

P-51C aircraft model 103CA only.

Installation of Throttle Stop Control Quadrant – P-51B and P-51C Technical Order No. 01-60JD-22, 8 April 1944)

To prevent damage to the throttle control system.

P-51B – up to model 104AW model

P-51C – up to model 103AD inclusive.

Relocation of Battery Vent Inlet Line – P-51B, P-51C and P-51D (Technical Order No. 01-60J-19, 16 May 1944)

To reduce possibility of malfunction and improve the efficiency of the battery venting. All aircraft with 85 gallon tank installed and not modified during production.

Replacement of the Left Aileron Counterbalance Assembly – P-51B and P-51 C (Technical Order No. 01-60J-12, 20 May 1944)

To eliminate excessive compass deflection, the steel aileron counterbalance assembly installed in left wing of airplanes listed will be replaced by a non-magnetic counterbalance.

P-51B – up to model 104AW and P-51B-10 serial 43-7113

P-51C – up to 103AF inclusive.

Replacement of Contractor Installed Antenna Mast with Antenna Mast AN-104A

To improve the operation dependability of Radio Set SCR-522-A

Installation of the new antenna mast AN-104A type.

P-51B – up to model 104AW inclusive.

P-51C – up to model 103BD inclusive.

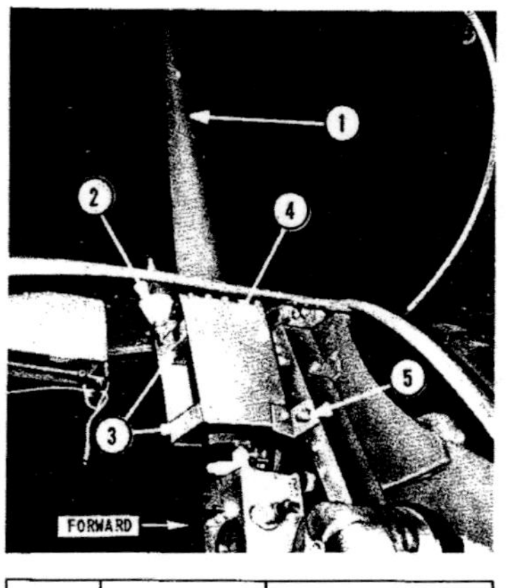

REF	PART NO.	DESCRIPTION
1	AN-104-A	Antenna Mast
2	IN-84	Insulator
3	43B7899	Antenna Clamp
4	43A9682	Support Bracket
5	44A2365-R	Angle Support

Figure 1 - Right Side of Plane

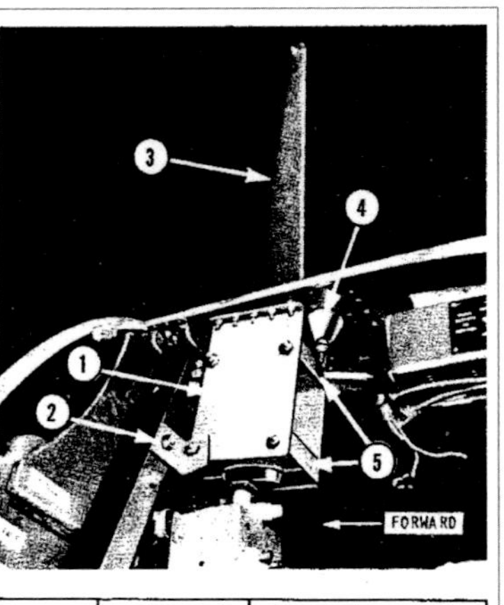

REF	PART NO.	DESCRIPTION
1	43A9682	Support Bracket
2	44A2365-L	Angle Support
3	AN-104-A	Antenna Mast
4	IN-84	Insulator
5	43B7899	Antenna Clamp

Figure 2 - Left Side of Plane

Photos from Technical Order showing new antenna mast, AN-104A installation.

Rework of Oil Breather System – P51B and P-51C

(Technical Order No. 01-60JD-37, 16 September 1944)

To prevent throwing of excessive oil through the breather exit and to eliminate the bulkhead canvas previously installed, the following P-51B and P-51C airplanes will be modified in accordance to the drawings.

Model	Serial Nos.	Kits Required
P-51B	42-106429 to 42-106986	A
	43-6313 to 43-7112	A, C
	43-7113 to 43-7202	A
	43-12093 to 43-12114	A, B, C
	43-12115 to 43-12492	A, C
	43-24752 to 43-24901	A
P-51C	42-102979 to 42-103178	A, C
	42-103179 to 103978	A

P-51C serial 43-24902 and later will be modified by the contractor prior to delivery.

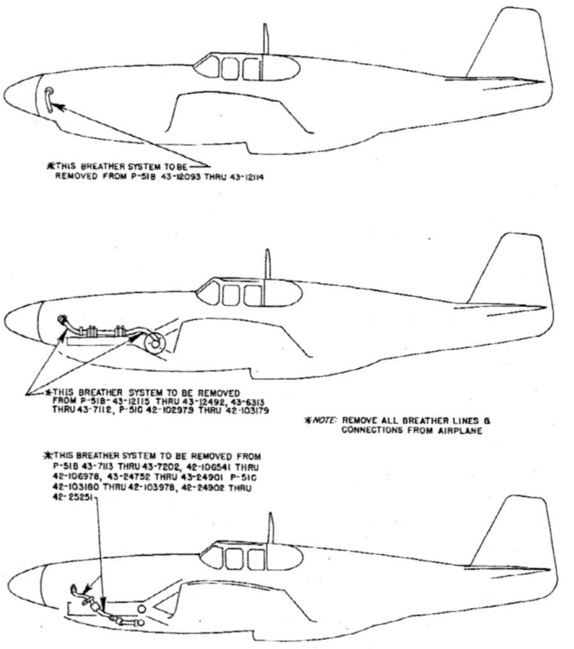

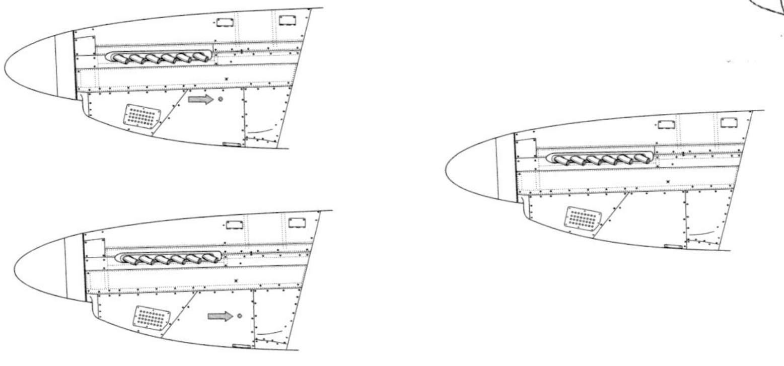

Above: Drawings from Technical Order showing oil breathing exit.

Left: Scale plans of the Mustang nose with different versions of the oil breathing exit. 1/72 scale.

Nose of the Mustang without exhaust stacks shroud and dust filter covered with metal plate. (US National Archives)

Replacement of the Propeller Blade Packings – P-51B, P-51C and P-51D 51C (Technical Order No. 01-60J-16, 17 July 1944)

To avoid oil leakage through the blade packings the new Chevron type packing should be installed.
All P-51B and P-51C.

Rework of Tail Wheel Idler Camshaft Declutching Cable Guide (Technical Order No. 01-60J-15, 21 August 1944)

P-51B models 102, 104A to 104BA,
P-51C models 103A.

Installation of Improved Enclosure Rear Panel Attaching Spring – P-51B and P-51C, (Technical Order No. 01-60JD-39)

To reduce the possibility of loss of the cockpit enclosure rear panels during flight, improved attaching springs will be installed.
P-51B – up to model 104AU inclusive.
P-51C – up to model 103BB inclusive.

Drawing of exhaust stacks from Technical Order.

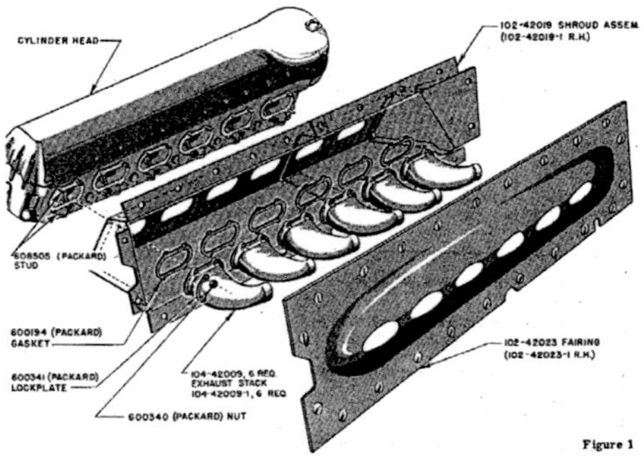

Replacement of Exhaust Stacks – P51B and P-51C (Technical Order No. 01-60JD-32, 1 July 1944)

To provide a more satisfactory exhaust system installation, removing a serious fire hazard. The new improved stacks will be installed.
P-51B – up to model 104BA and 104BB serial 43-106438
P-51C – up to serial 42-103178 inclusive.

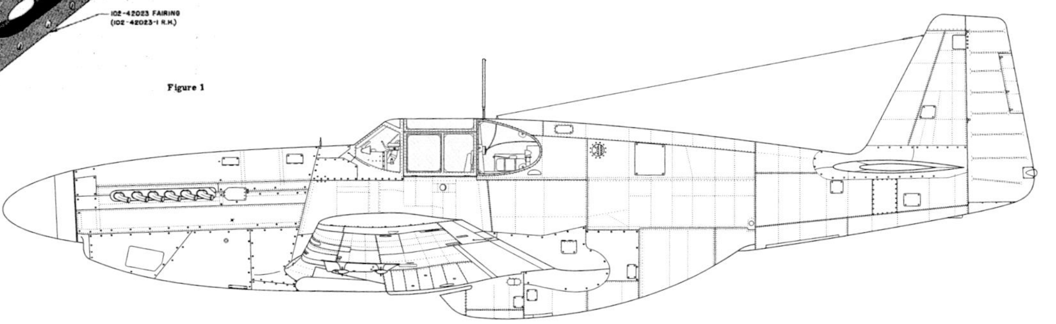

Right: P-51B-5-NA shown without exhaust stacks covers. Note sand filter louvers covered with the metal plate. 1/72 scale.

P-51B-5-NA, "Ticket Home" with oil breathing exit in upper position. Note also dust filter covered with metal, ("blank door" probably used in the cold weather). (US National Archives)

Additional Support for Relief Valve Vent Line – P-51B and P-51C
(Technical Order No. 01-60JD-30, 10 October 1944)
To prevent leakage of the header tank relief valve due to vibration of coolant header tank vent line. Two additional clips will be installed.
P-51B – up to model 104AV inclusive.
P-51C – up to model 103AF inclusive. (serial 43-103128 inclusive.)

Installation of the fuselage Fuel Tank Grounding Jack – P-51B, P-51C and P-51D
(Technical Order No. 01-60J-17, 11 September 1944)
To reduce the possibility of fire or explosion when filling the fuselage fuel tank.
P-51B models up to model 104BC.
P-51C models up to 103BD.

Installation of Elevator Inertia Weight
(Technical Order No. 01-60-90, 20 November 1944)
Such installation should be done to prevent reversal of the elevator control stick forces during manoeuvres on all produced P-51B/C.

Reinforcement of Horizontal Stabilizer and Fin – P-51B, P-51C
(Technical Order No. 01-60J-18, 8 April 1944) and later

Rework of Coolant and Oil Cooler Exit Flap Actuators, Types R-4250 and R-4310 – P-51 series,
(Technical Order No. 01-60J-24, 2 November 1944)
To prevent overheating resulting in failure of engines resulting from malfunctions of the engine oil and coolant exit flap, the actuator units installed will be modified.
P-51B – up to model 104BD.
P-51C – all models.

Operation of P-51 Series Airplanes with 85-gallon Fuselage Fuel Tank
(Technical Order No. 01-60H-20)
"The publication of this T.O. has been expedited as the instructions contained herein are of vital importance and should be disseminated to all affected personnel without delay...

1. Due to aft center of gravity position on P-51 series airplanes having 85 gallon fuselage fuel tank serviced and resultant reversal of stick forces when entering tight turns or attempting pullouts, extreme care will be exercised while operating the airplane until center of gravity is restored to a favourable position by using fuel from the fuselage tank
2. Take-off will be made on fuselage tank and continue to use fuel from fuselage tank until approximately 25 gallons of fuel remains. The airplane assumes optimum stability and flying characteristics with approx. 25 gallons of fuel in the fuselage tank...
3. Flights in rough air, instrument flying and manoeuvres involving high acceleration will be avoided whenever possible until at least one half of fuel is used from the fuselage tank..."

Dive limitation – P-51B, P-51C and P-51D
(Technical Order No. 02-60J-25, 10 July 1944)
P-51B, P-51C Limit Diving Speeds

Pressure Altitude (feet)	Pilot's Indicated Air Speed (mph)
40,000	270
35,000	305
30,000	340
25,000	385
20,000	420
15,000	465
10,000	505
5,000	505
0	505

Flight Characteristics and Restrictions – P-51 series
(Technical Order No. 01-60J-28, 17 August 1944)

1. In order to reduce the possibility of structural failures of wings on P-51 series airplanes, two commonly held misconceptions regarding fighter type aircraft must be corrected. They are:
    a. The belief that fighter airplanes are designed to such high load factory "g" that they are practically indestructible by any readily applied air load.
    b. That since the possible loading conditions are relatively few, that unbalance resulting in instability is impossible.
2. The increase in weight of the P-51 airplane through the addition of navigation and radio equipment, armour and armament and extra fuel, has decreased the load factor to which it was originally designed.
3. Reference Table will show that the optimum available load factors in usable combat condition are obtained under Conditions (...)

Replacement of Main Fuel Cell Drain Nipple – P-51B, P-51C, and P-51D
(Technical Order No. 69J-27, 20 October 1944)

To prevent failure of the nipple in the main fuel cell drains assembly, with resultant loss of fuel and possible fire hazard, the currently installed nipple will be replaced with a heavier type.
P-51B – up to 104B model inclusive.
P-51C – up to 103BD model inclusive.

Rework of Coolant Lines – P-51B, P-51C, and P-51D
(Technical Order 01-60J-36, 20 November 1944)

To prevent coolant lines from chafing at the fire wall and the aft edge of carburettor air scoop filter, all airplanes will be inspected to determinate if rework is required.
P-51B – all models.
P-51C – all models.

Rework of Feed Chutes and Installation of Split Belt Holding Pawls – P-51B and P-51C
(Technical Order No. 01-60JD-44, 21 December 1944)

To ensure feeding of the calibre .50 machine gun during combat manoeuvres in which the acceleration factor exceeds 3 g, the feed chutes will be modified and split belt holding pawl assemblies will replace present calibre .50 machine gun belt holding pawls and springs.
All P-51B and P-51C.

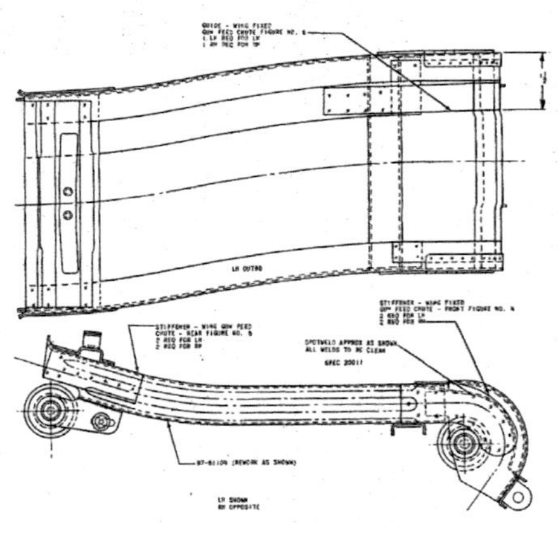

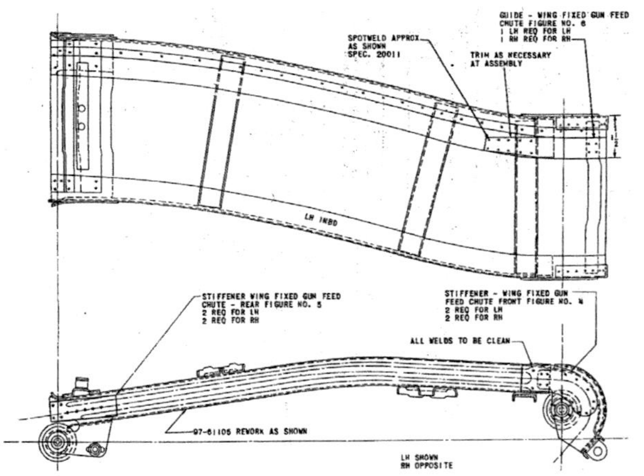

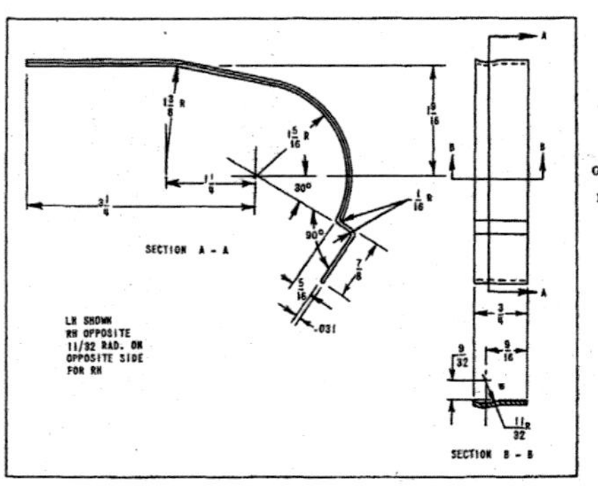

Figure 6
Guide - Wing
Fixed Gun
Feed Chute

Feed chutes as shown in the Technical Order manual.

Installation of Dorsal Fin and Reverse Rudder Boost Tab – P-51B and P-51C (Technical Order No. o1-60JD-43, 20 December 1944)

To correct the tendency, existing when certain manoeuvres are performed, for P-51B and P-51C airplanes to assume a high angle of yaw which may result in overloading the horizontal stabilizer, a dorsal fin will be installed. In conjunction with this the rudder trim tab will be converted to a reverse rudder boost.

P-51B – all models.

P-51C – up to model 103CC.

Installation of the dorsal fin and reverse rudder boost tab as shown in the Technical Order Manual.

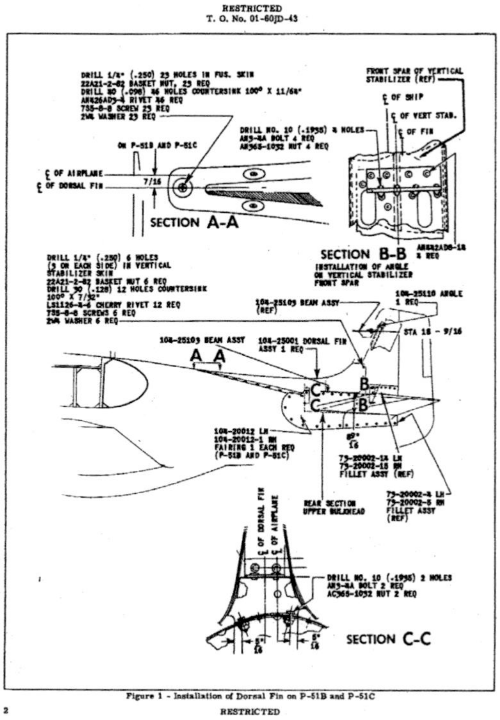

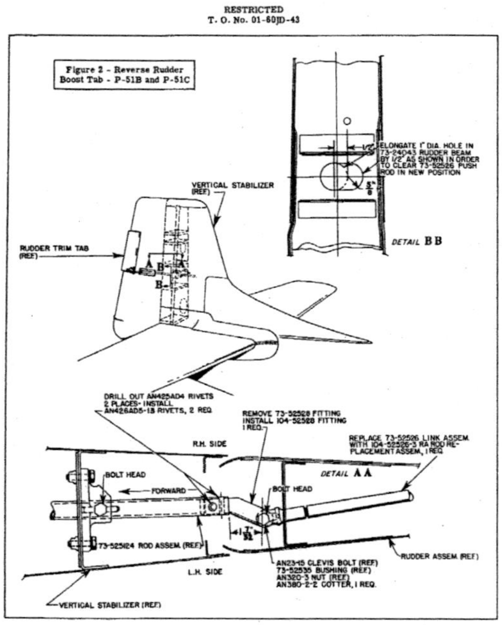

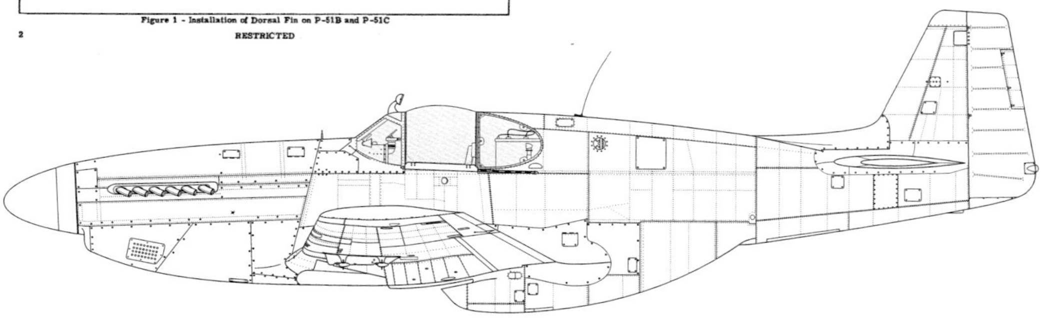

P-51B-10-NA with dorsal fin and Malcolm Hood installed. 1/72 scale.

Crew of the 353rd FG poses with "war weary" P-51B-1-NT s/n 43-12433 after being refurbished for use as a 351st FS "hack" aircraft. Obtained after it had flown a combat tour with the 359th FG, the aircraft was later recoded YJ-1. Aircraft with dorsal fin, Malcolm hood and antenna mast installed like on P-51D. (US National Archives)

Reinforcement of Horizontal Stabilizer and Fin – P-51B, P-51C
(Technical Order No. 01-60J-18, 15 January 1945)
To reduce the possibility of empennage failure the horizontal stabilizer and fin will be reworked.
P-51B – all models.
P-51C – all models.

Modification of Coolant Expansion Tank Assembly – P-51B. P-51C, and P-51D
(Technical Order No. 01-60J-23, 14 January 1945)
To prevent the efficiency of the desecrating scroll tubes being impaired, the extension tank will be inspected to determine if the tank has been modified.
P-51B/C – all models

Replacement of Fuel Hose from Selector Valve to Shut-off Valve – P-51B, P-51C, and P-51D,
(Technical Order No. 60J-34, 16 February 1945)
To prevent possibly chafing of the fuel hose by the tire on the LH landing gear wheel, the fuel hose will be replaced.
P-51B/C – all models.

Inspection and rework of the Elevator and Rudder Front Beams
(Technical Order No. 01-40-97, 27 February 1945)
To reduce the possibility of failure an inspection will be made of the elevator and rudder front beam.
All P-51B/C aircraft.

Replacement of Oil Drain Plugs – P-51B, P-51C, and P-51D
(Technical Order No. 01-60J-37, 5 March 1945)
To prevent leakage of oil at the oil system.
P-51B/C – all models. 24ST

Replacement of Propeller Spinner Seal – P-51B, P-51C, and P-51D
(Technical Order No. 01-60J-38, 16 March 1945)
To prevent cracking and spitting of the present two-piece spinner air seal. The new seal will be installed.
P-51B/C – all models.

Replacement of Tachometer Generator – P-51B, P-51C, P-51D, and P-51K
(Technical Order, No. 01-60J-40, 31 March 1945)
To eliminate the oscillation and general unsatisfactory operation of the tachometer on P-51 airplanes. The new model 2CM5ACZ will be installed.
P-51B/C – all models.

Reposition of Fuel Booster Pump Resistor Generator – P-51B, P-51C, P-51D, and P-51K,
(Technical Order, No. 01-60J-41, 16 January 1945)
To prevent breaking of the fuel booster pump resistor.
P-51B/C – all models.

Replacement of Fuel Selector Switch – P-51B, P-51C, P-51D, and P-51K
(Technical Order, No. 01-60J-42, 2 July 1945)
To provide a more reliable fuel selector switch.
P-51B/C – all models.

Installation of type C-1 gun Camera Mount and Camera Window – P-51A, P-51B and P-51C
(Technical Order, No. 01-60J-44, 24 April 1945)
To provide a more substantial and more easily and accurately adjusted gun camera mount and to provide a protective window for the gun camera.
P-51B/C – all models.

Inspection and replacement of Coolant Header tank inlet hose clamps – P-51B, P-51C, P-51D, and P-51K

(Technical Order, No. 01-60J-45, 22 February 1945)

To prevent breakage of hose clamps and loss of the coolant solution, inspection and modification, if necessary, will be made.

P-51B/C – all models.

Addition of Booster Spring to Carburettor Air Control Linkage System – P-51B, P-51C, P-51D, and P-51K,

(Technical Order, No. 01-60J-48, 8 May 1945)

To assist the pilot in moving the operating control lever from the unrammed "Filtered' air position to the 'Rammed' air position, a booster spring will be added.

P-51B/C – all models.

Rework of Main Landing Gear Brake Assemblies – P-51B, P-51C, P-51D, and P-51K,

(Technical Order, No. 01-60J-52, 26 March 1945)

To reduce the possibility of brake drag after pedal pressure has been released with consequent fusing and locking of the brakes.

P-51B/C – all models.

100/150 GRADE FUEL

In late winter of 1943 – 1944 the Allied Expeditionary Air Force (A.E.A.F.) decided, pending further trials, not to employ 150 Grade Fuel for Overlord due to spark plug issues, however, it was intended that 150 Grade Fuel would be used when proved satisfactory. The Production Division was directed on 28 March 1944, under the authority of the Commanding General, Army Air Forces, to modify all P-38, P-47 and P-51 airplanes in the United Kingdom for the use of Grade 150 fuel, with the necessary modification kits to be shipped to the European Theatre of Operations. It was decided that Grade 150 fuel was to be the only fuel available for USAAF fighter airplanes in the UK.

Successful service tests led in May 1944 to the 8th AF Fighter Command requesting that it "be supplied immediately with grade 150 aviation fuel for use in P-47, P-51 and P-38 planes".

Deliveries of Grade 100/150 aviation fuel to USAAF Stations commenced within a week of the landings in France. The change to 150 grade fuel necessitated the resetting of all aneroid switches on the P-51s.

150 grade fuel continued to be used by 8th AF units through 1944.

With 130 grade fuel, the average operational P-51B/C could last 5 missions (about 25 hours) before fouling required a plug change. With 150 grade fuel, it was reduced to 10 to 12 hours, or just 2 missions. As a result of excessive maintenance required on the V-1650 engines, General Doolittle of the 8th AF decided in late March 1945 to revert to the normal 100/130 (1 T) grade fuel.

Crashed Mustang showing dorsal fin, Malcolm hood and aerial installed on the starboard side of the fuselage. (US National Archives)

Above: P-51B-1-NA, s/n43-12335 of 30th Tactical Reconnaissance Squadron, 75th Tactical Reconnaissance Group, airborne from Meridian, MS. This airplane was written off in an accident 1-miles north of Key Field, MS.

Below: P-51B-7-NA, (built as B-5 and with added fuselage tank) serial 43-7055, 587, "Lady Jane" transferred to the 118th TRS (tail number 587 is a 118th TRS block number) from the 26th FS, 51st FG. This airplane was shot down by AA south of Stonecutter's Island, Hong Kong, 16 January 1945. The pilot, 1st Lt. John F. Egan was reported safe with the Chinese guerillas on 20 January 1945 and returned to duty at Luliang on 26 March 1945. (Both photos R. Bourlier coll.)

Above: *Photo from Technical Order manual showing installation of the ground jack.*

Left: *P-51B-15-NA with ground jack under fuselage fuel tank filler cap. (US National Archives)*

Below: *P-51B-15-NA, s/n 42-106775, R4+E with additional formation lights (indicated with black arrows) installed on the both sides of the fuselage. Aircraft started its combat career with the 368th FS, 359th FG at East Wretham. At some point it found its way to the 803rd BS (Provisional), which was redesignated 36th Bomb Squadron Radar Countermeasures Unit. It was used here as a formation assembly & command aircraft. The gun pod is a Douglas DGP-1 Twin 50 cal. gun pod. (US National Archives)*

F-6C Photo-Reconnaissance Mustang

By Robert Bourlier

During World War Two the US Army had a great need for photographic reconnaissance and mapping airplanes to support ground combat operations. One of the most successful of these was the F-4/5 variant of the P-38 "Lightning" but it had one major drawback: being unarmed the pilot had to rely on altitude and speed to survive against enemy airplanes. In the tactical and armed reconnaissance role there was no better airplane then the F-6 version of North American Aviation's P-51 "Mustang". With cameras added to the airplane the F-6 retained its armament of .50-cal machine guns and bomb racks and was able to defend itself against enemy attack. Several F-6 pilots became high scoring aces.

The F-6C was the photo-reconnaissance version of the Merlin engine P-51B/C Mustang. The airplanes were manufactured on the P-51 production line where several openings were added in the aft fuselage behind which cameras could be added. After production, the airplanes were sent to the Dallas modification center at Love Field (Lockheed Aircraft) or to the Kansas City, KS modification center where the airplanes received their cameras. Between December 1943 and July 1944 North American Aviation produced 230 F-6C airplanes, one at the Inglewood, CA facility and 229 in the Dallas, TX facility as indicated:

Dallas Modification Center

F-6C-5-NA	1	43-6785	delivered	12/3/43
F-6C-1-NT	59	42-103195 to 42-103383	delivered between	1/15/44 and 2/25/44
F-6C-5-NT	100	42-103386 to 42-103762	delivered between	2/15/44 and 4/25/44

Kansas City Modification Center

F-6C-10-NT	35	43-24990 to 43-25175	delivered between	6/20/44 and 7/25/44
F-6C-10-NT	29	44-10875 to 44-10911	delivered between	6/20/44 and 7/25/44
F-6C-11-NT	6	44-10796 to 44-10858	delivered between	6/20/44 and 7/25/44

In addition to factory modified airplanes, additional P-51B/C airplanes were modified at overseas depots or in the field by the squadron engineering section to suit operational needs. At least 53 P-51B/C airplanes (and probably more) were converted to F-6C configuration by depots in the ETO, MTO or CBI after initial delivery to the USAAF. Not all of these modifications were standard though as some squadrons preferred to have a third camera location added behind the pilot's headrest.

Early Mustangs carried up to two cameras, one behind the pilot's headrest and one in the aft fuselage. The F-6C used only one camera bay for camera installation providing for a single camera as dictated by mission requirements. Three types of cameras could be installed in the F-6C depending upon the mission. The Fairchild K-17 for combat photomapping and reconnaissance or the K-22 or K-24 for tactical reconnaissance.

The camera bay was located in the aft fuselage between the radiator exhaust and the tail wheel doors and contained two windows covered with optical glass, one at the left oblique and one vertical. On some of the airplanes a protective cover was added to protect the vertical window from dirt during takeoff and landing.

Access to the camera bay was made through an access door on the right side of the fuselage and by removing the window access door on the bottom of the fuselage, directly aft of the radiator exhaust. Further entry could be made through the tail wheel doors. Cameras were mounted in the fuselage using special mounting brackets designed to handle the g-forces of

F-6C-5-NT, s/n 42-103624, 599 is the first 118th TRS airplane to be painted with the black lightning markings, Chengkung, China, October 1944. Note the oblique camera opening below the national insignia. (family of Wallace Moyle via R. Bourlier)

combat maneuvering. Each camera could be fitted with a variety of lenses to suit mission requirements.

For vertical photography the F-6C would normally carry a K-17 camera. This was used for aerial mapping and provided finely detailed photographs up to 30,000 feet. For missions requiring oblique images the F-6C carried the K-22 or K-24 camera. The K-24 camera was the U.S. adaptation of the British F-24. Built by Eastman Kodak the K-24 was a vast improvement over the F-24 and was 10 pounds lighter. The K-24 with a 7-inch cone was most often used during tactical reconnaissance low-altitude oblique coverage to photograph rail lines, convoys, enemy aerodromes and installations and to locate enemy troop concentrations. These photos could be quickly processed at the local level, often by the tactical reconnaissance (Tac-R) squadron, for exploitation by the fighter-bomber pilots. Because the F-6C had the same performance and armament as the P-51 fighters, they would often accompany the fighters on ground attack missions and photograph the results for bomb damage assessment (BDA).

Camera Operation

The basic components for camera operation consisted of the camera with electric motor drive, camera master control panel, intervalometer and the radio transmitter push-to-talk switch on the throttle quadrant. The master control panel consisted of two switches, a master "On-Off" switch to turn the camera on or off and a selector switch to select manual operation or automatic timed interval operation.

F-6C-5-NT, 590, s/n 42-103623. Landing accident at Chengkung, China. (R. Bourlier coll.)

F-6C-1-NA, s/n 43-12191, "Hun Flusher" of 12th TRS. The low oblique camera port has been painted over and an oblique camera mount has been added behind the pilot's headrest. (IWM, Freeman Collection)

When selecting interval operation with the selector switch the pilot set the time interval desired between photographs by depressing and turning the interval knob on the intervalometer. Placing the master switch to "ON" started camera operation and placing the master switch to "Off", stopped the camera.

To operate the camera manually, the pilot placed the selector switch in the "Manual" position and the master switch to "ON". This allowed the pilot to use the radio transmit push-to-talk switch on the throttle to operate the camera. For a single exposure the pilot momentarily depressed the radio transmit switch. For a continuous series of exposures the pilot depressed and held down the radio transmit switch. While in "Manual" operation the radio transmitter was inoperative. Normal operation was restored by turning the master switch to "Off".

For oblique photography the pilot had to align the oblique camera with the target to be photographed. The K-24 camera was one of the most widely used cameras for this purpose and could be mounted in the camera bay at several different angles. To assist the pilot in properly aligning the oblique camera with the photo target several oblique camera alignment marks were painted on the airplane. On the left wing a 30° + camera sighting mark was painted at the gun bay doors and a 6° + camera sighting mark was painted at the junction of the left aileron and wing tip connection joint.An additional sighting mark + was etched into the left canopy glass. Looking through the canopy alignment mark, the pilot would line up the appropriate wing mark with the target then start the camera to collect the photographs.

Reconnaissance Aces

Capt. Clyde B. East, 15th TRS, 9th AF. With 13 victories he was the top reconnaissance ace in the ETO.

Capt. John H. Hoefker, 15th TRS, 9th AF. With 10 1/2 victories he was the number two reconnaissance ace in the ETO.

Capt. William A. Shomo, 82nd TRS, 5th AF. 8 aerial victories.Over Northern Luzon, Philippines, Capt. Shomo and his wingman attacked 13 Japanese airplanes. Capt. Shomo shot down 7 and his wingman 3. Capt. Shomo received the Medal of Honor for this action.

LtCol Edward O. McComas, CO 118th TRS, 23rd FG, 14th AF. 14 aerial victories, 4 airplanes destroyed on the ground and a Japanese destroyer sunk in Victoria Harbor, Hong Kong. All of his victories came while flying F-6C-5-NT s/n42-103604 "Miss Revenge". The 4th highest scoring ace in the 14th AF he was also the only ace-in-a-day shooting down 5 Japanese Oscars near Ehr Tao Kow airfield, China, 23 December, 1944.

Installing a K-17 vertical camera in an F-6C, 9th AF. (US National Archives)

Loading K-24 film, F-6C-11-NT s/n 44-11102 of 118th TRS, 23rd FG, 14th AF, China. Aircraft flown by 1st Lt. Ray Crowell and named "Duchess". (via R. Bourlier)

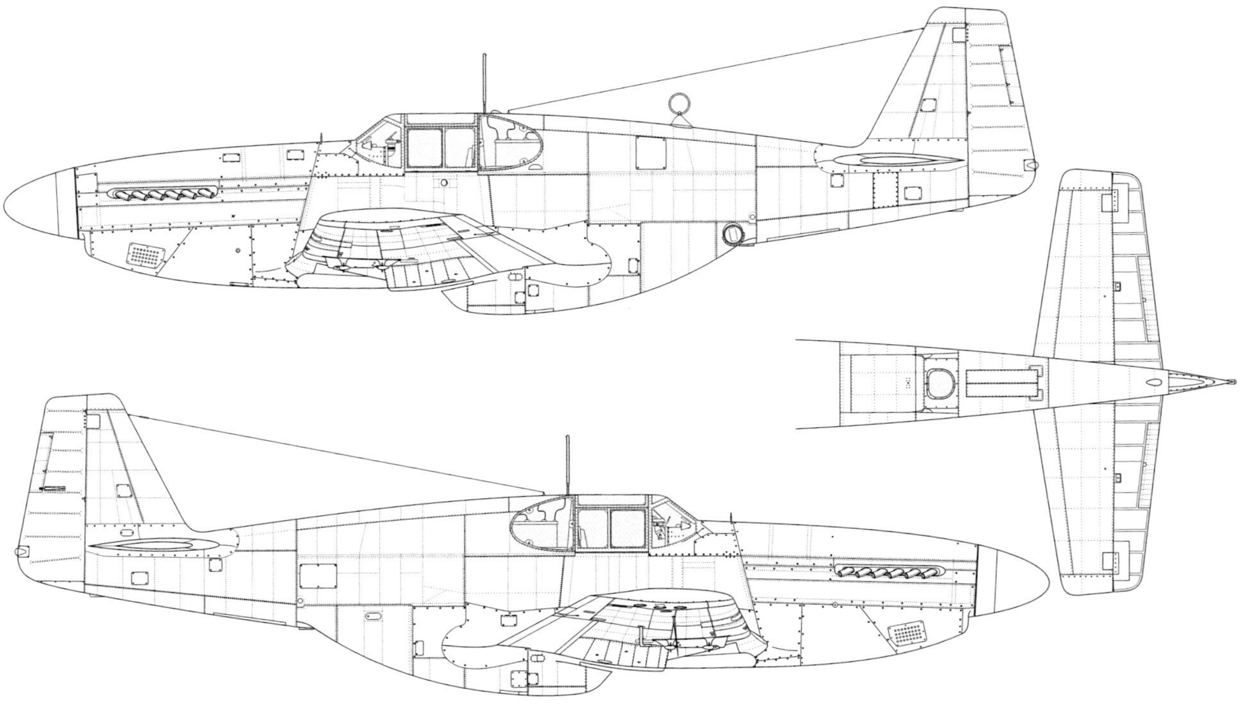

F-6C-10-NT, no fuselage tank, scale plans. 1/72 scale.

F-6C Production & Conversions

As with any research project the conclusions are only as accurate as the material that provides the data. The primary source material for this project was the North American Aviation Individual Aircraft Record Cards which tracked the production and delivery of the Mustangs. As the cards were not always carefully annotated as to production modifications it must be assumed that some airframes converted to the F-6C reconnaissance version were not properly documented. This means that the total production numbers listed here are most likely low.

The Research Project

The F-6C is the photo-reconnaissance version of the P-51B/C Mustang manufactured by North American Aviation (NAA) at the Inglewood, CA facility (P-51B suffix NA) and at Dallas, TX (P-51C suffix NT). These airplanes were not converted by NAA at its manufacturing facilities but were sent to the Lockheed modification center at Love Field, Dallas, TX or to the Kansas City modification center for conversion to the F-6 photo-reconnaissance configuration.

In the 1969 publication "Mustang – The Story of the P-51 Fighter" by Robert W. Gruenhagen, several statements are made concerning F-6C production and delivery. On page 83 he states that in preparation for operation "Point Blank" prior to operation "Overlord" "production schedules through December of 1943 called for 673 P-51B/C aircraft. Three hundred thirty-three of these aircraft would be photo recon variants. The action of October 30 (1943) by General Arnold cancelled further photo recon modifications and only a token number of B/C aircraft were modified as F-6 aircraft."

Additionally, in this book's section of "Serial Number and Production Data", on page 199 detailing P-51B-NA production and on page 200 detailing P-51C-NT production the following statements are made, respectively, concerning F-6C production;

"F-6C-10-NA, 71 aircraft modified from the P-51B-10-NA series" – (Inglewood)

"F-6C-10-NT, 20 aircraft modified from the P-51C-10-NT series" – (Dallas)

These two statements seem to sum up the total F-6C production by North American Aviation for a total of 91 F-6C photo-reconnaissance Mustangs.

The two production statements have been repeated many times in other publications such as the 1998 "Production Line to Frontline – North American Aviation P-51 Mustang" by Michael O'Leary, 1999 "The Mustang Story" by Ken Delve, 2009 "North American P-51 Mustang" by Malcolm V. Lowe, 2010 "Building The P-51 Mustang" by Michael O'Leary, 2012 "Mustang – Thoroughbred Stallion of The Air" by Steve Pace and in magazine articles about the Mustang's development and production. These statements raise two questions:

1 – What was the delivery timeline for the F-6C?
2 – How many F-6C airplanes were actually produced by North American Aviation?

The primary source consulted for NAA production was the Individual Aircraft Record Cards (IARC) on digital CDs obtained from the Air Force Historical Research Agency, Maxwell Air Force Base, Alabama. The results of a search of the record cards are very interesting.

First – in accordance with General Arnold's order of 30 Oct 1943, only one F-6C was delivered by NAA to the U.S. Army Air Forces (USAAF) prior to January 1944, F-6C-5-NA (P-51B-5-NA) 43-6785, delivered Dec. 3, 1943.

Second – of the 71 F-6C-10-NA airplanes to be produced from the P-51B-10-NA series, the record cards indicate that no P-51B-10-NA airplanes were converted to F-6C-10-NA. Only P-51B-5-NA, 43-6785, was converted at the Lockheed modification center in Dallas, TX, and delivered to the USAAF.

Third – of the 20 F-6C-10-NT airplanes to be produced at Dallas from the P-51C-10-NT series, the aircraft record cards reveal the following production and conversion by the Lockheed and Kansas City modification centers;

F-6C-5-NA	1	delivered	12/3/1943
F-6C-1-NT	59	delivered between	1/15/44 and 2/25/44
F-6C-5-NT	100	delivered between	2/15/44 and 4/25/44
F-6C-10/-11-NT	70	delivered between	6/20/44 and 7/25/44
Total F-6C-NT	229		
Total F-6C-NA/-NT	**230**		

Conclusions: No P-51B-10-NA airplanes were converted to F-6C recon Mustangs by the modification centers.

70 P-51C-10/-11-NT airplanes were converted to F-6C-NT, not the 20 indicated in the above referenced statements.

An additional 159 P-51C-NT airplanes were converted to F-6C-NT for a total production of 230 F-6C-NA/-NT airplanes, not the 91 suggested by the two commonly referenced statements.

NAA Inglewood & Dallas F-6C-NA & F-6C-NT Production
Primary Source – Individual Aircraft Record Cards

Inglewood P-51B-NA Production (Dallas Mod Center)
NA-104 AC-304 79
F-6C-5-NA 43-6785 Total: 1

Dallas F-6C-1-NT Production (Dallas Mod Center)

NA-103 AC-33940
42-103195, 196.
42-103198 to 42-103230.
42-103281, 304, 311, 344, 355, 356, 357, 358, 360, 364, 365, 366, 367, 368, 370, 371, 374, 375, 376, 378, 380, 381, 382, 383.
Total: 59

Dallas F-6C-5-NT Production (Dallas Mod Center)

NA-103 AC-33940
42-103386, 388, 391, 397, 399, 402, 403, 404, 405, 406, 407, 409, 411, 412, 413, 414, 415, 417, 418, 419, 421, 422, 425, 427, 428, 429, 430, 433, 435, 437, 438, 440, 442, 444, 447, 448, 449, 451, 452, 453, 457, 481, 482, 484, 486, 487, 488, 490, 491, 493, 494, 495, 496, 497, 504, 506, 509, 511, 512, 555, 568, 572, 573, 576, 577, 578, 579, 594, 604, 607, 610, 614, 615, 618, 619, 620, 621, 622, 623, 624, 625, 626, 628, 632, 734, 736, 738, 739, 740, 744, 745, 746, 748, 751, 754, 755, 757, 759, 760, 762.
Total: 100

Dallas F-6C-10-NT Production (Kansas City Mod Center)

NA-103 AC-33940
43-24990
43-25063, 081, 107, 121, 134, 139, 143, 145, 146, 147, 148.
43-25153 to 43-25175
Total: 35

NA-111AC-40063 (Kansas City Mod Center)

44-10875, 876, 877, 878.
44-10880 to 44-10887.
44-10889 to 44-10898.
44-10900, 902, 903, 904, 906, 907, 911.
Total: 29

Dallas F-6C-11-NT Production (Kansas City Mod Center)

NA-111 AC-40063
44-10796, 854, 855, 856, 857, 858. Total: 6

Total F-6C-NA/-NT Production: Total: 230

F-6C Conversions after Entering Air Force Service

After entering service with the USAAF, some P-51B-NA and P-51C-NT airplanes were modified as F-6Cs at Army Air Force depots or in the field. Several secondary sources were consulted for evidence of these conversions. These secondary sources included Missing Air Crew Reports (MACR), Aircraft Accident Reports (AAR), photographs from several private collections and photographs from the Imperial War Museum and the National Archive collections.

This secondary source evidence reveals that at least 35 P-51B-NA and 18 P-51C-NT Mustangs were converted to the F-6C reconnaissance configuration after entering Army Air Force service. These numbers should be considered as minimums only as more airplanes were probably modified as operations dictated.

Conclusion: With North American's production of 230 F-6Cs and, at a minimum, 53 depot/field conversions, there were at least 282 F-6C Mustangs provided to the Army Air Forces, and probably more.

Secondary Source Evidence of F-6C Conversions

Inglewood P-51B-1-NA to F-6C
NA-102, AC-33923
43-12160, 164, 191, 207, 301, 302, 329, 330, 355, 365, 391, 396, 397, 398, 403, 404, 409, 413, 426, 467, 474.
Total: 21

P-51B-5/-10/-15-NA to F-6C
NA-104, AC-30479
F-6C-5-NA 43-6360, 6370, 6383, 6505, 6524, 6642, 6699, 6702, 6713, 6744, 6797, 6954, 7001
Total: 13

F-6C-10-NA 42-106728
F-6C-15-NA 42-106740 Total: 2

Dallas P-51C-1-NT to F-6C
NA-103 AC-33940
42-102991
42-103001, 005, 006, 013, 018, 131, 134, 233, 304, 349.
Total: 11

Dallas P-51C-5-NT to F-6C
NA-103 AC-33940
42-103396, 408, 460, 616. **Total: 4**

Dallas P-51C-10-NT to F-6C
NA-103 AC-33940
43-25129 **Total: 1**

Dallas P-51C-11-NT to F-6C
NA-111 AC-40063
44-11102 Total: 1

Secondary Source Identification of F-6C Conversions

Missing Air Crew Report (MACR)
Aircraft Accident Report (AAR)
Imperial War Museum (IWM)
Photograph – from private collections or publications.

P-51B-1-NA CONVERSIONS (F-6C)

43-12160	MACR 10875	109th TRS 67th TRG IX TAC	11 Dec 1944	10 mi W. Bonn, Germany
43-12164	MACR 13108	15th TRS 10th PG XIX TAC	14 Mar 1945	Gr. Gerau, Germany
42-103191	IWM	Photograph Freeman Collection	FRE_10209 "Hun Flusher"	
43-12207	MACR 6651	15th TRS 10th PG XIX TAC	11 Jul 1944	France
43-12301	Photograph,	Page 105, Development of the P-51 Long-Range Escort Fighter "Ludwig"		
43-12302	AAR	109th TRS 67th TRG IX TAC	26 Nov 1944	Gosselies, Belgium
43-12329	MACR 8156	109th TRS 67th TRG IX TAC	15 Aug 1944	7 mi WSW. L'Aigle, France
43-12330	Photograph	26th FS 51st FG 14th AF	1944	China
43-12355	MACR 9818	109th TRS 67th TRG IX TAC	6 Oct 1944	10 mi E. Roermonde, Holland
43-12365	Photograph	Page 77, Aerial Reconnaissance, The 10th Photo Recon Group In World War II "Tom Ivie". "Puff", the personal mount of the 12th TRS CO, Maj. Woodrow.		
43-12391	MACR 7655	12th TRS 10th PG XIX TAC	30 Jul 1944 5 mi	SE Tessy-Sur-Vire, France
43-12396	Photograph	Page 105, Development of the P-51 Long-Range Escort Fighter "Ludwig"		
43-12397	AAR	109th TRS 67th TRG IX TAC	23 Feb 1945	Charleroi, Belgium
43-12398	AAR	109th TRS 67th TRG IX TAC	1 Mar 1945	Honsfeld, Belgium
43-12403	MACR 6479	12th TRS XIX TAC	29 Jun 1944	3 mi SW. Beuzeville, France
43-12404	Photograph	26th FS 51st FG 14th AF, China		
43-12409	AAR	12th TRS 10th PRG, 9th AF	24 Feb 1945	France
43-12413	MACR 14405	109th TRS 67th TRG IX TAC	10 May 1945	5 mi N Eschwege, Germany
43-12426	AAR	12th TRS 10th PRG, 9th AF	3 Oct 1944	Saint Dizier, France
43-12467	IWM	Photograph	Freeman Collection FRE_7014	
	AAR	15th TRS 10th PRG, 9th AF	18 Mar 1945	Hettange Grande, France
43-12474	AAR	109th TRS 67th TRG IX TAC	29 Dec 1944	Gosselies, Belgium

P-51B-5-NA CONVERSIONS (F-6C)

43-6360	MACR 10275	162nd TRS Prov. RG XII TAC	29 Oct 1944	20 mi E. Epinal, France
43-6370	AAR	107th TRS 67th TRG	31 Mar 1944	Middle Wallop, England
43-6383	Photograph	Page 105, Development of the P-51 Long-Range Escort Fighter "Ludwig"		
43-6505	AAR	31st TRS 9th TRG	3 May 1945	Wiesbaden Airfield, Germany
43-6524	AAR	160th TRS 363rd TRG	9 Oct 1944	Stenay, France
43-6642	AAR	162nd TRS	7 Apr 1945	Haguenau, Germany
43-6699	MACR 12412	162nd TRS Prov. RG XII TAC	1 Dec 1944	Neufreistett, Germany
43-6702	AAR	160nd TRS 363rd TRG	13 Mar 1945	Venlo Airfield, Holland
43-6713	AAR	162nd TRS	30 Jan 1945	Azelot, France
43-6744	AAR	161st TRS 363rd TRG		10 Feb 1945
43-6797	AAR	161st TRS 363rd TRG	20 Jan 1945	Kumtich, Belgium
43-6954	AAR	161st TRS 363rd TRG		5 Dec 1944
43-7001	AAR	160th TRS 363rd TRG	5 Dec 1944	Le Culot, Belgium

P-51B-10-NA Conversions (F-6C)

42-106728	MACR 13151	160th TRS 363rd TRG	18 Mar 1945	Gumer, Germany

P-51B-15-NA Conversions (F-6C)

42-106740	AAR	161st TRS 363rd TRG	14 Mar 1945	Venlo Airfield, Holland

P-51C-1-NT Conversions (F-6C)

42-102991	MACR 6193	12th TRS 10th PRG XIX TAC	30 Jun 1944	La Hutte, France
42-103001	AAR	162nd TRS 10th PRG	27 May 1945	Furth, Germany
42-103005	Photograph			
42-103006	Photograph			
42-103013	AAR	111th TRS	30 Jan 1945	Azelot, France
42-103018	IWM	Photograph Freeman Collection FRE_008780		
42-103131	AAR	15th TRS 10th PRG	10 Apr 1945	Ruppertenrod, Germany
42-103134	MACR 7485	107th TRS 67th TRG IX TAC	26 Jul 1944	France
42-103233	Photograph	118th TRS 23rd FG 14th AF	"Black Lightning" w/shark mouth.	China
42-103304	MACR 11739	111th TRS XII TAC	29 Jan 1945	near Karlsruhe, Germany
42-103349	AAR	160th TRS 363rd TRG	9 Nov 1944	La Culot, Belgium

P-51C-5-NT Conversion (F-6C)

42-103396	AAR	111th TRS	15 Jan 1945	Azelot, France
42-103408	AAR	107th TRS 67th TRG IX TAC	18 Aug 1944	1.5 mi SW. Le Molay, France
42-103460	MACR 11619	111th TRS Prov. RG XII TAC	25 Dec 1944	SW of Frankfurt, Germany
42-103616	AAR	107th TRS 67th TRG IX TAC	1 Jan 1945	Gosselies, Belgium

P-51C-10/-11-NT Conversions (F-6C)

43-25129	AAR	CCTR (TR)	8 Dec 1944	Key Field, MS
44-11102	Photograph	118th TRS 23rd FG 14th AF #598 "Duchess" 1Lt Ray Crowell	Nov 1944	Chengkung, China

F-6C-1-NA, s/n 43-12330 of 26th FS, the 118th TRS was not the only squadron to have reconnaissance airplanes. Most squadrons had one or two airplanes assigned. This airplane is from the 26th FS, 51st FG (tail code 263). Note the Chinese "coolies" building the runway in the background, all done by hand labor. (R. Bourlier coll.)

1st Lt. Crowell & collapsed Gear, Suichuan, China. F-6C-11-NT, s/n 44-11102 landing accident. The right landing gear did not lock down due to a rivet bucking bar that had been left in the wing. The airplane was repaired and would be named "Duchess" after 1st Lt Crowell's wife. When the airplane was reassigned to Lt. Fred Poats it was renamed "Lady Marion".

1st Lt. Ray Crowell and F-6C-11-NT "Duchess". He was a flight leader of "Red Flight". The airplane, an F-6C-11-NT, s/n 44-11102 was converted to reconnaissance configuration after leaving the United States, not by North American Aviation. (R. Bourlier coll.)

NAA Mustang III

The Mustang III was the British designation for the Merlin-powered P-51B and P-51C. The aircraft were virtually identical to the American versions, with some changes made after aircraft had arrived in Britain.

The RAF ultimately received 274 P-51Bs and 626 P-51Cs. These served with the RAF and four Polish squadrons, three RCAF and one Free French.

A total of 59 Mustang IIIs was diverted to the Royal Australian Air Force.

Mustang III, FX8??, (P-51B-1-NA) in delivery markings and British camouflage. (NAA)

Mustang III, serial FX982, (P-51B-5-NA, s/n 43-6342) awaiting delivery to the UK. (via R. Wallsgrove)

British modifications.

Mustang III, serial FX876, WC+D, (P-51B-1-NA, s/n 42-12146) of 309 Squadron PAF. (via W. Matusiak)

Malcolm Hood

The view from the cockpit of the Mustang was considered inadequate by the RAF, so a replacement for the original folding centre sections was designed.This was a bulged canopy very similar the that of the Spitfire, which greatly enhanced the pilot's view. The firm of Robert Malcolm was assigned the task of manufacturing production kits for this improved (bubble) canopy section. This firm specialized in blown plexiglas (Perspex) and already made the Spitfire canopy, among others.Malcolm refined the design and began production.About 135 man hours was the expected time needed to fit a Malcolm hood. Antenna work, structural work, skin riveting, parts installation, all added up to a surprising amount of detail work needed to convert a Mustang.

The actual production Malcolm hood was first fitted on Mustang III FX893 in February 1944.However, the hood was in the test stage as early as December 1942 and was being considered for Allison-engined TacR Mustangs. The first RAF Mustang III Squadron, No 19, went operational in February 1944 with Malcolm hoods on their aircraft.The Malcolm canopy was also fitted to key USAAF Mustangs at about the same time.In addition to greatly improving the pilot's view, the rearwards-sliding Malcolm hood also made it easier to exit the aircraft in emergency.

Malcolm hood canopy of the Mustang III, serial HB861, UZ-B, (P-51C-5-NT, s/n 42-103710). Personal aircraft of Flt. Lt. J Jeka, 306 Squadron PAF, March 1945. (Stratus coll.)

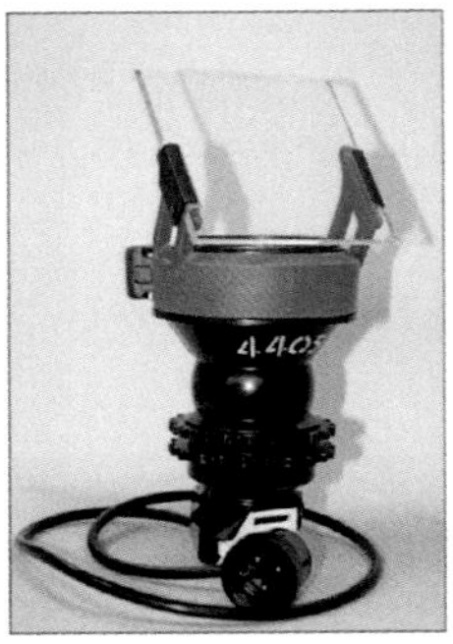

British gunsight

Most of the Mustang IIIs received British Mark II (and Mark IIL) gunsights. Many USAAF pilots also retrofitted Mark II gunsights in their Mustangs.

Antiglare panels.

The first deliveredoperational Mustangs IIIs had anti-glare panels, but these panels were removed very quickly. Just a few photos exist showing such panels, or traces after removing them.

Louvred cowl sand filters panels

Early Mustang IIIs also received louvred cowl sand filters panels, also seen on some Mustang IVs. These features existed much longer than anti-glare panels and are seen in many photos.

Two photos of the Mustang III with antiglare panels and louvered cowl sand filters panels. It is Mustang III serial FZ175, WC-Y, (P-51B-5-NA, s/n 42-6596) of 306 Squadron PAF. (via W. Matusiak)

Nose of the Mustang III, serial FZ128, UZ-A, (P-51B-5-NA, s/n 42-6469) of 302 Squadron PAF. Note removed exhaust shrouds and louvered sand filters. (via W. Matusiak)

Mustang III of 315 Squadron PAF with traces of the removed antiglare panels. (Stratus coll.)

High grade fuel (100/150 grade)

During 1942 and 1943 the RAF was testing aviation fuels that allowed for higher engine power in their fighter aircraft than was possible using the standard 100/130 grade aviation fuel then in use.

Similar test were later made by the US Army Air Force in 1944.

Following successful testing, the Spitfire IX's Merlin 66 was cleared in March 1944 to use +25 lbs boost, obtainable with 150 grade fuel. In early May, 1 and165 Squadrons were the first to convert their Spitfires to +25 lbs boost and employ 150 grade fuel on operations.

By 12 August 1944, 16 Squadrons in Air Defense Great Britain (ADGB) had been modified to operate with 150 grade fuel.

The increased performance obtained with 150 grade fuel was important for Mustangs, Tempests, Spitfires and Mosquitos in intercepting V-1 flying bombs launched against Britain in June.

Mustang III performance increases at sea level were as follows:

Aircraft	130 grade	150 grade
Mustang III (V-1650-3)	360 mph	390 mph +25 lb

Using 100/150 grade fuel led to excessive maintenance required on the V-1650 engines. Very often engine exchanges forced the RAF to make frequent rotation of aircraft between units.

On 18 September 1944 ADGB positively summarized the experience gained to date using 100/150 grade fuel. However, due primarily to logistical difficulties, such as the interchange of squadrons between ADGB and 2nd TAF, it was decided that UK-based fighter squadrons should revert to the use of 130 grade fuel.

In November 1944 S.H.A.E.F cleared 100/150 grade fuel for use by the Second Tactical Air Force.

Mustang III. serial FX893 during tests with rockets. (Stratus coll.)

British rockets installation

The RAF tested installation of underwing rockets.

Additional modifications

Mustang IIIs of early series never received the additional fuselage fuel tank.

Mustang III as reconnaissance aircraft

541 Squadron used three Mustang III aircraft – FB182, FX855 and FX952 – taken on strength in June 1944 and used until May 1945. They were modified with the installation of an oblique camera in the lower rear fuselage and a vertical camera in the rear fuselage ahead of the tail wheel – similar to the US F-6C modification. At the end of June 1944 three South African pilots "trained in low level photography" were attached to 541 Sqn at Benson in the UK. In June and July 1944 541 Squadron was heavily committed to Operation Crossbow, the search for and destruction of German V weapon installations and depots in France and the Low Countries.

Mustang IIIs of 309 Squadron PAF. Aircraft serial FZ124, (P-51B-5-NA, s/n 43-6465) still without fuselage tank, but with dorsal fin. Photo was taken in late 1945. (via W. Matusiak)

Mustang III serials.

Mustang III	FB100	FB124	P-51B-5 s/n 43-6659 to 43-6683
	FB125	FB350	P-51C-1-NT s/n 42-103019 to 42-103280
	FB351	FB370	P-51C-5-NT s/n 42-103461 to 103480
	FB370	FB399	P-51C-5-NT s/n 42-103521 to 103549
	FR411	-	P-51B-5 s/n 43-6565 Returned to USAAF Dec 13, 1943, no RAF service.
	FX848	FX852	P-51B-1-NA s/n 43-12113 to 12127
	FX853	FX872	P-51B-1-NA s/n 43-12305 to 12324
	FX973	FX997	P-51B-5-NA s/n 43-6333 to 6357
	FX998	FX999	P-51B-5-NA s/n 43-6398 to 6399
	FZ100	FZ122	P-51B-5 s/n 43-6400 to 43-6423
	FZ123	FZ147	P-51B-5 s/n 43-6464 to 43-6488
	FZ149	FZ172	P-51B-5 s/n 43-6532 to 43-6553
	FZ173	FZ197	P-51B-5 s/n 43-6618 to 43-6618
	HB821		P-51C-5-NT s/n 42-103550
	HB822	HB921	P-51C-5-NT s/n 42-103671 to 103890
	HB922	HB941	P-51C-10-NT s/n/ 43-24914 to 24933
	HB942	HB961	P-51C-10-NT s/n/ 43-24994 to 225013
	HK944	HK947	Ex 12th AF USAAF
	HK955	HK956	Ex 12th AF USAAF
	KH421	KH430	P-51C-10-NT s/n/ 43-25014 to 25022
	KH431	KH460	P-51C-10-NT s/n 44-10753 to 10782
	KH461	KH510	P-51C-10-NT s/n 44-10818 to 10873
	KH511	KH530	P-51C-10-NT s/n 44-10913 to 10932
	KH531	KH610	P-51C-10-NT s/n 44-10956 to-11035
	KH611	KH640	P-51C-10-NT s/n 11123 to 11152
	SR406	SR438	Ex USAAF 43-12162, 43-12407, 43-12412, 43-12473, 43-12484, 43-12427, 43-70114(?), 43-12189, 43-12177, 43-7039, 43-6831, 43-12155, 43-12188, 43-12456, 43-12480, 43-12399, 42-10663(?), 42-106683, 42-106630, 42-106687, 43-7071, 43-7144, 43-5595, 43-7171, 43-6829, 43-12420, 43-7152, 43-7135, 42-103209, 42-106478, 42-106431, 43-7007, 43-12420, 43-7159
	SR440	-	P-51B-10-NA s/n 43-7159 From USAAF

Mustang III, serial FZ149, UZ-W, (P-51-B-5-NA, s/n 43-6530) of 302 Squadron PAF, photographed in October 1944. Note lack of the fuselage tank. (via W. Matusiak)

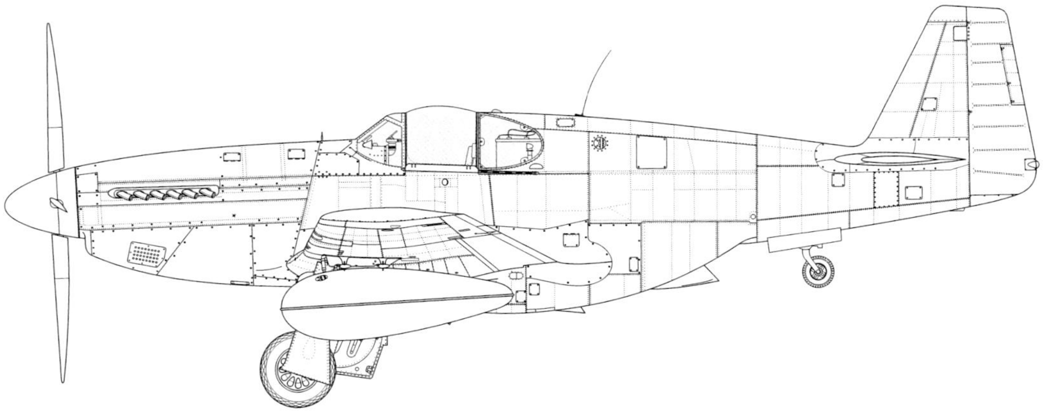

Side view of the standard RAF Mustang III with Malcolm hood. 1/72 scale.

Mustang III with antiglare panels and louvred cowl sand filter panels. 1/72 scale.

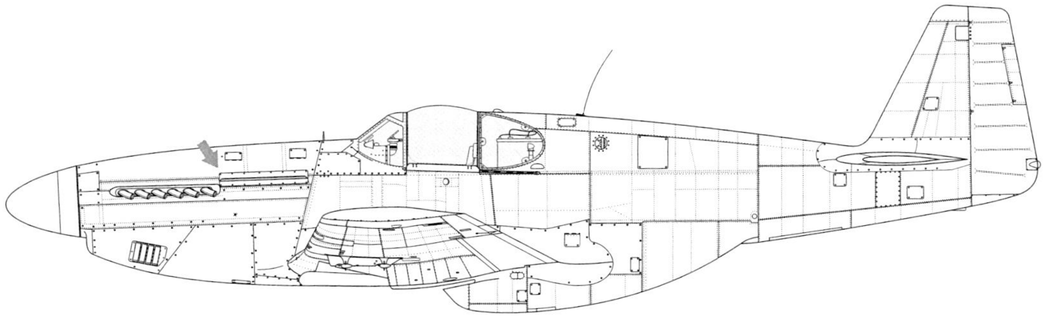

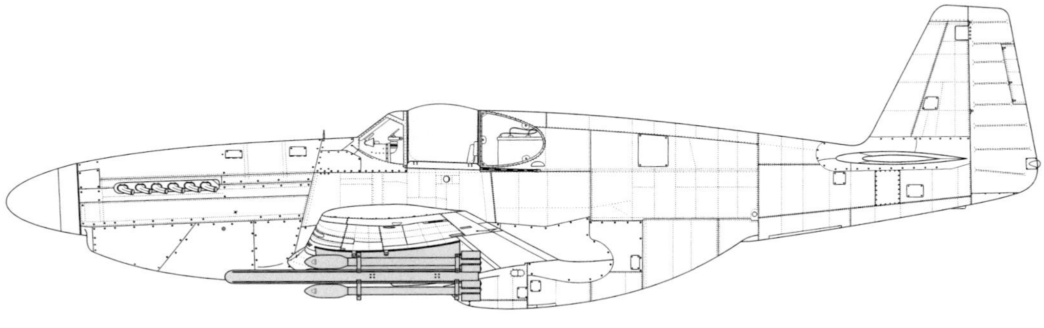

Mustang III rockets installation. 1/72 scale.

Mustang III of 315 Squadron PAF. (via W. Matusiak)

P-51B/C Technical Description

Wing.

Tapered, all-metal, two-spar wings. Dihedral angle 5°, laminar-flow wing section NAA-NACA, thickness ratio of 15.1 percent at the wing root at 39 percent of the chord, tip ratio 11.4 percent at the 50 percent chord line. Wing sweep 0° at 25 percent of the chord. Both wings attached with bolts to the central rib in the airframe centreline. Wing upper surface in the cockpit area formed the cockpit floor. Each wing had 19 ribs and two spars of 24ST Alclad. Removable wingtips, attached to wings with screws. Wing skin made of Alclad light alloy, riveted to ribs and longerons with countersunk rivets. Ailerons and flaps of metal structure hinged on rear spar, covered with light alloy skin. Ailerons of two-spar structure with 12 ribs, flaps of similar structure with 13 leading edge ribs and 15 central ribs. Statically and dynamically balanced ailerons fitted with trim tabs: port – adjustable, starboard – fixed. Ailerons operated mechanically with a system of tie rods, cranks and cables. Aileron deflection: 15° upwards and downwards. Hydraulically powered flaps deflected in the range of 0°–50° at 10° intervals.

Fuselage.

Semi-monocoque fuselage made of duralumin (mainly Alclad – plated duralumin skin), divided into three sections joined with bolts. Front part housed the engine mount, central part the pilot's cockpit and engine radiator and the rear part the tail attachment points. Fuselage structure consisted of four main longerons drawn from duralumin plate, frames and additional longerons, and was covered with stressed Alclad skin. Between front and central fuselage parts was the armour plate firewall separating the engine compartment from the cockpit. Front part of the fuselage was covered with four removable elements and a three-part lower cowling. Engine cowling was attached to the structure with special quick-release locks. In the lower part of the cowling were three carburettor air intakes with air filters. The engine mount consisted of two box girders with auxiliary transverse struts. Both girders were joined with two U-shaped transverse frames. The entire unit was attached to the firewall with four bolts. Such a structure allowed quick removal of the engine from the airframe after removal of the engine cowling only. The central fuselage was made of two halves joined at the fuselage centreline. Upper longerons of the central fuselage I-shaped at the front and T-shaped at the rear. Lower longerons also I-shaped at the front and C-shaped at the rear. Behind pilot's seat was a steel frame, which formed the turnover protection. Structurally, the central section consisted of eight parts joined with bolts and rivets.

Cockpit enclosure consists of upper and side plastic panels, each in two sections, forward one forming a sliding window with locking handle. Right upper panel hinges upward; left panel hinges downward against fuselage. Both have locks controlled from inside and outside. Hood is attached by four hinges on upper longerons. An emergency release permits the enclosure to be removed or jettisoned in an emergency.The

P-51B/C station diagram, drawing from Airplane Parts Catalog.

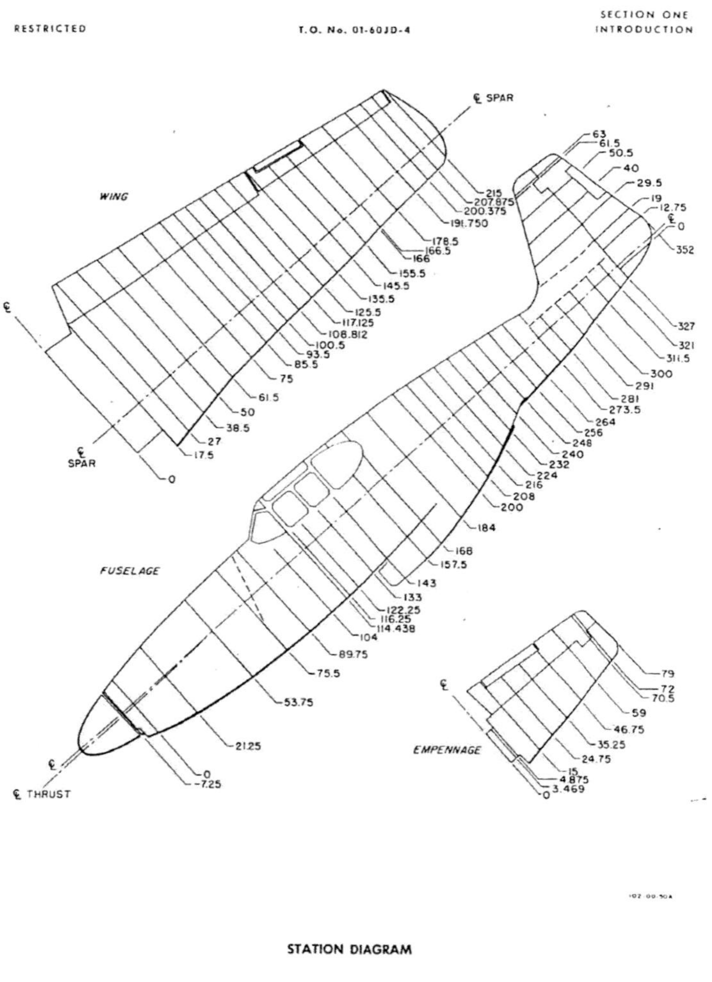

opening centre section was often replaced with a one-piece Malcolm hood of blown perspex, sliding aft.

Aft windows of moulded Lucite fit the fuselage contour and are removable for access to the radio behind the pilot. Aft of the radio, abulkhead prevents drafts and keeps objects from rolling aft and fouling controls. Plates at centre of the bulkhead secured the oxygen bottles.

Adjustable pilot's seat adapted for seat-type parachute. Adjustable rudder pedals. Behind the pilot's seat were two armoured plates protecting the pilot's head and back.

Semi-monocoque rear fuselage consisted of two 24ST longerons, three frames (walls), five auxiliary frames and a closing wall with tail attachment points.

Tail.

Tapered, two-spar cantilever horizontal tail unit covered with Alclad. Stabiliser fitted with removable tips facilitating installation and removal of elevators. Fabric covered elevators deflected 30° upwards and 20° downwards. Elevators mass and aerodynamically balanced (with adjustable trim tabs). Two-spar fin covered with light alloy skin. Fin set 1° to port in relation to the airframe longitudinal centreline. Someaircraft were retrofitted with an additional dorsal fin. Rudder was covered with mercerised cotton fabric and fitted with a trim tab. The elevator was operated with push-pull rods, bell cranks and cables. Elevator trim by cables and the rudder and rudder trim also by cables.

Landing gear.

Conventional landing gear with tail wheel. Single-leg main landing gear fitted with oleo-pneumatic shock absorbers, retractable in the direction of the longitudinal fuselage centreline. Retraction system powered hydraulically. Hydraulic disc brakes, controlled by the rudder pedals. Main wheels of 68.5 cm diameter. Two-piece main wheel door. One piece was fastened to the wheel leg, the other one to the fuselage, covering the entire landing gear when fully retracted. Hydraulically retractable tail wheel with oleo-pneumatic shock absorbers. The tail wheel controlled by the rudder pedals via control cables. The tail wheel steering system could be disconnected during parking or taxiing by moving the control stick forward. The tail wheel is fully castoring with the stick forward. When the stick is back, movement, via rudder pedals, is limited to six degrees either side of fore & aft. Tail wheel bay fitted with two doors covering the bay when the tail wheel was fully retracted. Tail wheel diameter 32 cm.

P-51B/C fuel system. Drawing from Technical Manual.

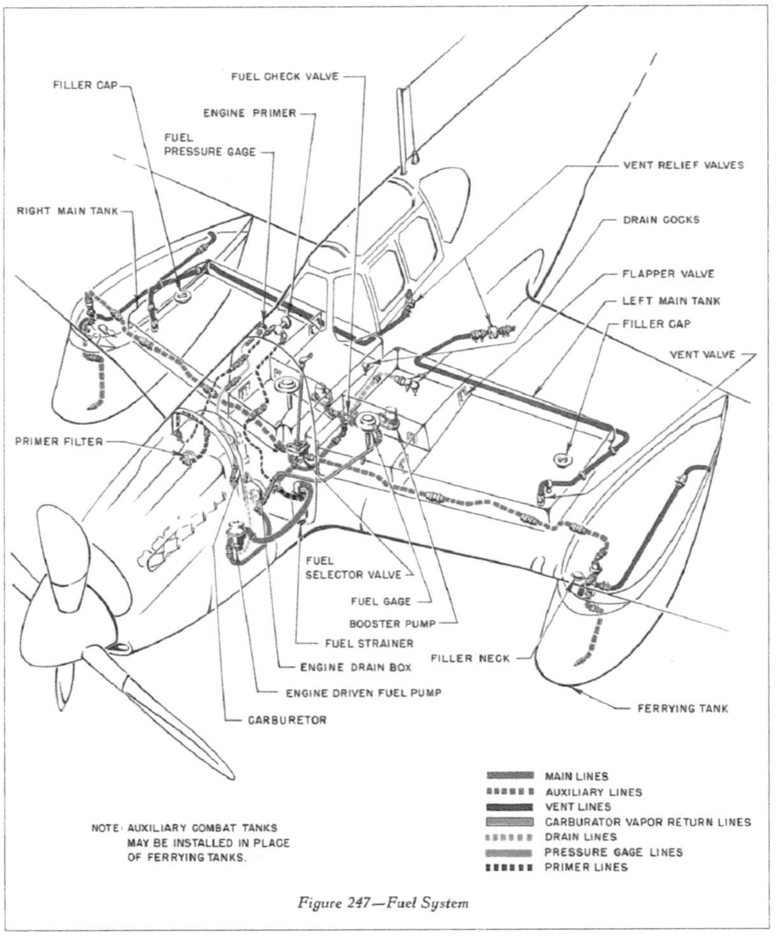

Figure 247—Fuel System

Powerplant.

The aircraft was powered by a V-12, four-stroke, liquid-cooled, Packard V-1650-3, later V-1650-7 engine, or Rolls-Royce Merlin 68 licence-built by Packard Motor Car Co., Detroit.

Technical notes – Packard V-1650-7 engine

Cylinder banks angled at 60°, displacement 1,649 cu. in (27,029 cm3), piston stroke 6 in (152.4 mm), cylinder bore 5.4 in (137.16 mm), compression ratio 6:1. The engine was fitted with reduction gear (0.479:1) and a two-stage, two-speed supercharger, which retained take-off power up to 25,590 ft (7,800 m). The supercharger was switched automatically to high blower between 15,700 and 19,700 ft (4,785 m & 6,000 m) and was variable depending on rate of climb and descent, speed and the ram air at the carburettor intake.

Normal take-off power – 1,490 hp (1511 KM);

War emergency – 1,720 hp (1744 KM)

Rated power – 1,315 hp (1,333 KM) (3000 rpm);

maximum power – 1,720 hp (1,744 KM) (3000 rpm)

Short-term, five-minute combat rating was 1,598 hp (1,620 KM) with boost pressure 2,065 hPa and 3,300 rpm.

Engine weight 1,690 lb (766,57 kg),

Length: 87.11 in. (2.21 m), Width: 29.97 in. (0.76 m), Height: 41.63 in. (1.057 m)

Equipment installed on the engine consisted of carburettor, two magnetos, propeller speed controller, fuel pump, oil pump, coolant pump, hydraulic system pump, generator, vacuum pump, starter and tachometer.

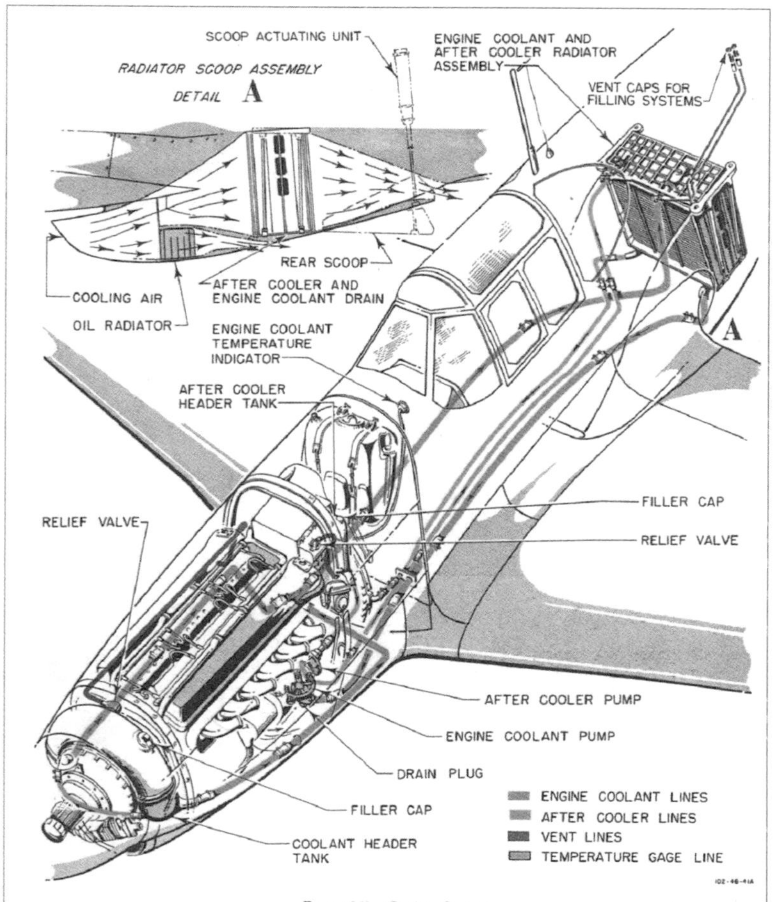

Figure 269—Cooling System

P-51B/C cooling system. Drawing from Technical Manual.

Fuel system.

Fuel system consisted of two 92 US gal (348 l) tanks installed in the wing roots between spars and an additional 85 US gal (321 l) tank in the fuselage just behind the pilot's seat.

The aircraft could carry two additional jettisonable underwing tanks. In the cockpit was a lever for mechanical jettisoning of underwing tanks in the case of failure of the electric release system. Recommended fuel octane rating 100/130. Float-less pressure injection carburettor, fed by a 600 gallon per hour engine driven fuel pump.

Engine control systems.

Merlin engines were fitted with a throttle lever mechanically connected to an Automatic Boost Controller (made by Packard or Simmons), which controlled engine boost. The device kept constant engine boost pressure irrespective of flight conditions. On the rear part of the throttle quadrant was the fuel mixture control lever. The supercharger was controlled automatically, with the help of an aneroid connected to the electric system of the supercharger control unit. The engine used an electric starter.

Propeller.

Four-bladed Hydromatic-type Hamilton Standard 24D50-65 or – 87 propeller. Propeller blades made of 6547-6, 6547A-6 or 6523A-24 aluminium alloy. Propeller diameter 11' 2" (3.40 m).

Engine cooling system.

The aircraft was fitted with two independent cooling systems. The main cooling system had a capacity of 16.7 US gal (63 l) of coolant (30% solution of ethylene glycol in water). This included a header tank of 5.2 US gal (19.6 l) installed on the front of the engine in the engine compartment. Both the main and after-cooler coolant system temperatures could be automatically or manually controlled via thermostat controlled electric actuators. The fuel mixture intercooler system was fitted with a separate radiator. Total volume of this system was 4.8 US gal (18 l) including the 0.5 US gal (1.9 l) header tank. Both the main and inter-cooler systems had individual engine driven coolant pumps. Radiator tunnel outlet flaps were controlled automatically. The pilot could set one of four working modes: automated, open, closed, control off.

Engine oil system.

The engine oil system had a total capacity of 21 US gal (79.4 l). The engine oil tank was mounted on the forward face of the main firewall between the cockpit and engine compartment, and had a capacity of 12.5 US gal (47.3 l) plus 1 US gal air space for expansion. The oil cooler was installed in the tunnel under the fuselage. Oil temperature was controlled automatically by a thermostatically controlled actuator and could be set in one of four modes, the same as the coolant actuator. The oil system limited the time of inverted flight to ten seconds.

Flight instruments.

Airspeed indicator, remote indicating compass, directional gyro, clock, vertical speed indicator, accelerometer and altimeter, artificial horizon, turn & bank indicator.

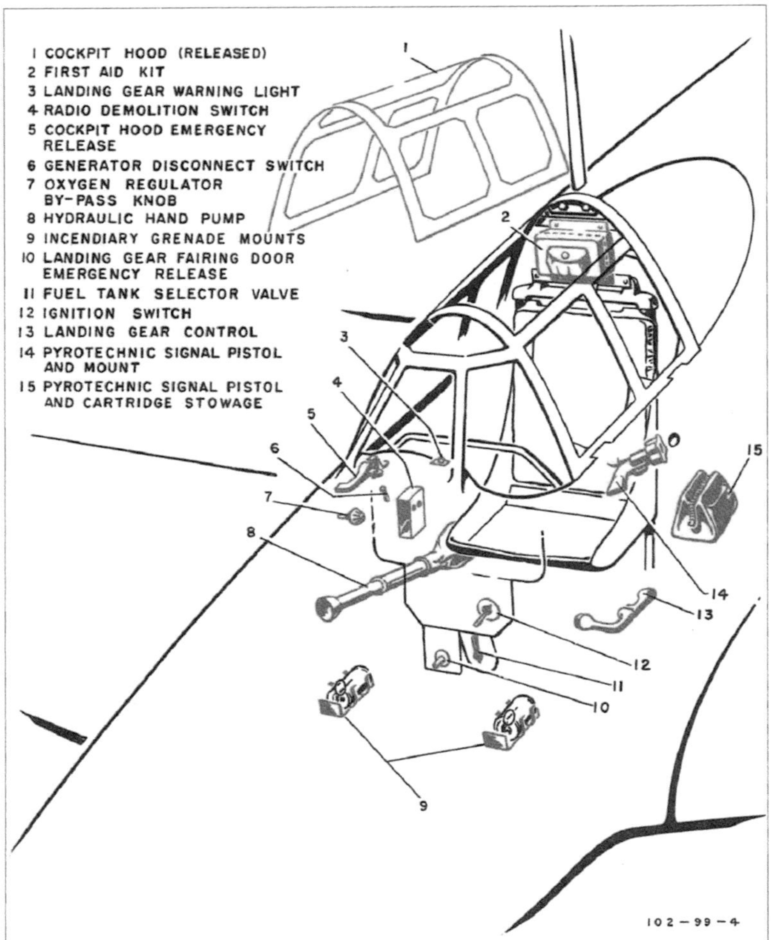

Figure 390—Emergency Equipment Diagram

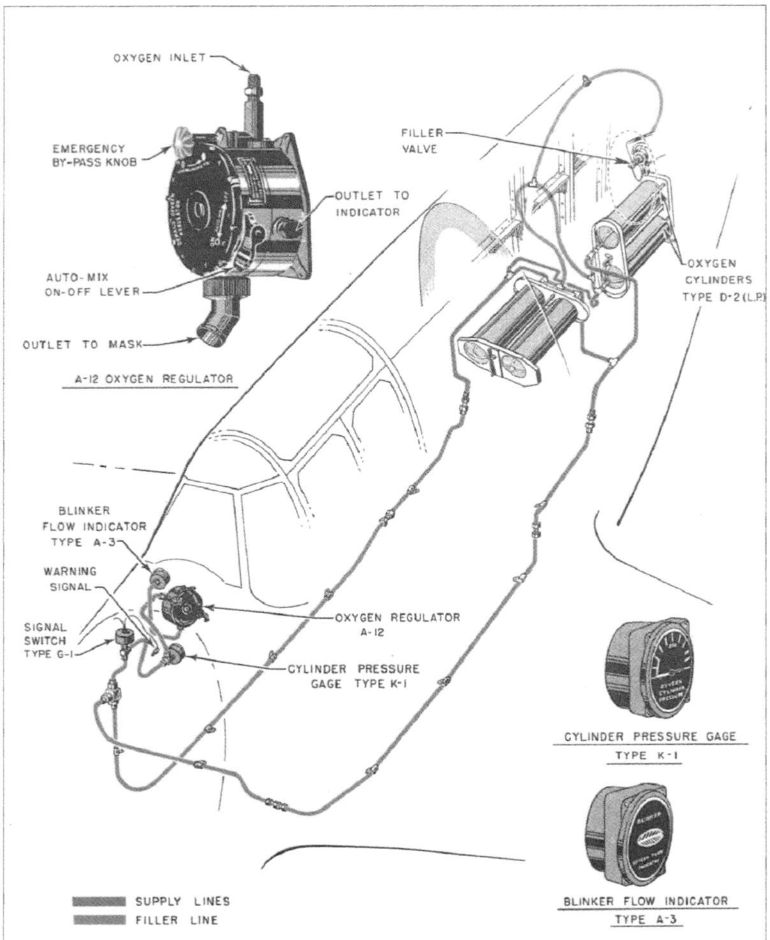

Figure 380—Oxygen System Diagram

Engine control instruments.

Manifold pressure (boost) gauge, coolant temperature gauge, rpm gauge, carburettor air inlet temperature gauge, oil temperature gauge and fuel pressure gauge.

Other instruments.

Oxygen pressure gauge, hydraulic pressure gauge, vacuum gauge and ammeter.

Electrical system.

24 volt, supplied from 28 volt, 100-Ampere generator driven by the engine. If the generator voltage fell below 26.5V, the system was supplied from a 24 volt battery of 34 Ah capacity. The battery was installed in the bay just behind pilot's seat armour. Additionally, the aircraft was fitted with a 26 V, 400 Hz alternator supplying power to the remote indicating compass. The electrical system included the supercharger control system, instrumentation, oil cooler and coolant radiator flap control system, landing gear warning system, engine starter, fuel boost pumps, machine gun triggers and gun sight, radio power supply, pitot heat and lighting. External lights included navigation lights and landing lights installed in the port wing.

Oxygen system.

The oxygen system consisted of two D-2 and two F-2 bottles and an AN6004 controller.

Equipment.

Above the instrument panel was an N-9 gunsight. Machine gun and bomb rack triggers were located on the control stick.

Radio equipment.

Radio equipment consisted of one transmitter and three receivers:

Communication – SCR-274-N and later SCR-522-A.

IFF (one of these): SCR-515 with AN-40 Antenna, SCR-535, SCR-695 with antenna AN-95.

Additionally, mostly for long distance ferry flights, a BC-1206 Beacon receiver (also called Detrola) was installed.

Radio equipment was accommodated in fuselage compartments behind the cockpit.

Armament.

P-51 B/Cs were armed with four 0.5 in (12.7 mm) Browning M2 machine guns. They are adjusted to converge fire with the centre line of airplane at 300 yd. Lateral adjustment of 1/2° is provided on either side, and guns are quickly removable through doors in the upper wing surface. Ammunition is fed to top sides of guns through stainless steel chutes. Cases and links are ejected through metal chutes in the lower wing skin. All four guns fire simultaneously, control being by a switch on the control stick. Electric heaters are attached to each gun, permitting them to function at temperatures as low as – 70°.

A removable, streamlined bomb rack was provided on each outer wing panel for bombs up to 500 lb, depth charges, chemical or auxiliary fuel tanks. Fusing of bombs is electrically controlled from the cockpit, and bombs can be dropped in a dive, level flight, or 30° climb. Sway braces are integral with the racks.

Dimensions

Span	37.03′
Length (overall)	32′ 2⅜″
Length (tail wheel on ground)	30′ 8″
Height (tail wheel on ground, propeller blade vertical at top)	12′ 6″
Wings	
Airfoil section	NAA-NACA low drag
Chord at root	8′ 8″
Chord near tip (215″ from fuselage centreline)	4′ 2″
Incidence (variable)	Approx. 1°
Sweepback	3° 35′ 32″
Dihedral (at 25% line)	5°
Stabilizer	
Span	13′ 2⅛″
Maximum chord	2′ 6″
Incidence	2°
Dihedral	none
Fuselage	
Width (max)	2′ 11″
Height (max)	6′ 3⁷⁄₁₆″
Length (without engine mount, front of heat exchanger to tip of tail)	24′ 2½″
Length (with engine mount, tip of propeller shaft to tip of tail	30′ 9″
Wings area (less ailerons)	220.55 sq ft
Aileronsarea (total)	12.64 sq ft
Flaps area (total)	32.6 sq ft
Stabilizer area (including elevators)	27.85 sq ft
Elevators area (including tabs)	13.05 sq ft
Elevator trim tabs area(total)	2.00 sq ft
Vertical stabilizer area	8.83 sq ft
Rudder area (including tabs)	10.25 sq ft
Rudder trim tabs area (total)	0.82 sq ft
Settings of Control Surfaces	
Stabilizer, fixed	2°
Vertical stabilizer, fixed offset (from fuselage centreline) Degrees In at max chord	1°
Landing Gear	
Type	Hydraulic, retractable, conventional 3-wheel
Tread	11′ 10″
Shock struts	Air-oil combination
Wheels (Magnesium alloy construction) diameter	27″
Tires (all-weather tread)	27″
Brakes	Disk, hydraulic
Oleo travel	8″
Tail Gear	
Type	Hydraulic, retractable, steerable
Shock strut	Air-oil combination
Wheel diameter	12.5″ × 4.5″
Tire (channel tread)	12.5″ × 4.5″
Oleo travel	7.50″

P-51B and P-51C Mustangs of the 361st Fighter Group with D-Day stripes, June 1944. (US National Archives)

Finish specification

Finish specification, excerpts from *Maintenance Manual P-51B&C Fighter Airplane, NAA, INC, Inglewood, Report No. NA-5692*, early 1944.

1. General Requirements

The finish for surfaces and parts is in accordance with Spec. 3-100, the markings are in accordance with Spec. 98-24105, and the insignia in accordance with Spec. 98-24102. Generally. The finish requirements may be summed up as follows:

Assembly	Finish Color
*Ailerons, Exterior	Camouflage
Ailerons, Interior and Interior Parts	No finish**
Castings, Forgings	To match
Cockpit, Antiglare	Flat bronze-green
Compartment, Pilot's	Yellow-green
Compartment, Landing Light	Fiat Black
*Cowling, Exterior	Camouflage
Cowling, Interior	No finish**
*Elevators, exterior	Camouflage
Elevators, interior	No finish**
Fairings, exterior	Camouflage
Fairings, interior	No finish**
*Fin, exterior	Camouflage
Fin, interior	No finish**
*Flaps, exterior	Camouflage
Flaps, interior	No finish**
*Fuselage, exterior	Camouflage
Fuselage, interior (except pilot's compartment)	No finish**
Horns, control	To match
Instrument Panel	Black
*landing gear	Camouflage
Propeller blades, both faces	Flat black
Propeller tips, both faces	Identification yellow
*Rudder, exterior	camouflage
Rudder, interior	No finish**
Pilot's seat	Bronze-green

*All camouflage painted surfaces are to be sanded and Pumiced until smooth to the finger tips. No. 400 sandpaper suitable for either wet or dry sanding may be used and all sanding strokes shall be made in the direction of normal flight. After sanding is completed, apply powdered pumice (Grade FFF) to a folded, dampened cheesecloth and rub the sanded surfaces in the direction of normal flight. Wash all pumiced areas clean ad free of all powdered pumice.

**Finish for corrosion prevention shall be in accordance with the detail sections listed below. Whenever the peculiarity of a particular part of assembly prohibits the use of the specific finish, the part or assembly shall be given as high a degree of protection as is consistent with its proper functioning and purpose.

2. Finish and Finish Material Specifications

The following are the AAF Specification numbers (except as noted) for the finish materials which are quoted in the following detail finish requirements:

Material	Specification No.
Cadmium plating	AN-QQ-P-4210
Camouflage finished for aircraft	24114
Chromium plating	AN-P-39
Cleaning aircraft surfaces	98-20007
Dope, cellulose nitrate, clear	AN-TT-D-514
Dope, pigmented nitrate camouflage	14106
Enamel, aircraft	3-98
Enamel, camouflage, quick drying	14109
Finishes, fire retardant	20023
Insignia for aircraft	98-24102
Lacquer, cellulose nitrate	AN-TT-L-51
Markings for aircraft	98-24105
Oil, linseed raw	JJJ-0-336
Primer, znic chromate	AN-TT-P656*
Protective finish, metal parts	3-100**
Protective treatment for magnesium alloys	98-20010
Sealer, wood, liquid	14113
Surfacer, wood, liquid	14115
Zinc plating	AN-P-32

*Zinc chromate primer may be tinted with a suitable tinting material.

**Yellow-green finish shall be formulated with a suitable tinting material.

P-51B-15-NA, s/n 42-106950 of the 354th FS, 355th FG at Steeple Morden. Originally assigned to Lt Clairborn H. Kinnard, Jr, the ship was nicknamed "Man O' War." Then aircraft was transferred to Lt Robert E. Hulderman, who renamed it "The Iowa Beaut", but still carried the ten kill marks compiled by its previous pilot. The "Beaut" went down on 11 September 1944, Capt Kevin G. Rafferty was KIA. (US National Archives)

NAA P-51B-1-NA, s/n 43-12201 during test at the factory. Aircraft Olive Drab uppersurfaces and Neutral Grey undersurfaces. Note very worn camouflage.

One of the first Mustang III delivered to RAF, serial FX864 (P-51B-1-NA, s/n 42-12316). Aircraft in RAF camouflage –Dark Green, Brown Earth and Sky with US delivery markings.

P-51B-1-NA, s/n 43-12434, AJ-T, "Short-fuse Sallee", usually flown by Capt. Richard Turner of 356th FS, 354th FG, 1944, UK. Aircraft Olive Drab uppersurfaces with Neutral Grey undersurfaces.

P-51B-1-NA, S/n 43-12152, GQ-S, "Killer". Personal aircraft of Capt. W. Stephens, 335th FS, 354th FG, Lashenden, May 1944. Aircraft Olive Drab uppersurfaces with Neutral Grey undersurfaces. Note that this aircraft received lower engine cowlings from a later Mustang version, with sand filter inlets.

P-51B-5-NA, s/n 43-7058, 261, "Jeanne III" of 26th FS, 51st FG. Aircraft Olive Drab uppersurfaces and Neutral Grey undersurfaces. Note very worn camouflage and older version of the radio set. Aircraft equipped with Bazooka launchers.

P-51B-7-NA, (built as P-51B-5-NA) s/n 43-6913, VF-T, "Shangri-La". Personal aircraft of Cpt. Dominic S. Gentile of 335th FS, 4th FG. Debden, UK, March 1944. Aircraft Olive Drab uppersurfaces with Neutral Metal undersurfaces.

P-51B-5-NA, s/n 43-6898, QP-J, "The Deacon", personal aircraft of Maj. Howard D. Hively, June 1944. Aircraft Olive Drab uppersurfaces with Neutral Grey undersufraces.

P-51B-10-NA, s/n 42-106647, C3+D, "BigMac Junior" of 382nd FS, 363rd FG. Personal aircraft of Capt. John R. Brown, May 1944. Aircraft natural metal overall with Olive Drab antiglare panel.

P-51B-15-NA, s/n 42-106872, PE-T, "Patty Ann II". Personal aircraft of Lt. John F Thornell Jr. 328th FS, 352nd FG, Bodney, UK, summer 1944. Aircraft natural metal overall with blue nose.

P-51C-1-NT, s/n 42-103896, 1078, of 530th FS, 311th FG China, 1944. Aircraft natural metal with Olive Drab antiglare panel.

P-51C-5-NT, s/n 42-103363, SX-M, "Lucky Leaky II" used as "hack" in 352nd FG, 353rd. Lt. LeRoy O. Pletz suffered an engine failure on 2 May 1945 and forced landed. Aircraft natural metal with Olive Drab antiglare panel. Note fin fillet and tail warning radar antenna on the fin.

P-51C-10-NT, s/n 42-103867, No. 52, 867, piloted by Lt Col "Chet" Sluder of 318th FS, 325th FG, June 1944. Aircraft natural metal with Olive Drab antiglare panel, red nose and black and yellow chequered tail surfaces.

P-51C-10-NT, s/n 42-103956, 7, "Miss-Pelt". Personal aircraft of Lt. Clarence D. Lester, 100th FS, 332nd FG. Aircraft natural metal with Olive Drab antiglare panel and red unit markings. Yellow bands only on wing uppersurfaces.

P-51B (s/n unknown), T9-PK, aircraft tested by Luftwaffe 1944. Aircraft natural metal overall with black antiglare panel.

P-51C-11-NT, s/n 44-10816, 278, "Evalina" of 51st FG. Personal aircraft of 1st Lt. Strawbridge, January 1945. Aircraft natural metal with Olive Drab antiglare panel.

P-51C-11-NT, s/n 44-10816, 278, "Evalina" in Japanese hands.

F-6C-11-NT, s/n 44-11102, 598, "Duchess" of 23rd FG, 118th TRS, China 1944. Usually flown by 1st Lt Ray Crowell. Aircraft natural metal with Olive Drab antiglare panel.

F-6C-5-NT, s/n 42-103624, 599. Aircraft natural metal with Olive Drab antiglare panel. It was the first 118th TRS airplane to be painted with the black lightning markings, Chengkung, China, October 1944.

F-6C, built as P-51C-10-NT, s/n 44-10894, R7+E of GR II/33, Luxeuil, 1945, Armée de l'Air (French Air Force). Aircraft natural metal with Olive Drab antiglare panel.

Mustang III, serial FX893, built as P-51B-1-NA, s/n 43-12382, during tests with British rocket rails. Aircraft in standard RAF camouflage of Dark Green, Ocean Grey and Medium Sea Grey. Standard RAF markings of the period.

Mustang III, serial FX865, (P-51B-1-NA, s/n 43-12317), PK+X of 315 Polish Squadron, June 1944. Standard RAF camouflage and markings.

Mustang III, serial FX865, (P-51B-1-NA, s/n 43-12317), YT-P of 65 Squadron RAF, August 1944, usually flown by F/Lt John, "Maxwell" Wauchope. Note that this P-51B-1-NA received sand air filters under engine, during overhaul. Standard RAF camouflage and markings.

Front of the Mustang III with antiglare panel.

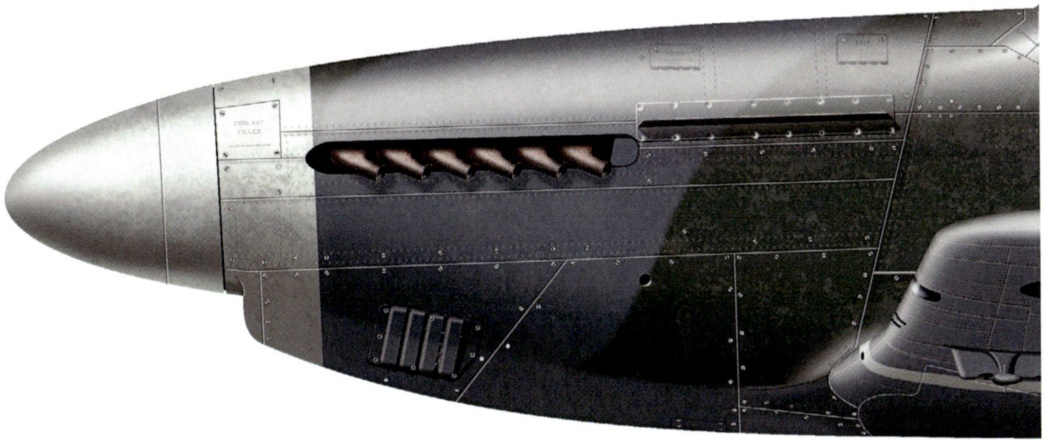

Mustang III, serial FB382, (P-51C-5-NT, s/n 42 – 103532), PK+G of 315 Polish Squadron, personal aircraft of S/Ldr Eugeniusz Horbaczewski, summer 1944. Standard RAF camouflage and markings.

Mustang III, serial HB866, (P-51C-5-NT, s/n 42-103715), JZ. Personal aircraft of W/Cdr Jan Zumbach when he led 2nd Polish Wing (No. 133 Wing). Standard RAF camouflage and markings.

Mustang III, serial FB182, built as P-51C-1-NT, s/n 42 – 103076 and then rebuilt to reconnaissance version. Aircraft belonged to 541 Squadron, June/July 1945. Aircraft PRU Blue overall with RAF markings and D-Day stripes.

Mustang III, (P-51C-10-NT, s/n 44-10823), serial KH466, 9G-Y of 441 Squadron RCAF, UK 1944. Aircraft in standard RAF camouflage. Note traces of the antiglare panel behind the exhaust.

Mustang III, (P-51C-10-NT, s/n 44-11130), serial KH618, CV-J of 3 Squadron RAAF, Italy 1944. Aircraft in standard RAF camouflage.

P-51B comparison.

P-51B (Mustang Mk III) / Fw 190 A-8

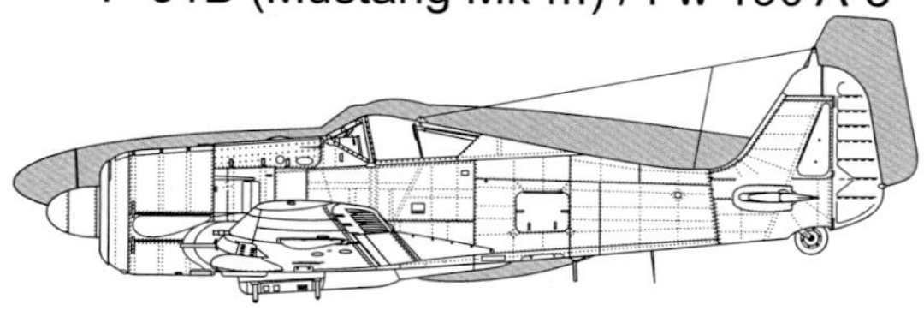

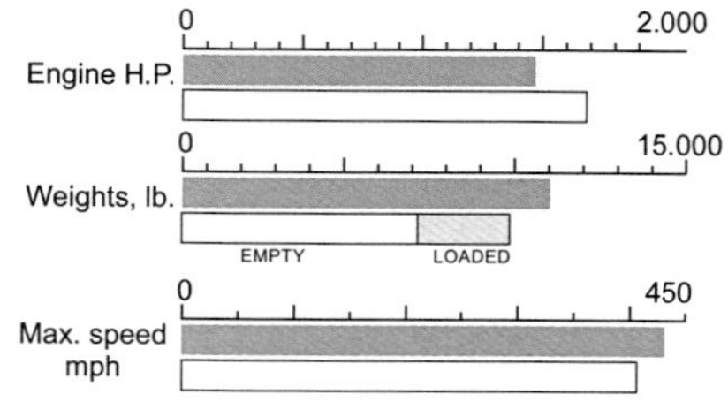

P-51B (Mustang Mk III) / A6M5 Zero

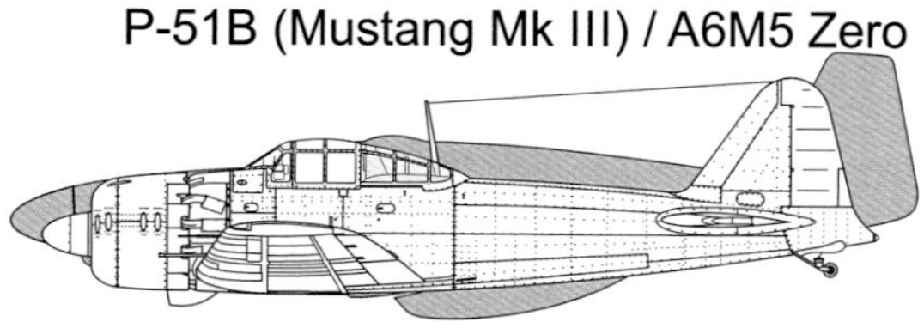

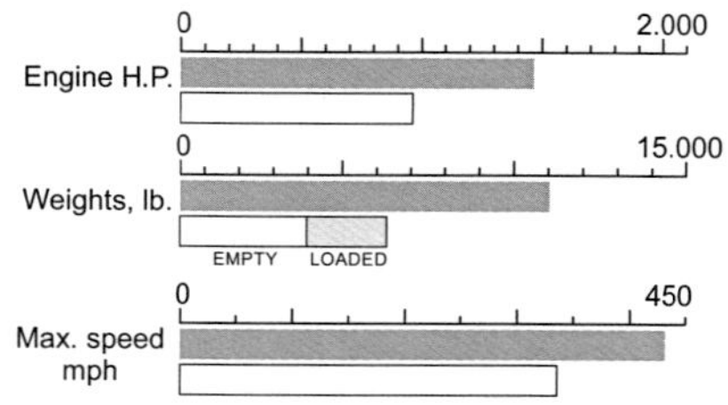

P-51B (Mustang Mk III) / Spitfire IXe

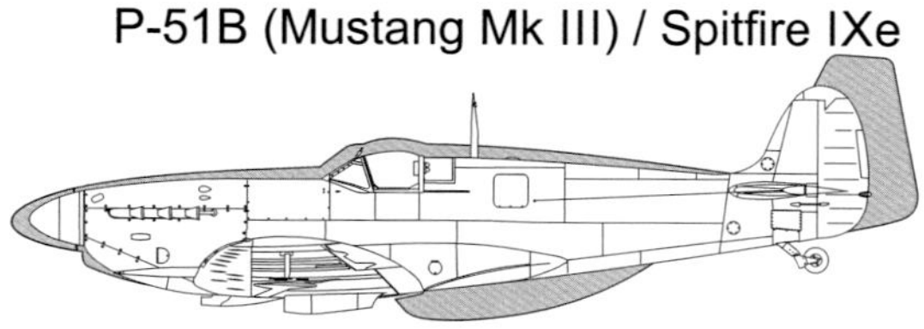

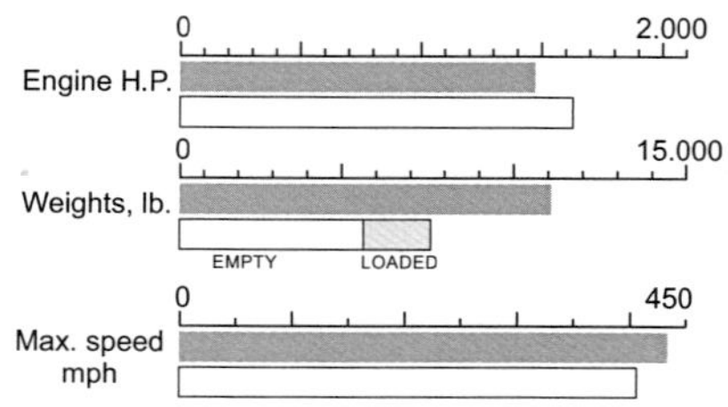

P-51B (Mustang Mk III) / Bf 109 G-6

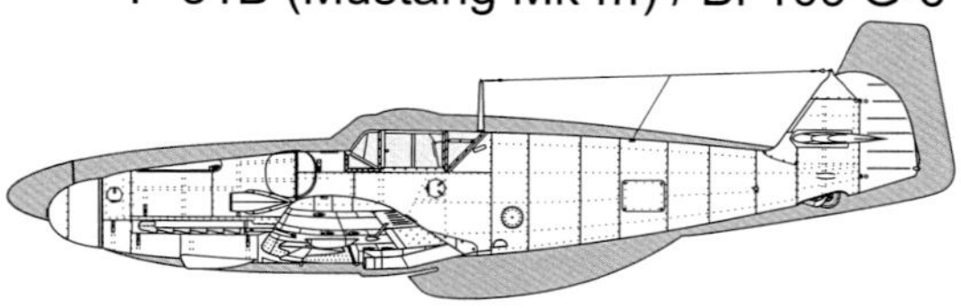

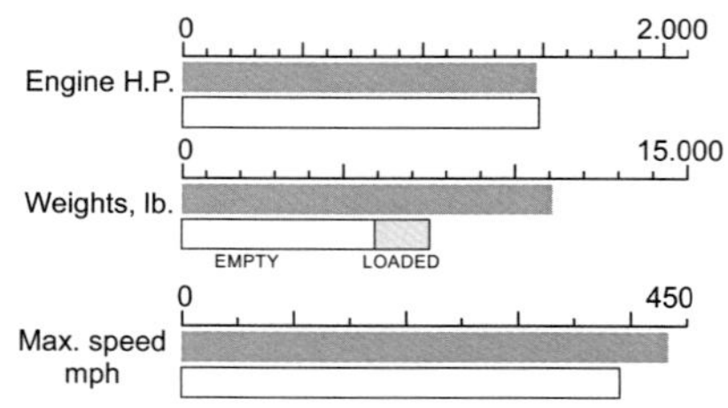

P-51B (Mustang Mk III) / P-47D-25

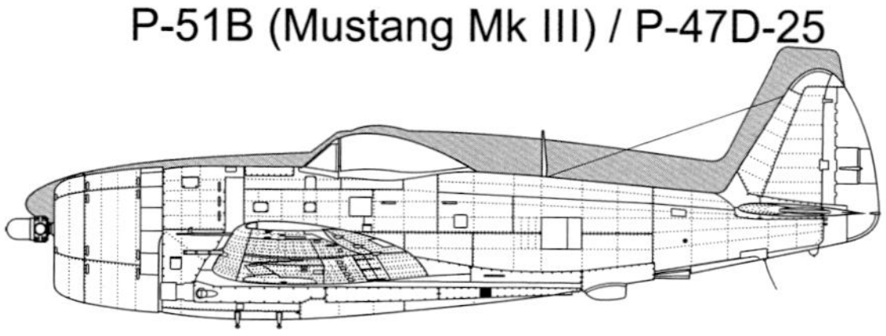

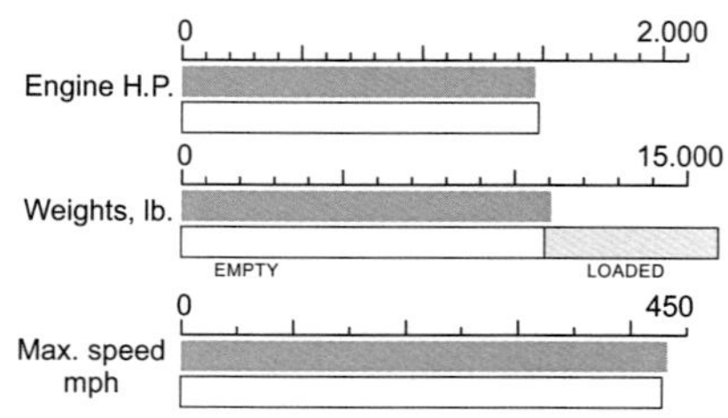

P-51B (Mustang Mk III) / Macchi MC.205

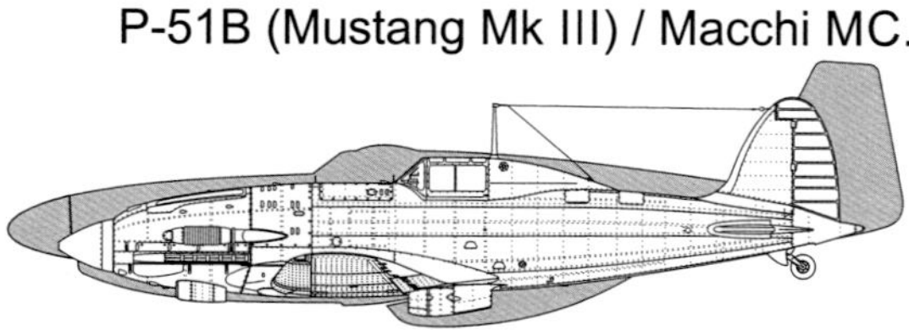

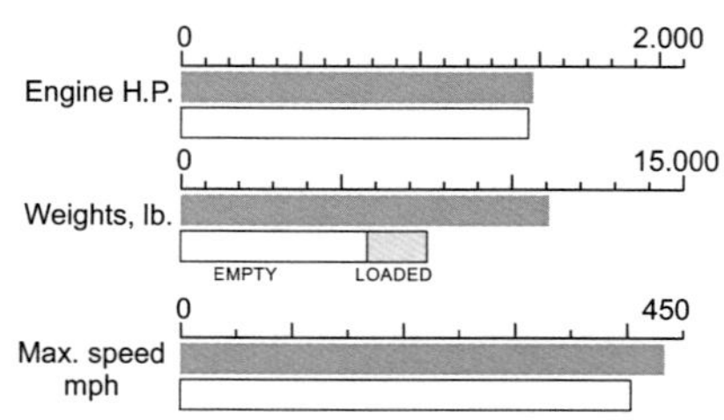

P-51B high speed performance. Gross weight ~ 8,500 lbs. 3,000 rpm. V-1650-3 and V-1650-7 engines Boost shown in inches of HG. P-51D-15-NA, s/n 44-15342 with racks. Data from official USAAF documents.

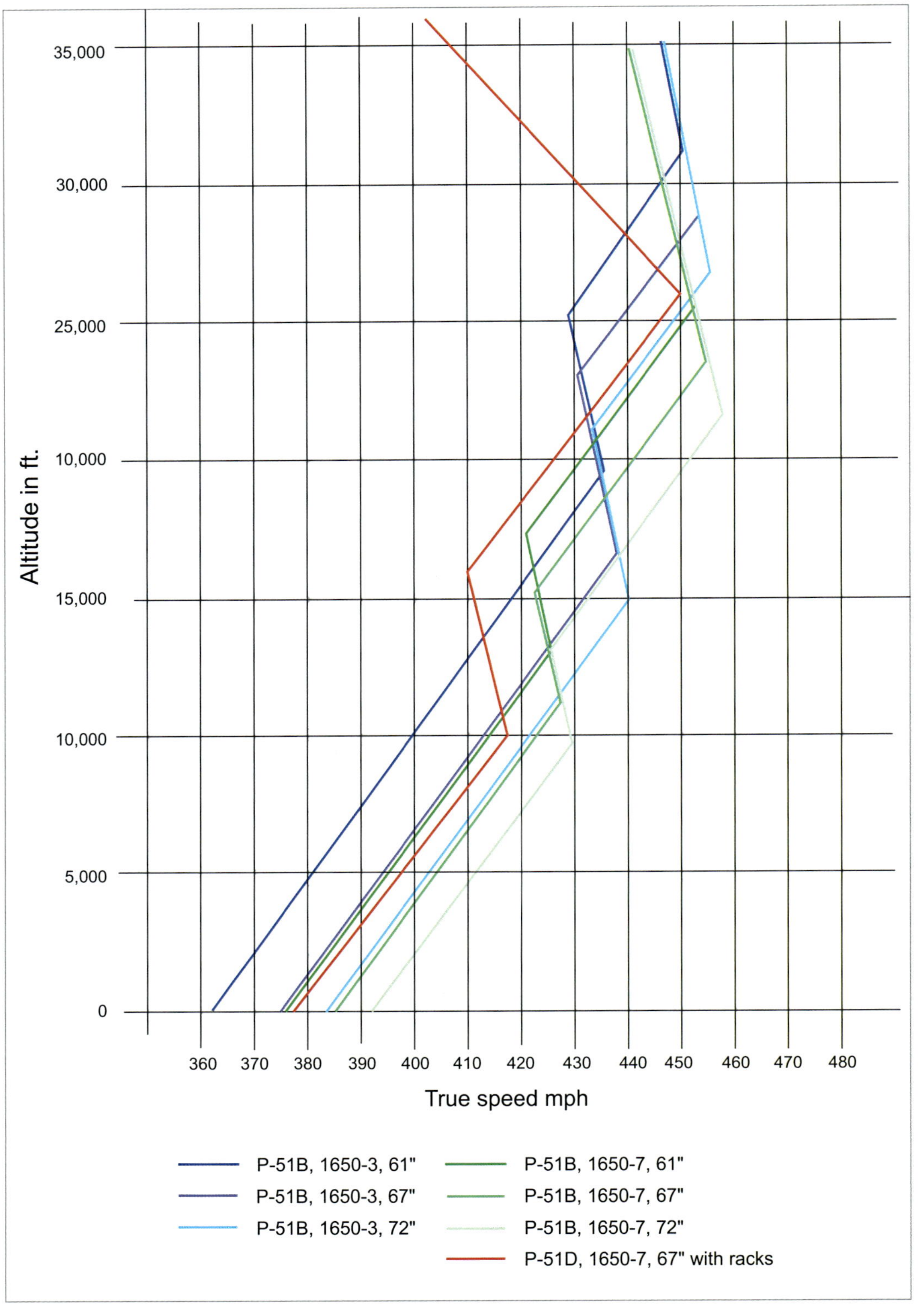

USAAF aircraft comparison data from official document by USAAF, 22 June 1944

Aircraft	Gross Weight lb.	Rate of Climb fpm	Limit Diving Speed (indicated) mpf	Radius of Turn ft.	Max rate of roll at 400 mph deg/sec
P-38J	15,000	2,960	420	838	39 120 (with boost)
P-47	13,000	2,165	500	990	63
P-51B	9,000	3,000	505	883	78
P-80A	10,000	5,800	580	1,170	-

Detail Photos

General view

P-51C-10-NT, s/n 42-103293, converted to dual control aircraft, registered as NL251MX. (R. Bourlier)

Colour wartime photo of P-51B-5-NA, s/n43-7058, 261, "Jeanne III" of 26th FS, 51st FG. Aircraft with added fuselage tank. (Jack Canary via R. Bourlier)

F-6C-5-NT, s/n 42-103506 of 118th TRS during maintenance engine run at Chengkung, China. (Jack Canary via R. Bourlier)

P-51B Mustang "Berlin Express" (N-515ZB). The restored fighter is based around the remains of P-51B-15-NA s/n 43-24837. This Mustang flew with the 363rd Fighter Group. (M. Wasielewski)

P-51C Mustang Tuskegee Airmen, registered N61429, saw service stateside as a trainer in 1945, then declared surplus after the war ended. (R. Boulier)

P-51B-10-NA, "Princess Elizabeth", s/n 42-106449. (J. Kightly)

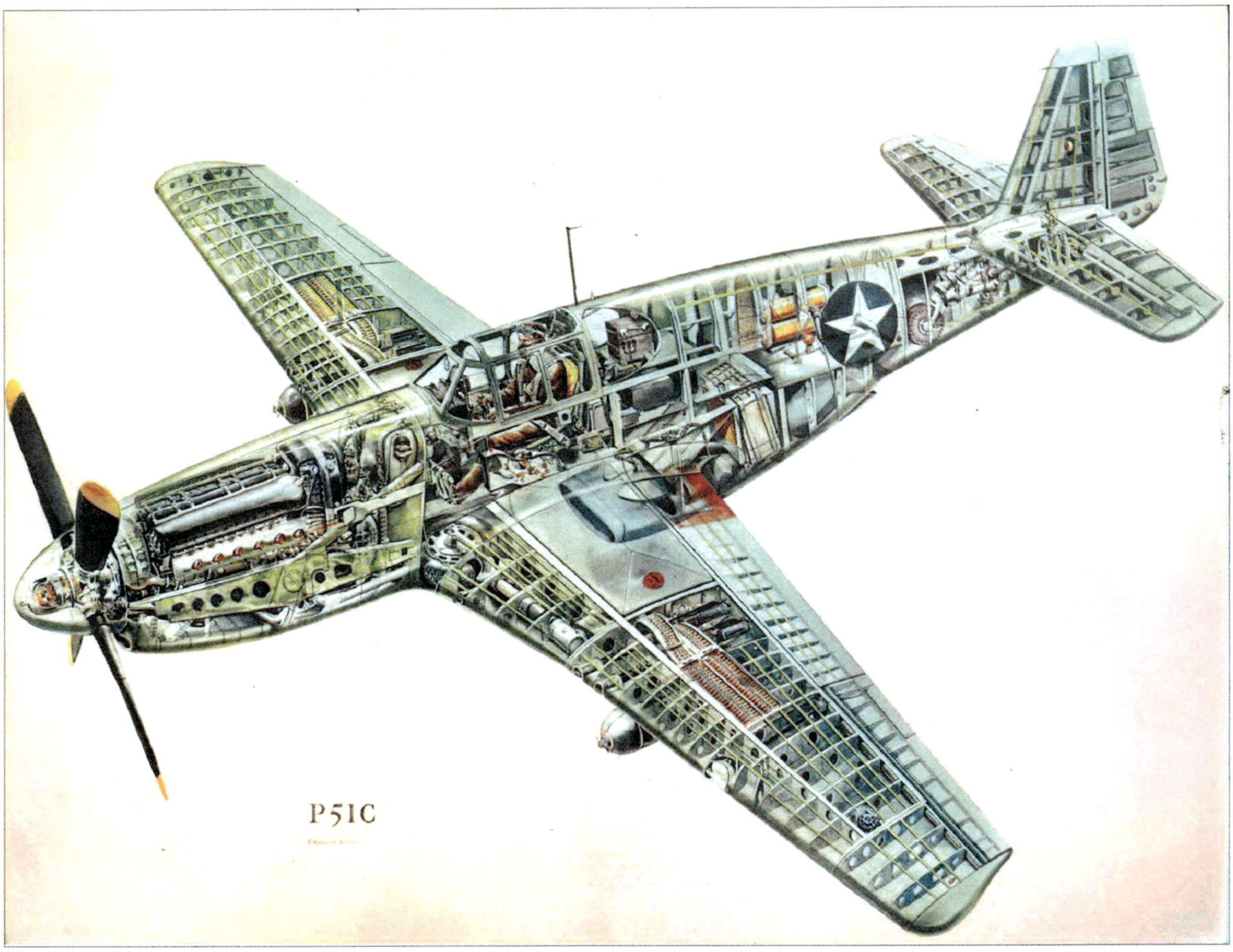

Above: *P-51B cutaway drawnig published in Maintenance Manual P-51B&C, Report No. NA-5692.*

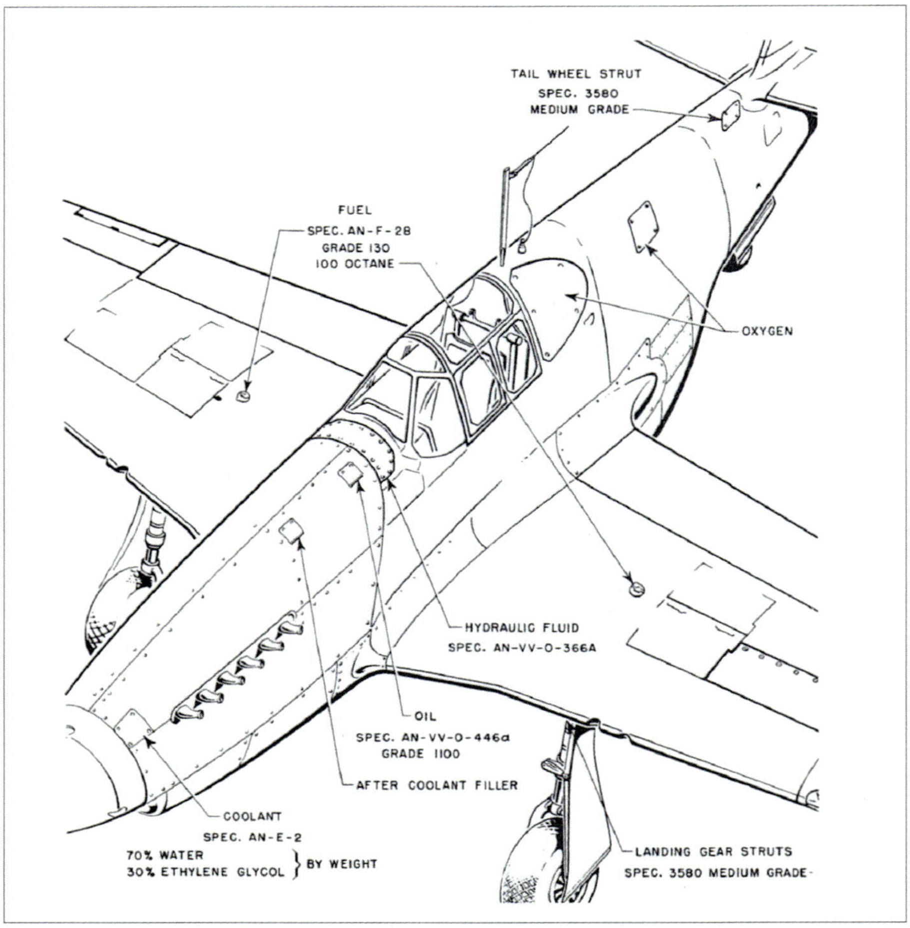

Servicing diagram from Maintenance Manual P-51B&C.

P-51B-5-NA, s/n 43-7106, 109 of 76th FS at Suichuan, China between December 1944 and January 1945. (via R. Bourlier)

P-51C-10-NT, s/n 43-25185, 586 of118th TRS. Revetment at Suichuan fighter base, January 1945. This airplane was shot down by AA over Lungwa airfield, Shanghai, China, 20 January 1945. The Pilot, 2nd Lt. Glenn J. Geyer, bailed out and was rescued by Chinese guerillas. (Jack Canary via R. Bourlier)

Access and inspections panels. Keys see opposite page. Drawing from Maintenance Manual P-51B&C.

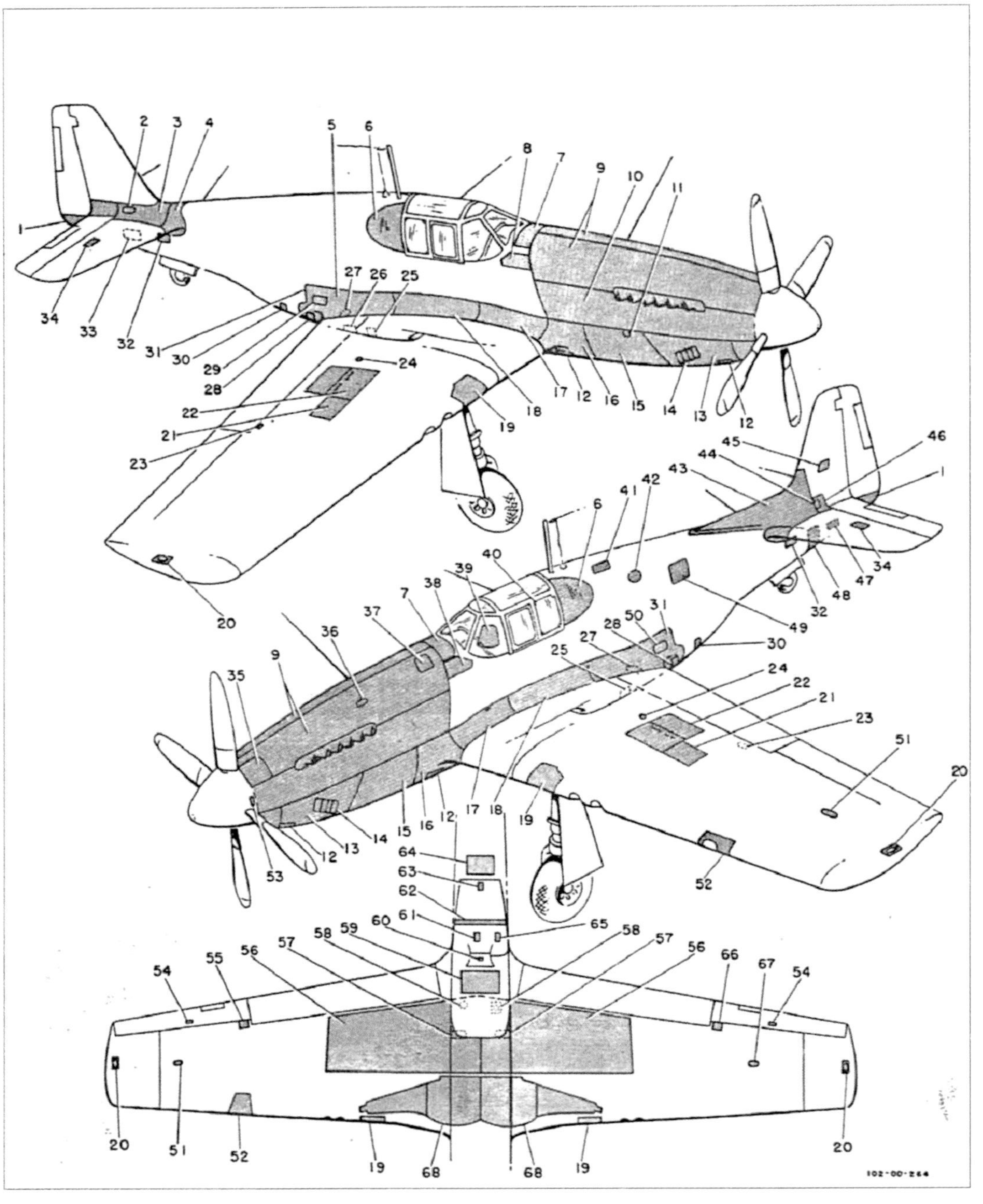

Remains of the P-51B "Hangar Queen" at 353rd FG base, being salvaged on 4 September 1944 fuselage with many panles removed. Oil tank is visible. Note also RAF serial FX8?? (US National Archives)

1. Rudder Lower Hinge Access Door
2. Vertical Stabilizer Aft Right-hand Fairing
3. Vertical Stabilizer Forward Fairing
4. Fuselage to Horizontal Stabilizer Fairing
5. Aft Wing to Fuselage Fairing
6. Radio Shelf and Battery Access Window
7. Hydraulic Reservoir Access Door
8. Oxygen Lines and Instruments
9. Upper Engine Access Cowling
10. Side Engine Access Cowling
11. Engine Crank Access Hole
*12. Engine Heating Access Door
13. Lower Forward Engine Access Cowling
*14. Carburettor Air Filter Access Door
15. Lower Intermediate Engine Access Cowling
16. Lower Aft Engine Access Cowling
17. Forward Wing to Fuselage Fairing
18. Intermediate Wing to Fuselage Fairing
19. Main Landing Gear Pivot Shaft Access Door
20. Running Light Access Plate
21. Ammunition Bay Access Door
22. Gun Bay Access Door
23. Aileron Cable Turnbackle Inspection
24. Wing Fuel Tank Filler Cap
25. Front Scoop Attachment Bolts Access Door
26. Oil Radiator Line Access Door
27. Aftercooler Line Hose Access Door
28. Radiator Cover Bolts Access Door
29. Extenal Power Plug Access Cover
30. Radiator Cover Attachment Bolts Access Door
31. Radiator Cover Assembly
32. Tail Gear Down-lock Access Door
33. Tail Gear Up-latch Access Door
34. Elevator Trim Tab Actuating Drum Access Door
35. Coolant Tank filler Neck Access Door
36. Aftercooler Tank Access Door
37. Oil Tank Filler Neck Access Door
38. Engine Controls and Instruments Access Door
*39. Clear Vision Panel
40. Cockpit Enclosure Access Handle
**41. Battery Access Door
**42. Fuselage Fuel Tank Filler Cap
***43. Dorsal Fin Installation
44. Rudder Trim Tab Cable Rollers
45. Rudder Trim Tab Actuating Cable Drum
46. Vertical Stabilizer Aft Left-hand Fairing
47. Rudder Bellcrank Access Door
48. Tail Gear Up-latch and Actuating Strut Access Door
49. Oxygen Cylinders and Filler Valve Access Door
50. Fuselage Fuel Tank Vent Line Access Door
51. Remote-reading Compass Access Door
52. Landing Light Access Door
53. Propeller Governor Access Door
*54. Aileron Center Hinge Access Door
55. Aileron Trim Tab Actuating Drum
56. Fuel Tank Doors
57. Fuel Booster Pump Access Door
58. Fuel Tank Drain Cock Access Door
59. Oil Radiator Access Door
60. Oil Radiator Rear Scoop Actuating Rod Access Plate
61. Coolant Drain Access Door
62. Rear Scoop Hinge Bolts Access Door
63. Rear Scoop Actuating Rod Access Plate
64. Control Cable and Oxygen Cylinder Access Door
65. Aftercooler Drain Access Door
66. Aileron Boost Tab Actuating Fitting Access Door
67. Remote Contactor Mast Access Door
68. Wheel Well Fairing Door

*P-51C and Late P-51B Airplanes Only.
***Late P-51C Airplanes Only.
**Late P-51C and P-51B Airplanes Only.

P-51B during overhaul after arrival in the UK. Note how panels are sealed for sea transport. (US National Archives)

Fuselage

Above: P-51B-5-NA, s/n 43-6845, YF-X of the 358th FS 355th FG after belly landing. Note exhaust cover removed and fuselage tank added after production (white cross on the fuselage). (US National Archives)

Two drawings from Spare Parts Catalog showing fuselage construction.

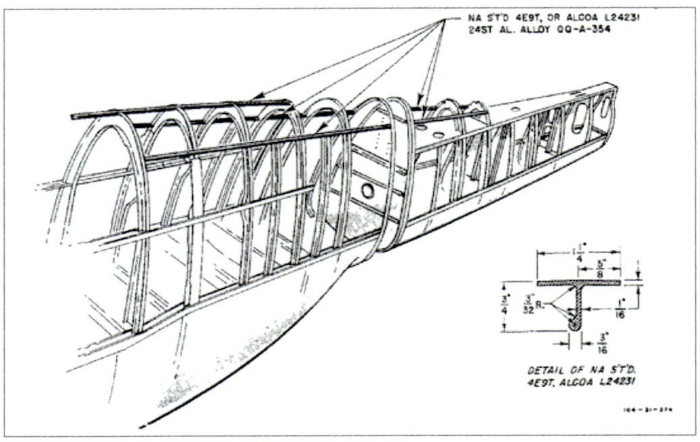

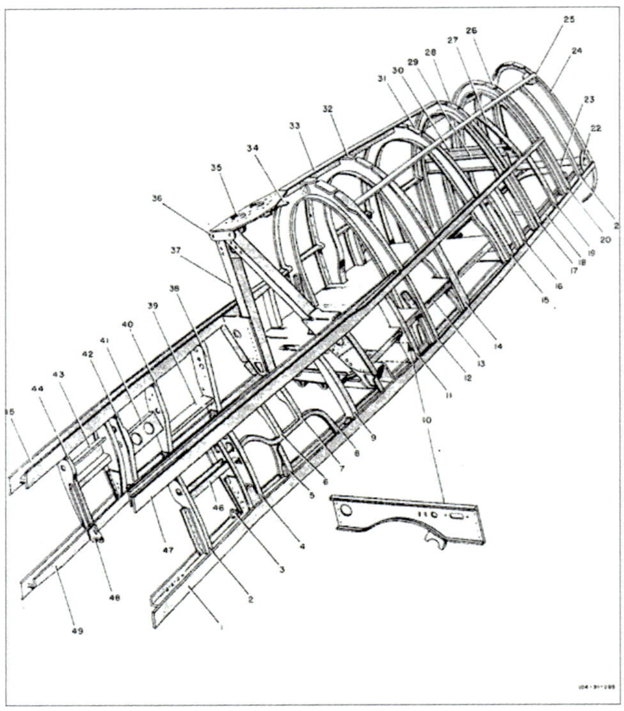

Rear, starboard side of the P-51B fuselage. (via R. Panek)

Starboard side of the fuselage just behind the cockpit. (via R. Panek)

Port side of the fuselage. Note fuselage fuel filler cap (red) and ground jack below (black). (via R. Panek)

P-51B fuselage during overhaul. (Bogdan Rogoziński)

Radiator air scoop. Photo from Maintenance Manual P-51B&C.

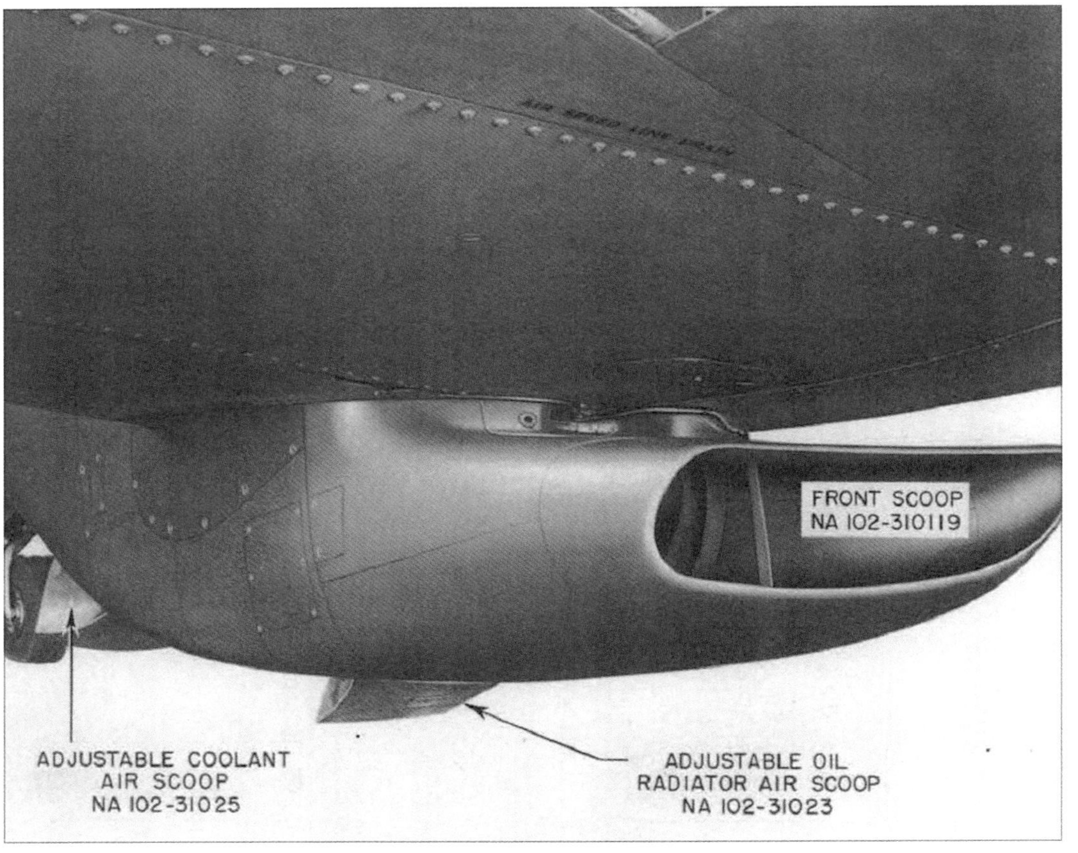

P-51B-5-NA, s/n 43-6876, SX-5 of 352nd FS, 353rd FG, 8th AF. Aircraft declared as 'War Weary' and sent to the "Clobber College". Damage is from a taxi accident on 27 February 1945 while being piloted by Maj. William M. Long. (US National Archives)

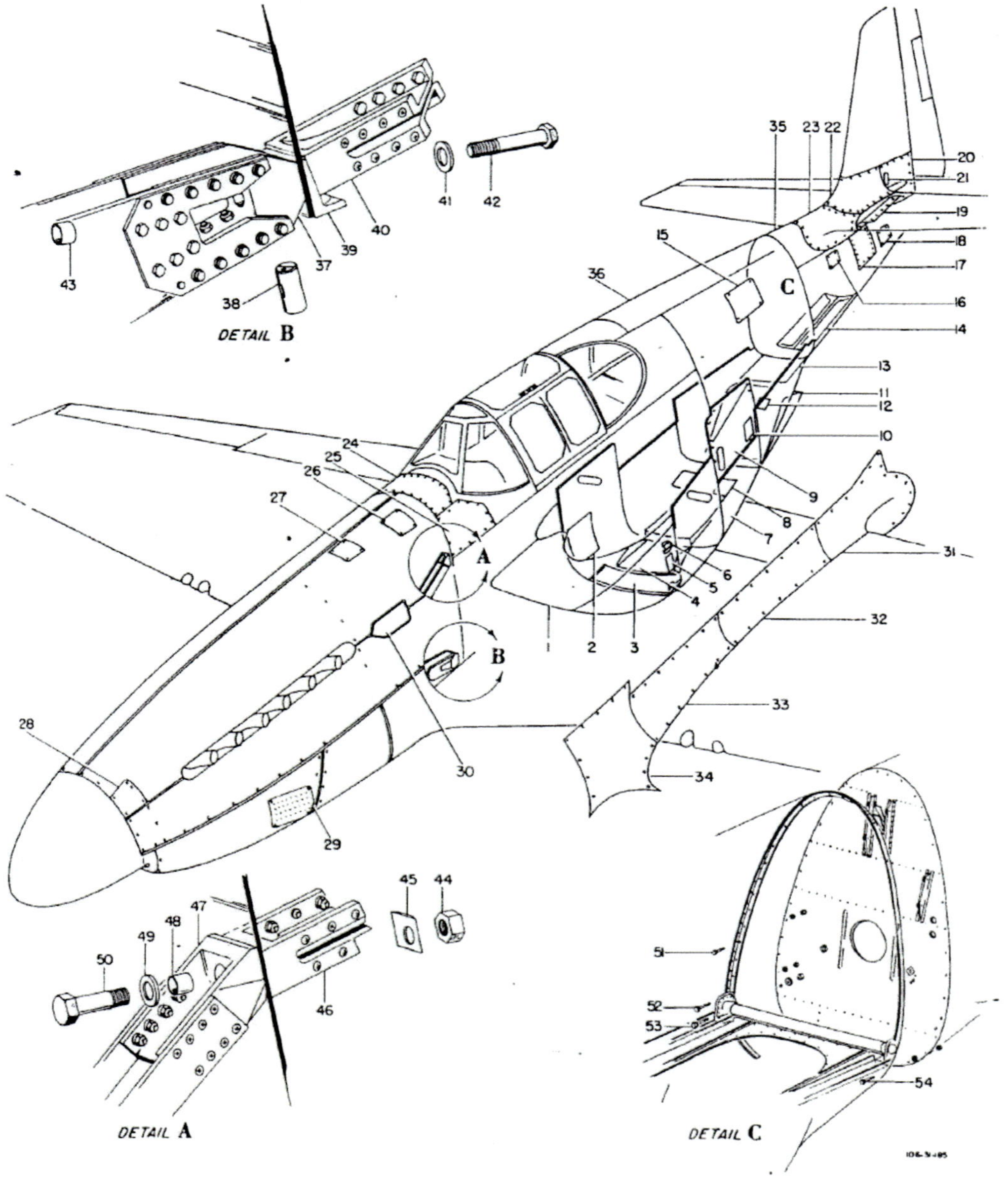

Fuselage cover fillets and sectional attachments for P-51B-1 and P-51B-5 without fuselage fuel tank installed. (Maintenance Manual P-51B&C)

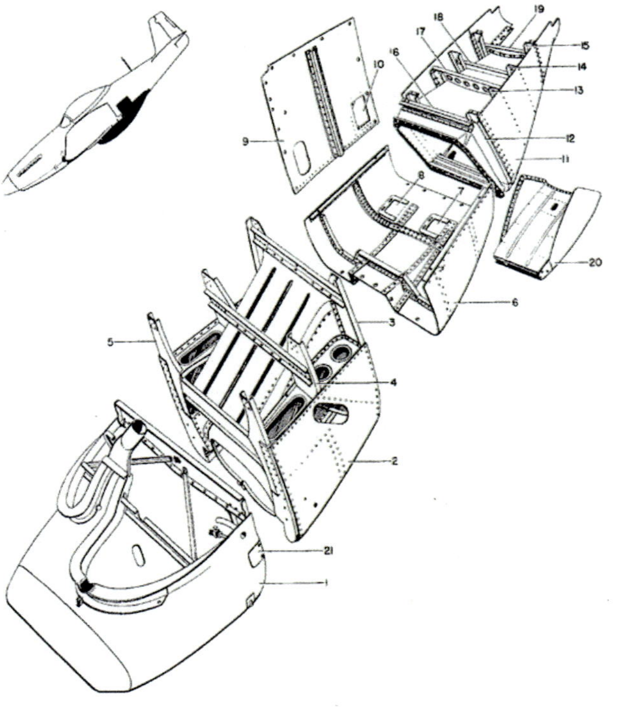

P-51B/C, radiator air scoop details. (Maintenance Manual P-51B&C)

P-51B, radiator air scoop with panels removed. (Bogdan Rogoziński)

Fuel, oil and coolant drains.
Maintenance Manual P-51B&C)

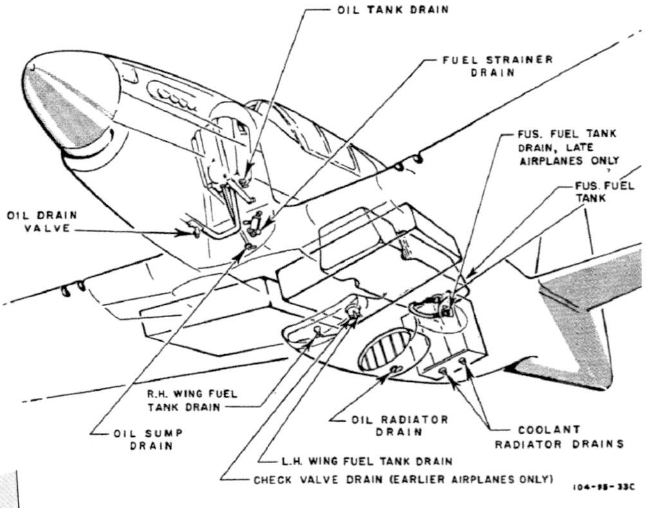

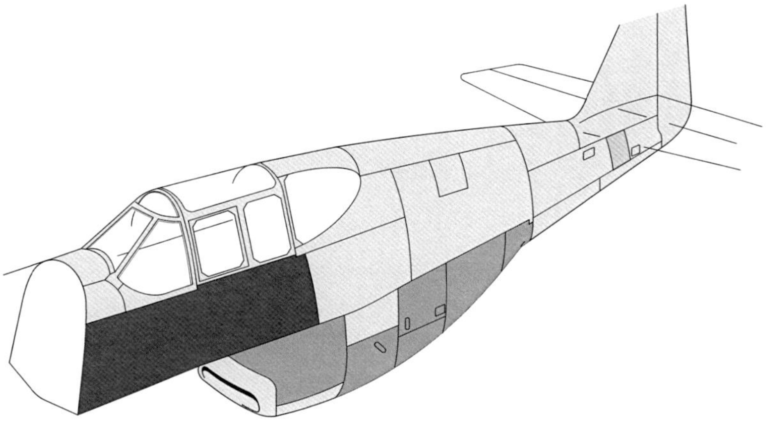

Fuselage skin arrangement of P-51B/C.
(based on Maintenance Manual P-51B&C)

.081 - INCH THICK 24ST ALCAD SHEET

.064 - INCH THICK 24ST ALCAD SHEET

.051 - INCH THICK 24ST ALCAD SHEET

.040 - INCH THICK 24ST ALCAD SHEET

.032 - INCH THICK 24ST ALCAD SHEET

Aircraft covers.
Upper drawing valid for P-51B-1.
Two lower drawings valid for later versions.
(Airplane Parts Catalog)

Wing

P-51C-10-NT, s/n 43-25050 assigned to Lt. Esteban A. Terrats of the 503rd FSquadron, 339th FG. Note the shape of the Mustang wings. (US National Archives)

Preserved P-51C in flight showing upperviews of the wings. (R. Bourlier)

P-51B/C wing structure.

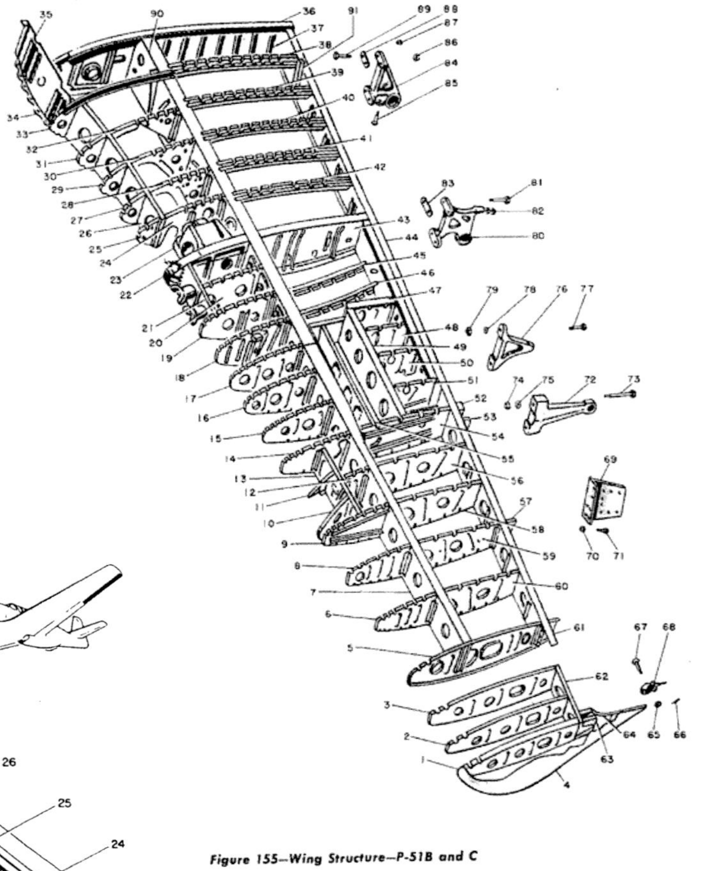

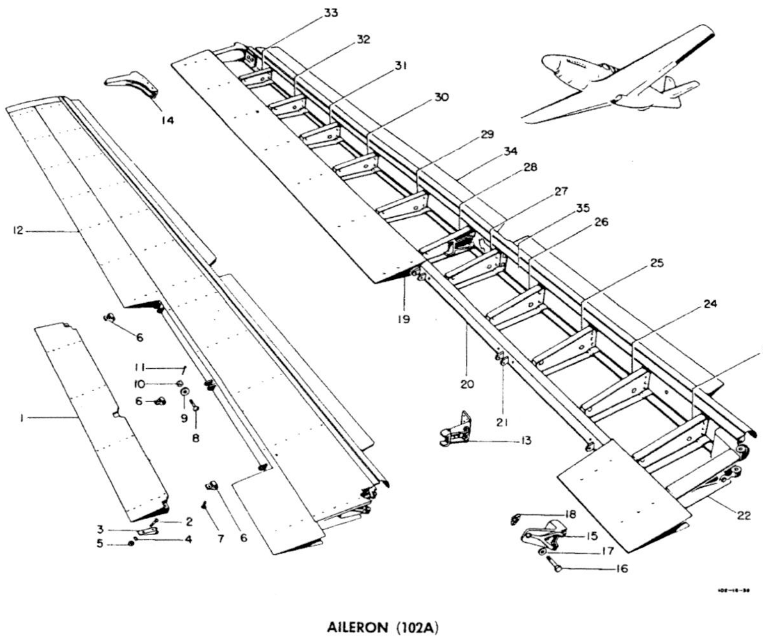

Above: *Aileron construction of P-51B-1-NA, model 102A.*

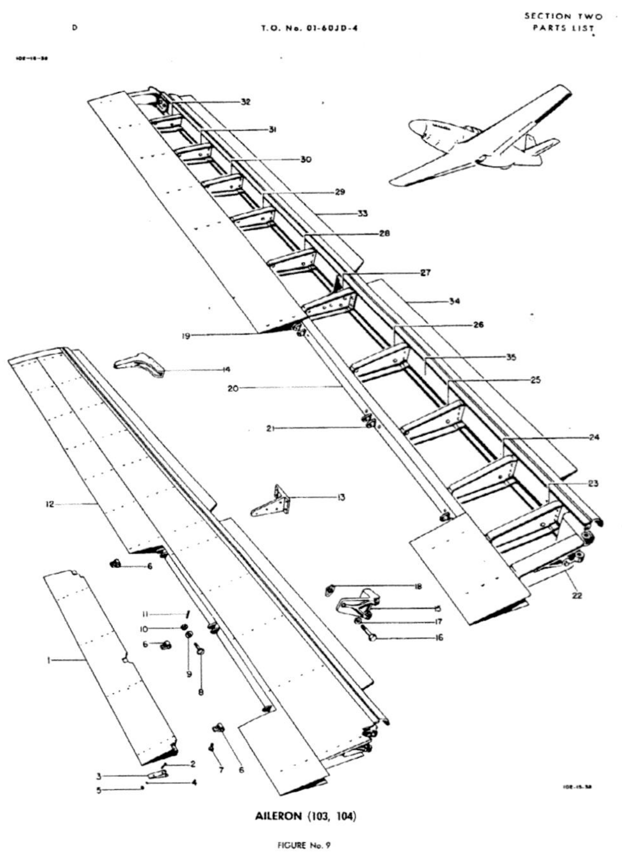

Right: *Aileron construction of P-51B/C, models 103, 104 & 111. All drawings from Airplane Part Catalog.*

P-51C-10-NT, s/n 42-103896 "Princess" of 530th FS, 311th FG. (US National Archives)

Left: Two photo sof the Pitot tube and underwing details.

Below: Upperside wing reinforcement. (All via R. Panek)

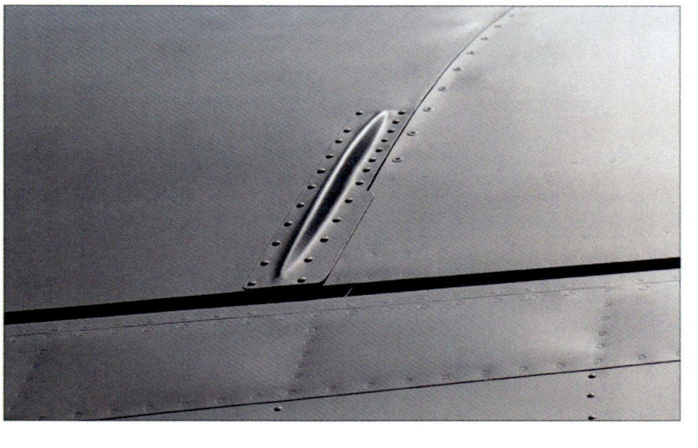

Starboard wing tip and navigation lamp.

Starboard, inner part of the flap.

Port aileron trim tab. (all via R. Panek)

Wing details, drawing from Parts Catalog.

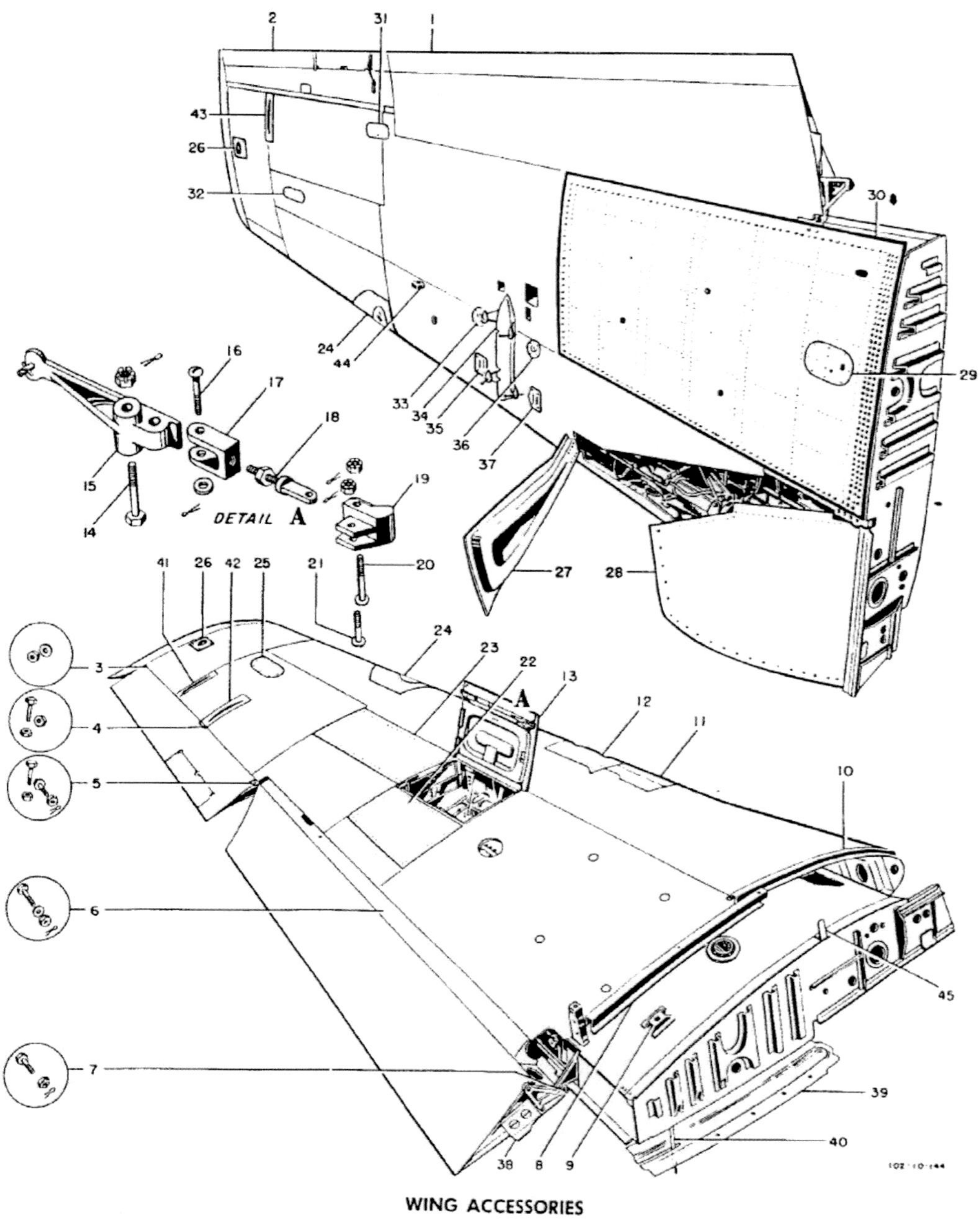

WING ACCESSORIES

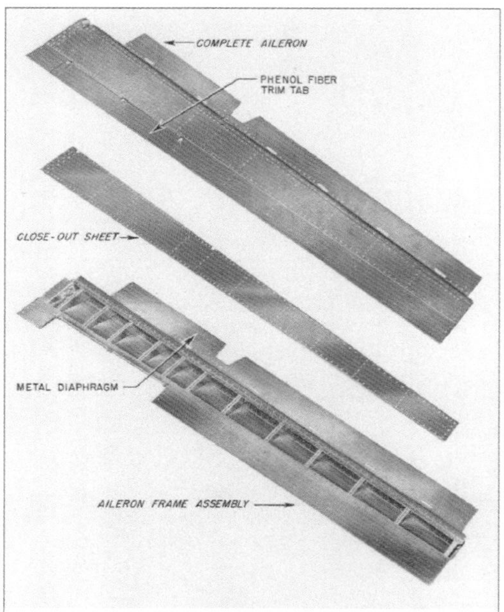

Figure 52—Aileron

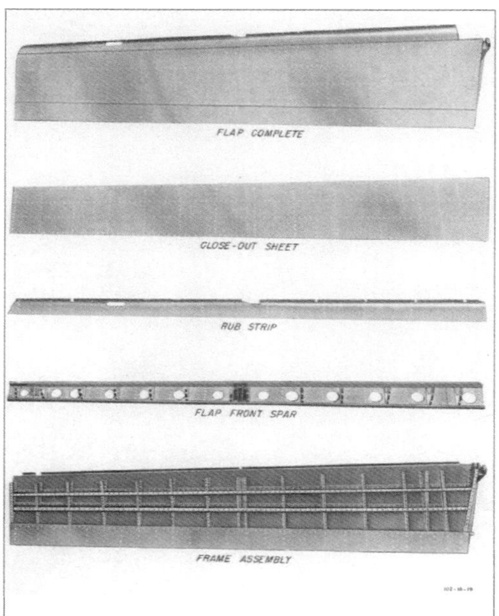

Figure 53—Wing Flaps

Left photo: *Aileron construction.*

Right photo: *Wing flap constructiom. (Both Erection and Maintenance Instructions)*

P-51B/C wing surface skins. (Airplane Spare Catalog)

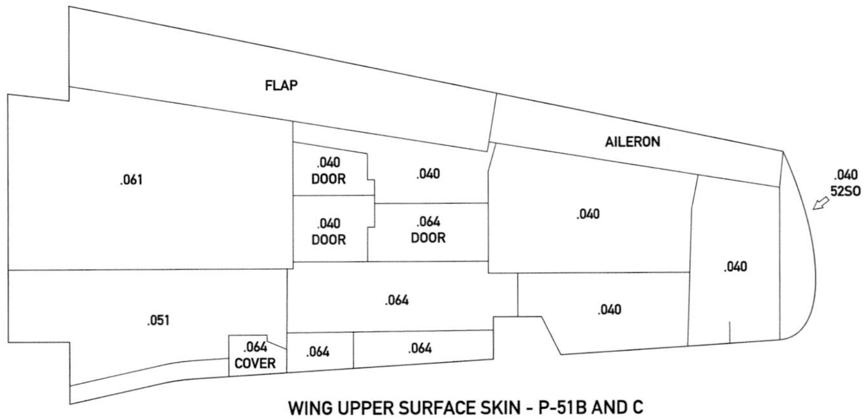

WING UPPER SURFACE SKIN - P-51B AND C

NOTE:
ALL SKIN IS 24ST ALCAD EXCEPT AS NOTED. DECIMAL FRACTIONS INDICATE SKIN THICKNESS IN INCHES

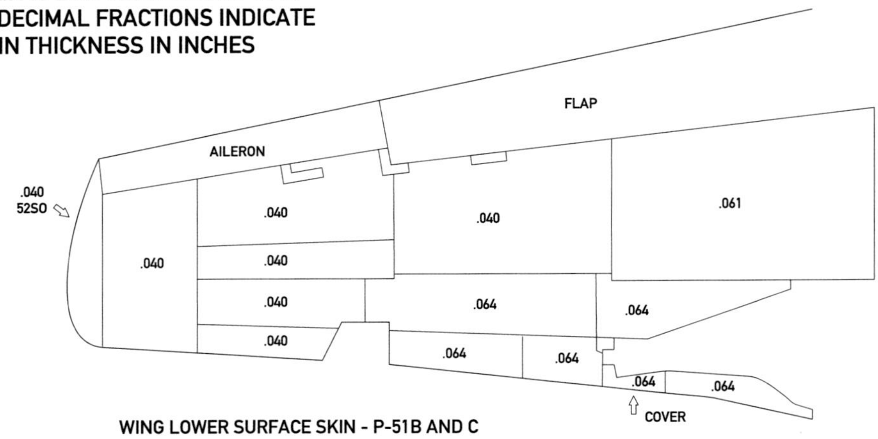

WING LOWER SURFACE SKIN - P-51B AND C

Wing structure. (Airplane Spare Catalog)

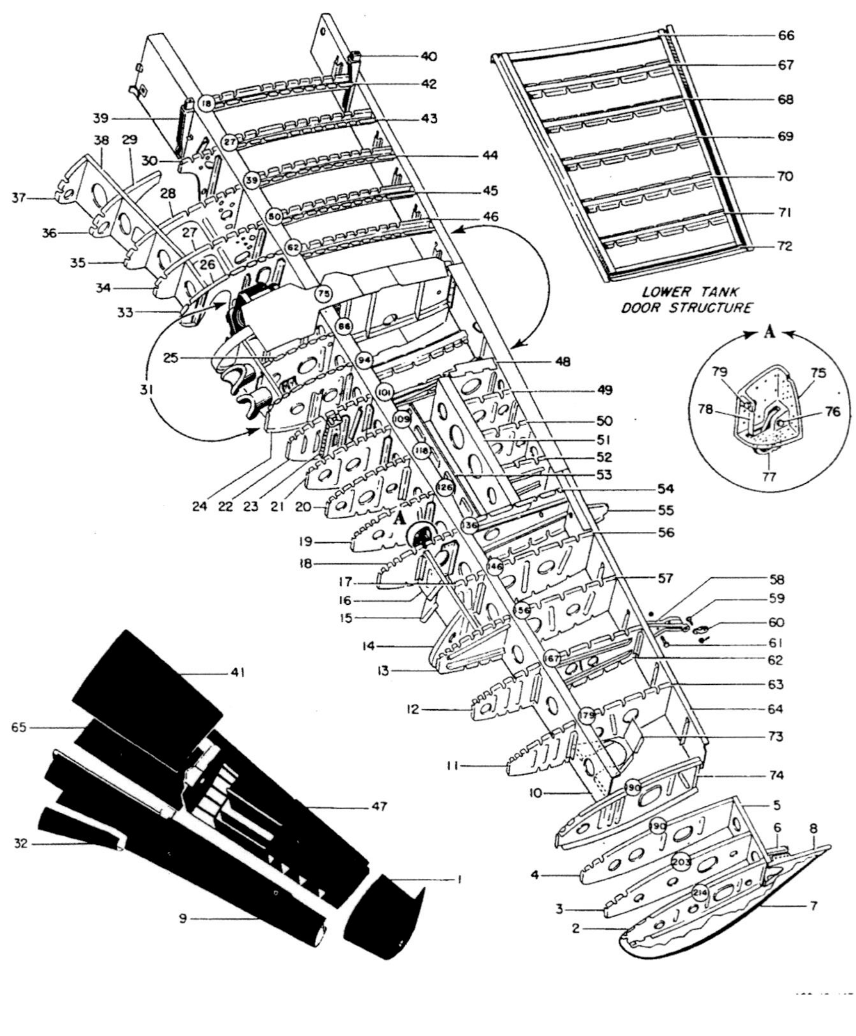

Port wing tio, aileron and navigation lamp. (via R. Panek)

P-51B-1-NA in flight, view from above, showing shape of the Mustang wings. (NAA)

P-51B/C in flight showing wings underside. (US National Archives)

P-51B-10-NA, s/n 42-106653. Note flap in down position and wing upper surfaces with wing fuel tank filler cap. (US National Archives)

P-51B, WZ-S "War Weary" of 84th FS, 78th FG after a landing accident at Duxford, England, UK. 10 Apil 1945. (US National Archives)

Another photo of P-51C-10-NT, s/n 42-103293, converted to dual control aircraft, registered as NL251MX. (R. Bourlier)

Drawing from Airplane Part Catalog showing empennage installation.

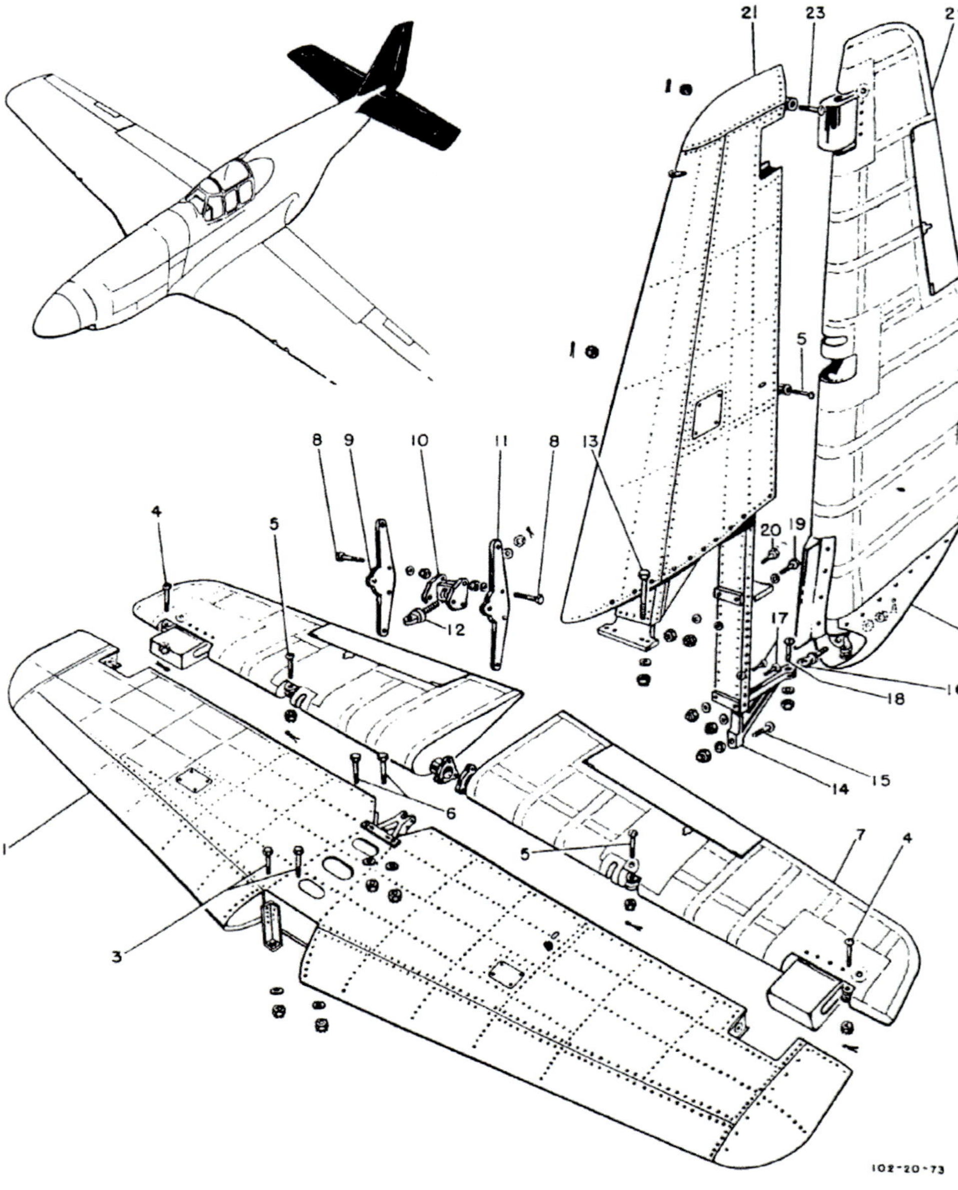

INSTALLATION OF EMPENNAGE

Starboard horizontal stabiliser and elevator details. (via R. Panek)

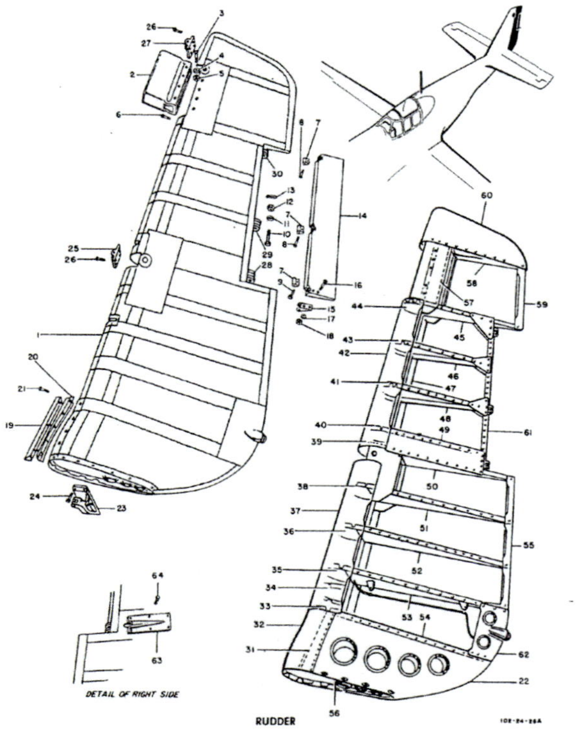

Rudder construction as shown in Airplane Parts Catalog.

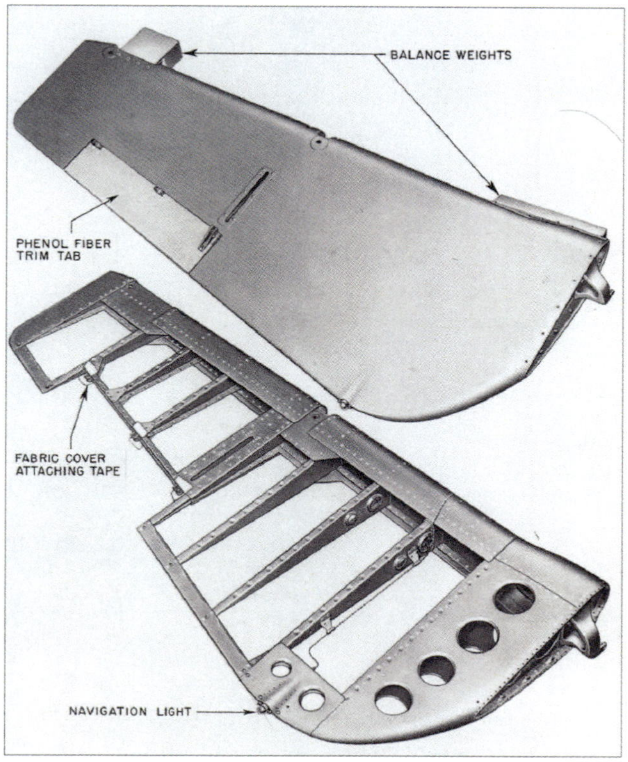

Rudder details, photo from Erection and Maintenance Instructions.

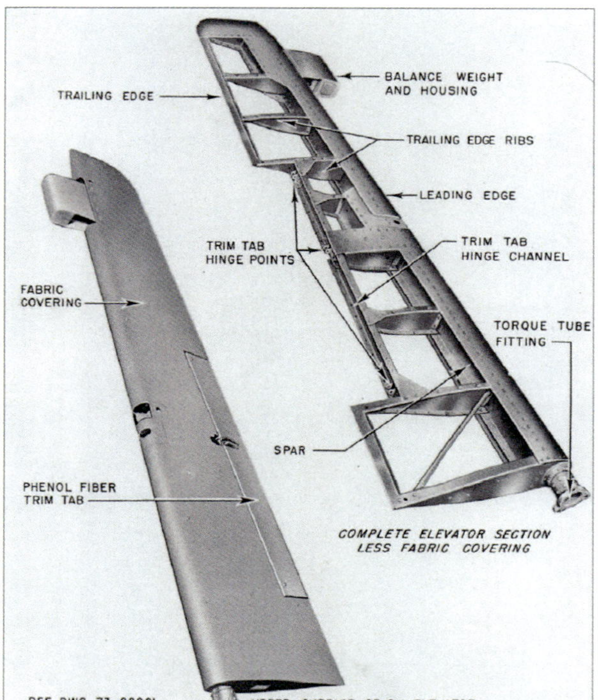

Above: *Elevator details, photo from Erection and Maintenance Instructions.*

Right: *Rudder details on prserved Mustang. (R. Malmstrom)*

Destroyed tail of the P-51C. Note elevator fairing just below the serial number. (US National Archives)

Crashed Mustang III, serial FB161, (P-51C-1, s/n 42-103055). Note, that fuselage tank is not installed. (The Polish Institute and Sikorski Museum)

Engine

P-51B-1-NA, note lack of the sand filters. One of the last of the Mustangs without sand filters under the engine. (US National Archives)

Engine cowlings of the P-51B-1-NA, s/n 43-12405, 267. Aircraft belonged to 26th FS, 51st FG. Note no air sand filter on the lower cowling. (US National Archives)

Engine cowling and formers shown in Airplane Parts Catalog.

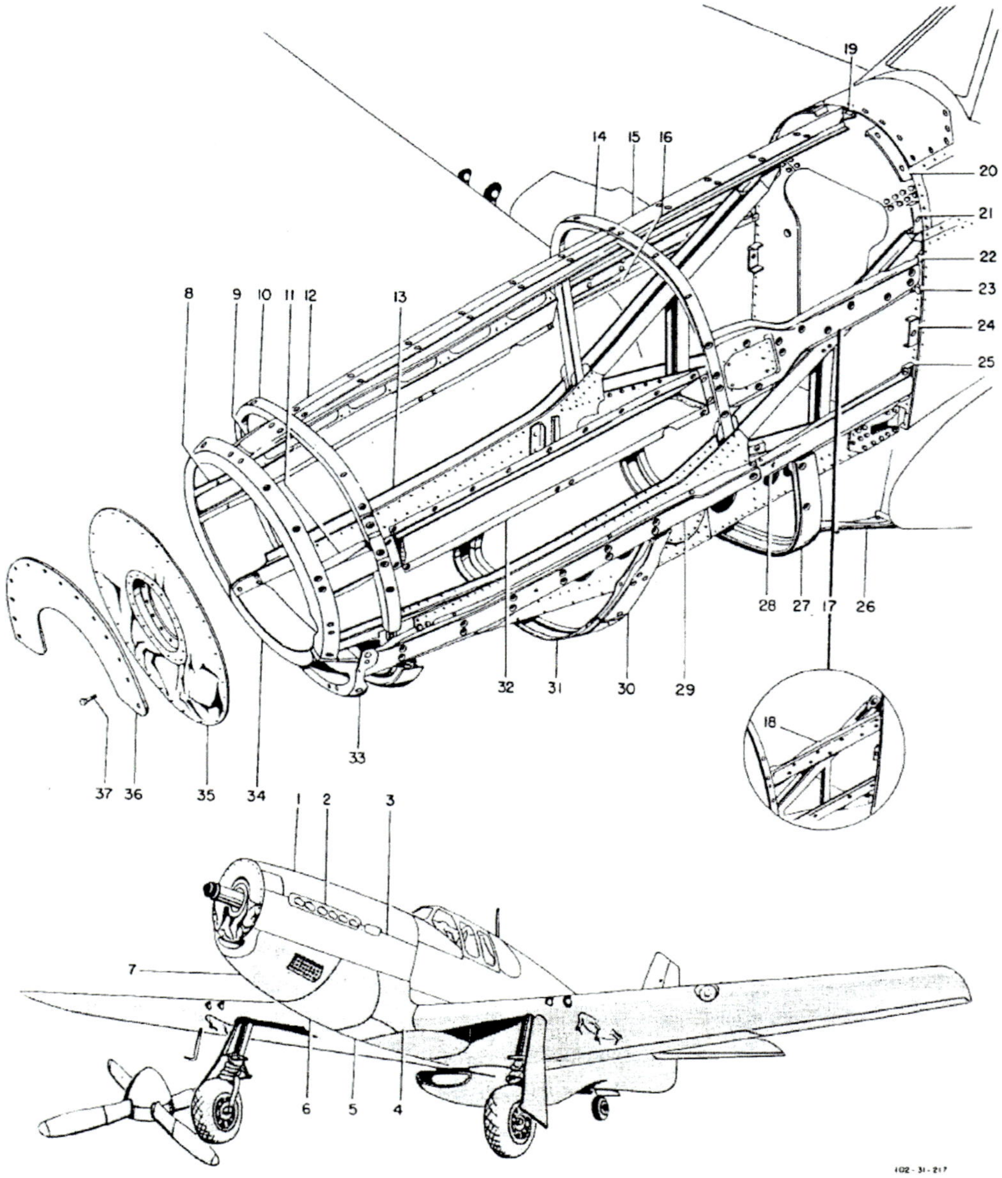

ENGINE COWLING AND FORMERS

Mustang's nose shown on a preserved aircraft. (M. Wasielewski)

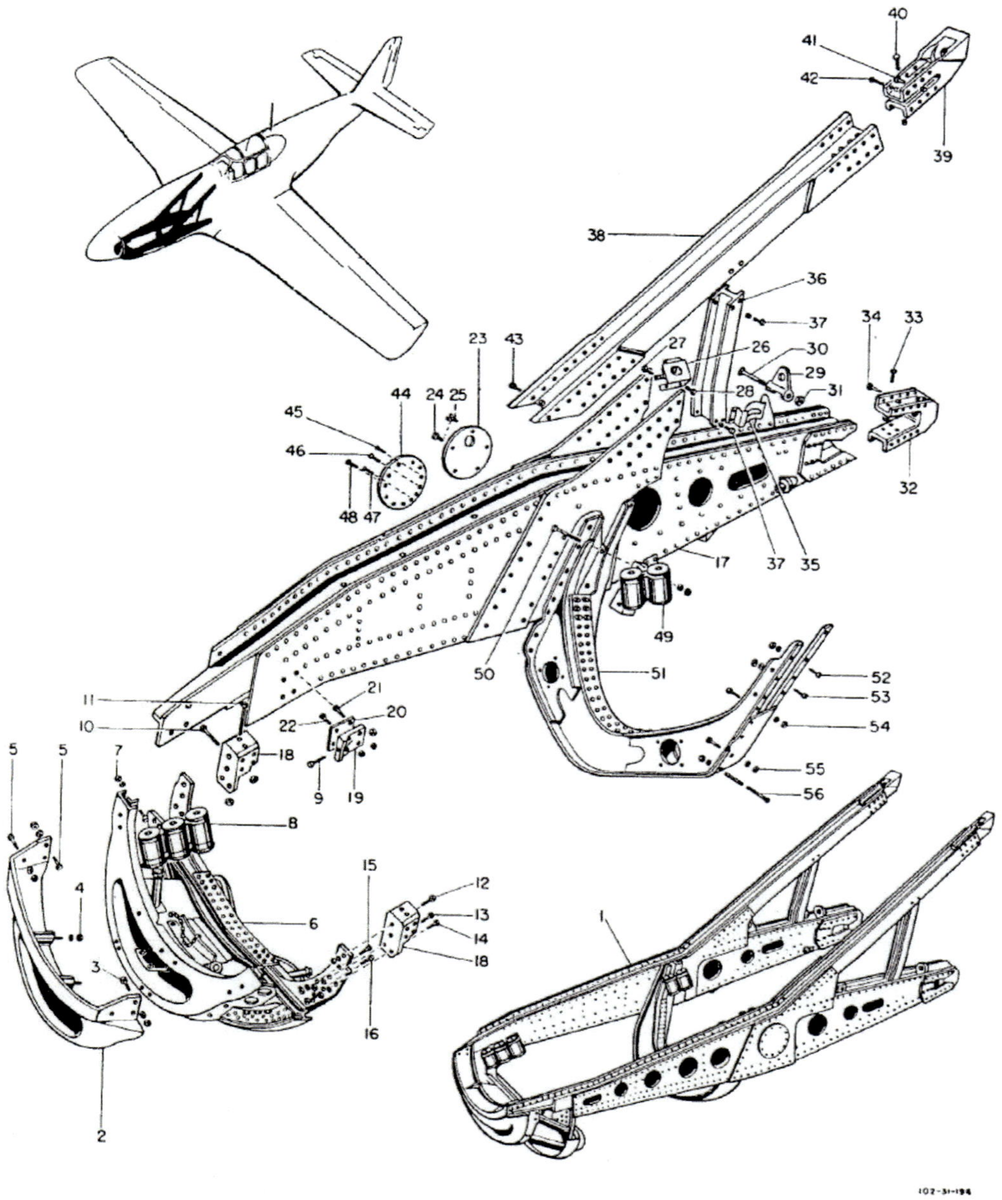

ENGINE MOUNT FRAME

Engine mount frame.
(Airplane Parts Catalog)

P-51B exhaust pipes.
(R. Malmstrom)

Packard-built Rolls-Royce Merlin V-1650-3 engine details. Photos from erection and Maintenance Instructions.

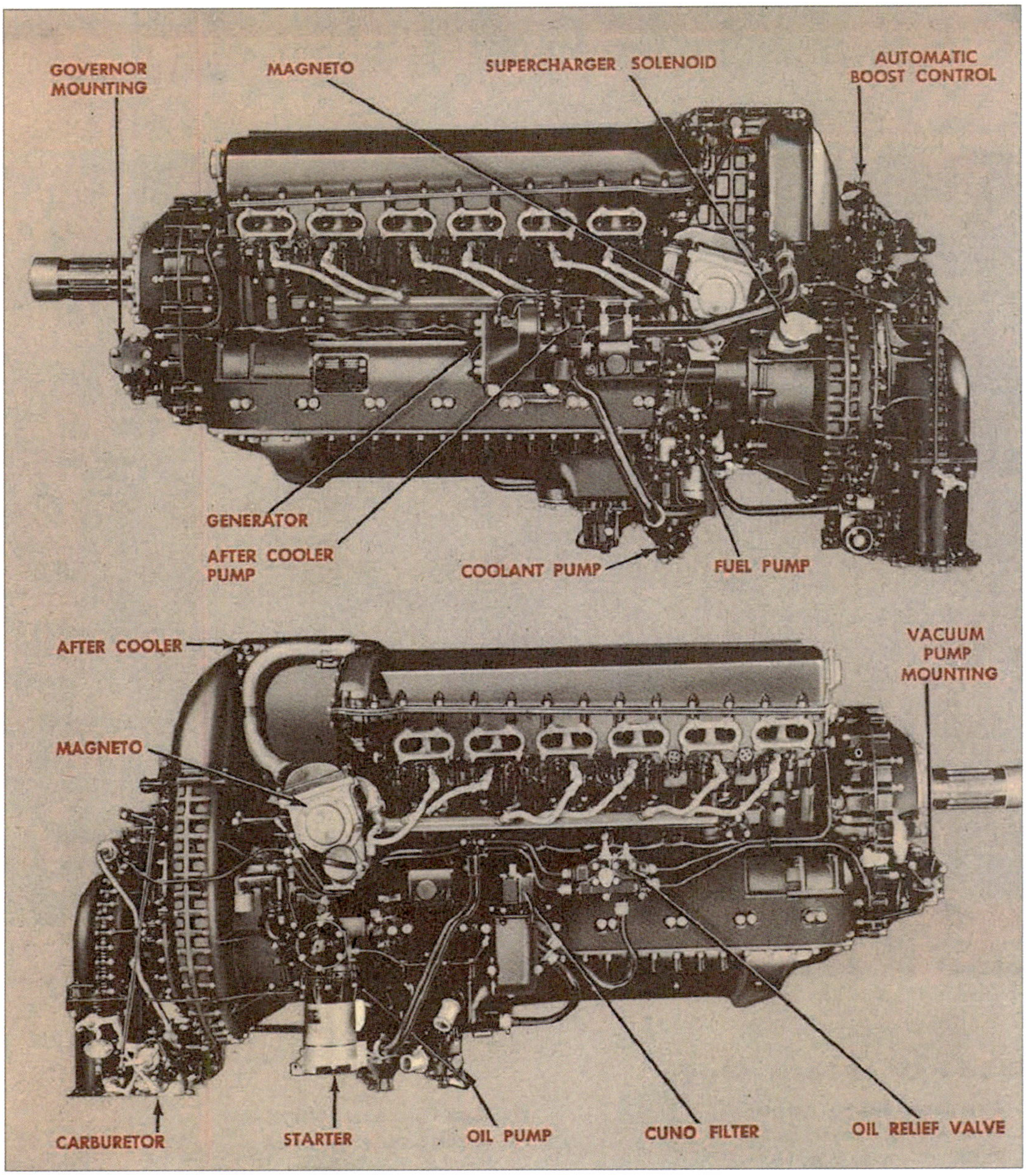

Starboard side of the Mustang engine. photo of a preserved aircraft. (Randy Malmstrom)

P-51B engine maintenance. (US National Archives)

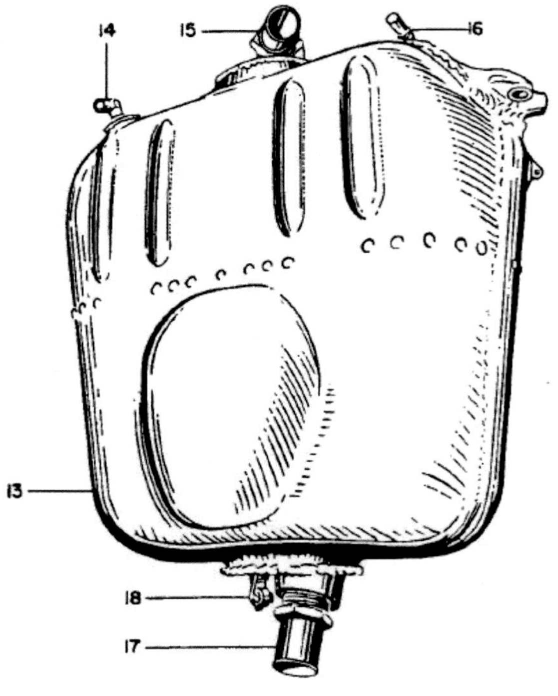

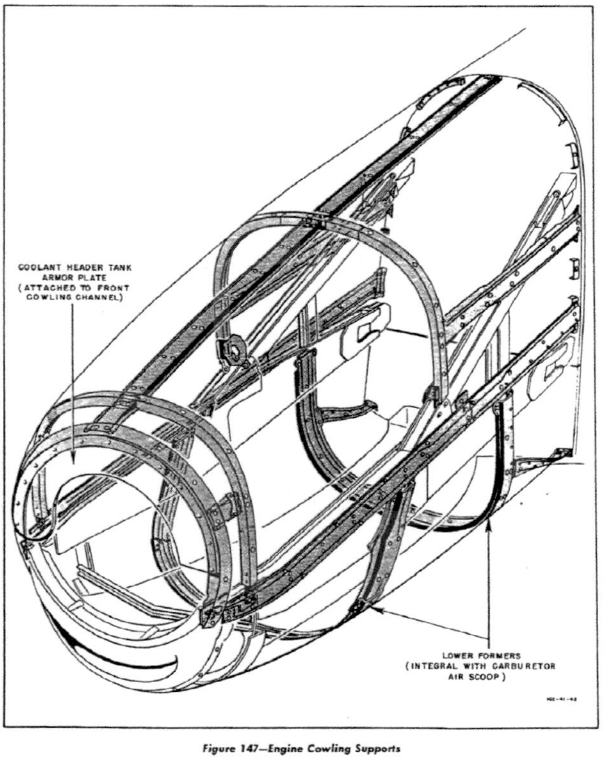

Figure 147—Engine Cowling Supports

Above, left: *Oil tank.*
Above, right: *Engine cowling supports. (Both drawings from Airplane Parts Catalog)*

Left: *Starter crank. (Erection and Maintenance Instructions)*

Above: *Engine cowling supports. (US National Archives)*

Below: *Engine cowling of P-51B, port side. (J. Kightly)*

Above: *Engine cowling of P-51B, starboard side.*

Below: *Engine details of P-51B-10-NA, note dust air filter visible. Compare to the photo on page 107. (Both US National Archives)*

Propeller – Hydromatic-type Hamilton Standard 24D50-65 and the spinner of the P-51B/C. (US National Archives)

P-51B-10-NA, s/n 43-7180, 5Q-F, "Ollie" of Maj. Edger B. "Skinny" Gravette of, 504th FS, 339th FG Note additional carburettor hot air duct inlet cover and exhaust covers removed. (US National Archives)

P-51B-5-NA, s/n 43-6913, VF-T, "Shangri LA". Personal aircraft of Capt. Don Gentile, 336th FS, 4th FG. Details of the propeller are visible. (US National Archives)

Undercarriage

P-51B undercarriage arrangement. Note dropped main undercarriage wheel well doors. (M. Wasielewski)

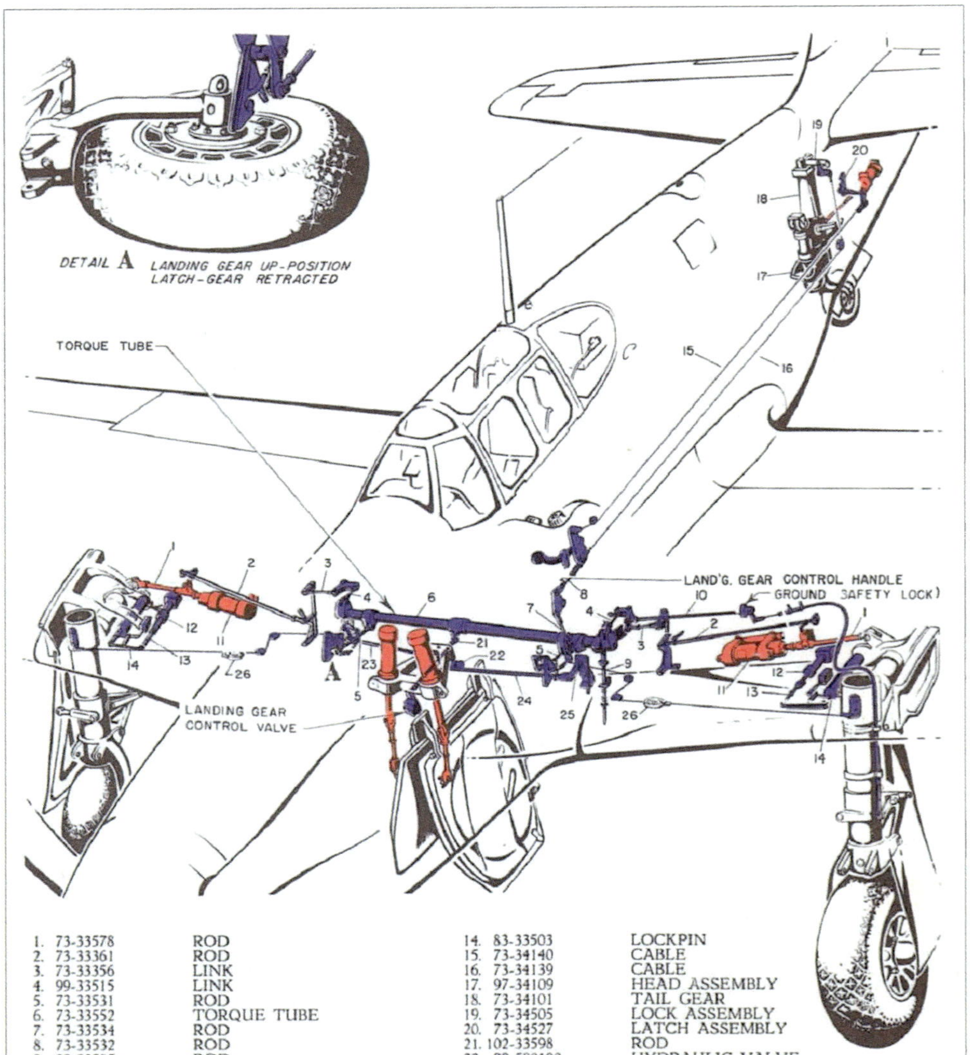

No.	Part No.	Name	No.	Part No.	Name
1.	73-33578	ROD	14.	83-33503	LOCKPIN
2.	73-33361	ROD	15.	73-34140	CABLE
3.	73-33356	LINK	16.	73-34139	CABLE
4.	99-33515	LINK	17.	97-34109	HEAD ASSEMBLY
5.	73-33531	ROD	18.	73-34101	TAIL GEAR
6.	73-33552	TORQUE TUBE	19.	73-34505	LOCK ASSEMBLY
7.	73-33534	ROD	20.	73-34527	LATCH ASSEMBLY
8.	73-33532	ROD	21.	102-33598	ROD
9.	99-33585	ROD	22.	99-580190	HYDRAULIC VALVE
10.	83-335101	ROD	23.	102-335133	ROD
11.	73-58027	STRUT	24.	102-33591	ROD
12.	83-58028	STRUT	25.	102-335126	BELLCRANK ASSEMBLY
13.	73-58454	ROD	26.	102-33592	LINK

Figure 107—Landing Gear Control System Diagram

Drawing of landing gear control system diagram. (Erection and Maintenance Instructions)

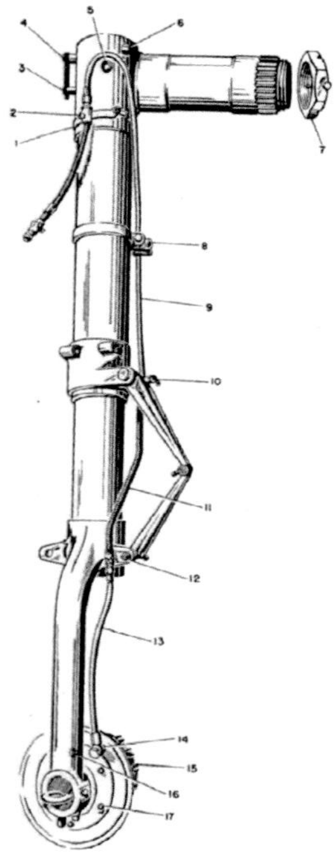

Above: *Main undercarriage leg. (Erection and Maintenance Instructions)*

Above, left: *Port main undercarriage and wheel well are visible. (US National Archives)*

Details of the starboard main undercarriage leg. (US National Archives)

Front view of the port main undercarriage leg. Note how the main leg door is attached. *(US National Archives)*

Two photos of the main wheel, inner view. Note brake line. (via R. Panek)

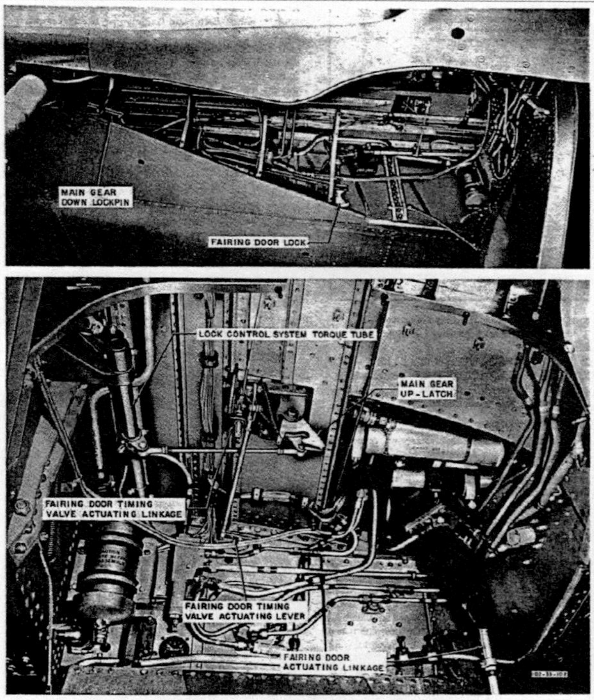

Figure 106—Landing Gear Controls—Right-hand Wing

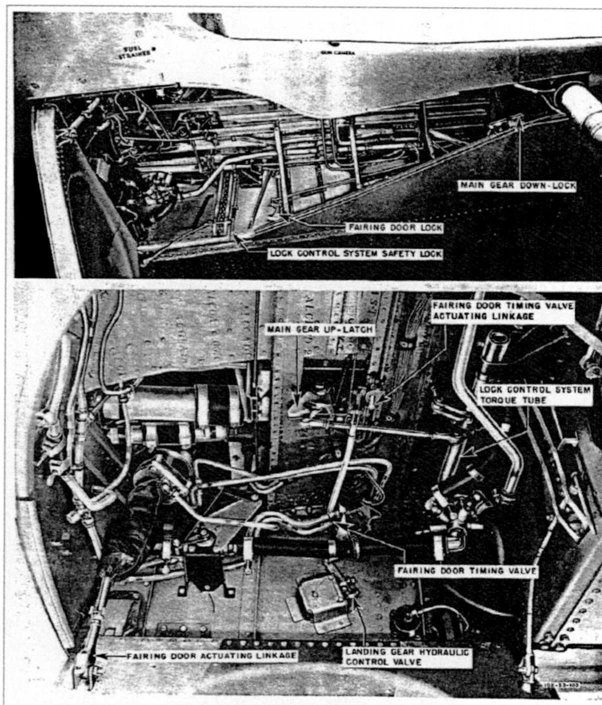

Figure 107—Landing Gear Controls—Left-hand Wing

Photos from Erection and Maintenance Instructions showing details of the main wheel wells.

***Below:** Main gear fairing door.*
(Erection and Maintenance Instructions)

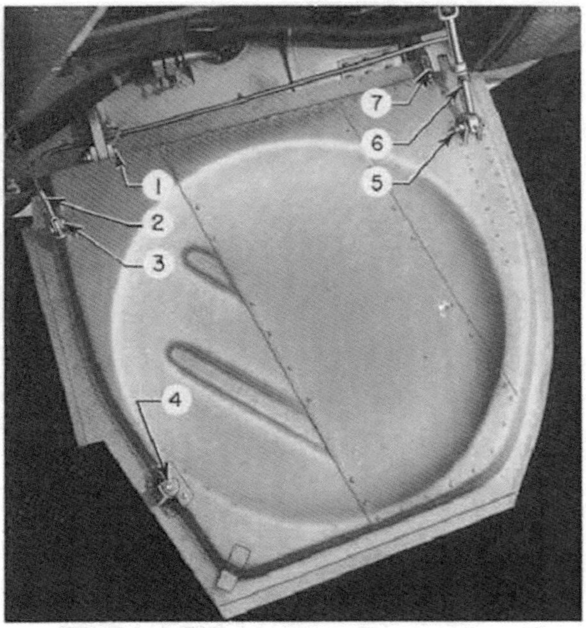

1. AN6-22 Bolt, AN310-6 Nut, and AN380-3-3 Cotter Key
2. 73-33340 Cable Assembly
3. AN5-10 Bolt, AN310-5 Nut, and AN380-2-2 Cotter Key
4. Fairing Door Locking Lug
5. AN6-16 Bolt, AN310-6 Nut, and AN380-3-3 Cotter Key
6. 73-33320 Link Assembly (LH)
   73-33320-1 Link Assembly (RH)
7. AN6-20 Bolt, AN310-6 Nut, and AN380-3-3 Cotter Key

Figure 111—Main Gear Fairing Door

Port main gear.
(US National Archives)

Tail wheel, view from the right. (via R. Panek)

***Faar right:** The tail wheel control diagram. (Pilot's Instruction)*

***Right:** Tail gear assembly. (Erection and Maintenance Instructions)*

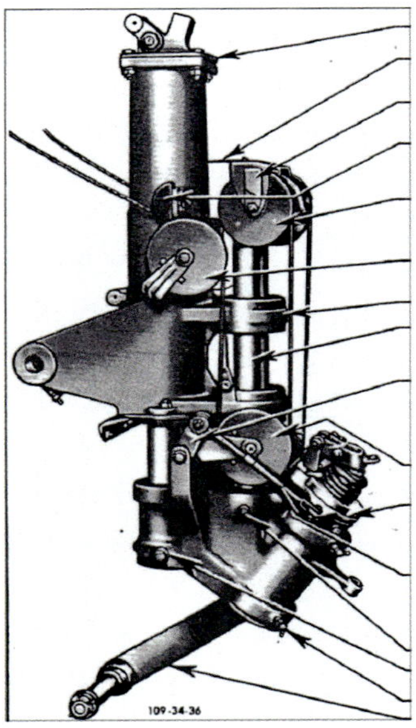

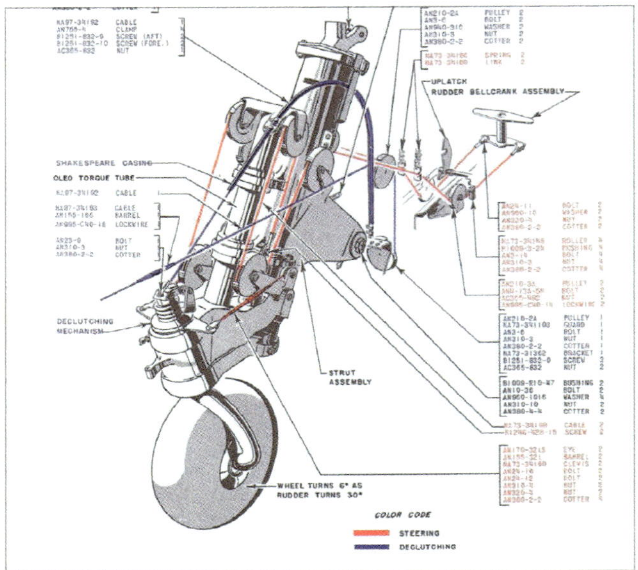

	Part Number	Name	No. Req.
1.	73-34515	BELLCRANK	1
	AN3-11A	BOLT	1
	AN365-1032	NUT	1
2.	73-34527	LOCK ASSEMBLY	
3.	AN155-16S	BARREL	1
	AN160-16S	FORK	1
	AN995C40-18	LOCKWIRE	1
	AN23-9	BOLT	1
	AN320-3	NUT	1
	AN380-2-2	COTTER KEY	1
4.	73-34528	SPRING	1
5.	TAIL GEAR UP-LATCH ACTUATING CABLE		

Figure 118—Tail Gear Up-position Latch-Gear Down

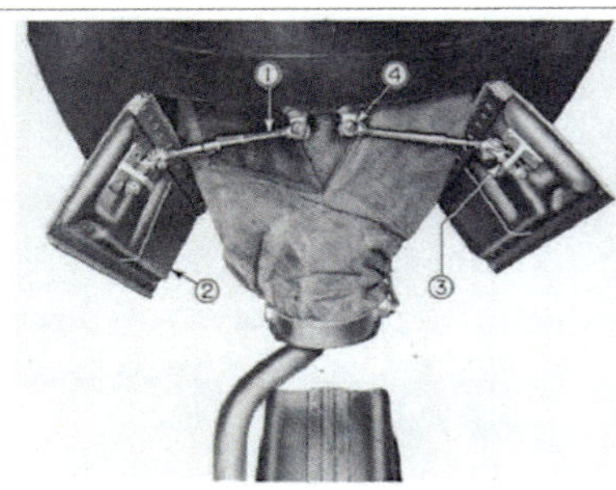

	Part Number	Name	No. Req.
1.	AN155-16S	BARREL	1
	AN161-16LS	FORK	1
	AN161-16RL	FORK	1
	AN995-6-40-24	LOCKWIRE	1
2.	TAIL WHEEL FAIRING DOOR		
3.	AN23-10	SCREW	1
	AN320-3	NUT	1
4.	AN43-7	EYEBOLT	1
	B985-12-20-63	WASHER	2
	B1009R-4-11	BUSHING	1
	AN310-3	NUT	1
	AN380-2-2	COTTER KEY	1

Figure 119—Tail Wheel Fairing Doors

Tail gear details, latch mechanism and fairing doors are shown. (Erection and Maintenance Instructions)

Front view of the P-51B showing undercarriage gears angles. (US National Archives)

P-51B, s/n unknown, 261 of 26th FS, 51st FB, 14th AF, China, 1944. (US National Archives)

Canopy

Above: *Open canopy of a preserved P-51C. (R. Bourlier)*

Below: *1st Lt. Walter J. Goehausen of the 308th FS, 31st FG in his P-51B-10-NA. See details of the canopy in open position. (US National Archives)*

P-51B/C original canopy. Drawings from Airplane Parts Catalog.

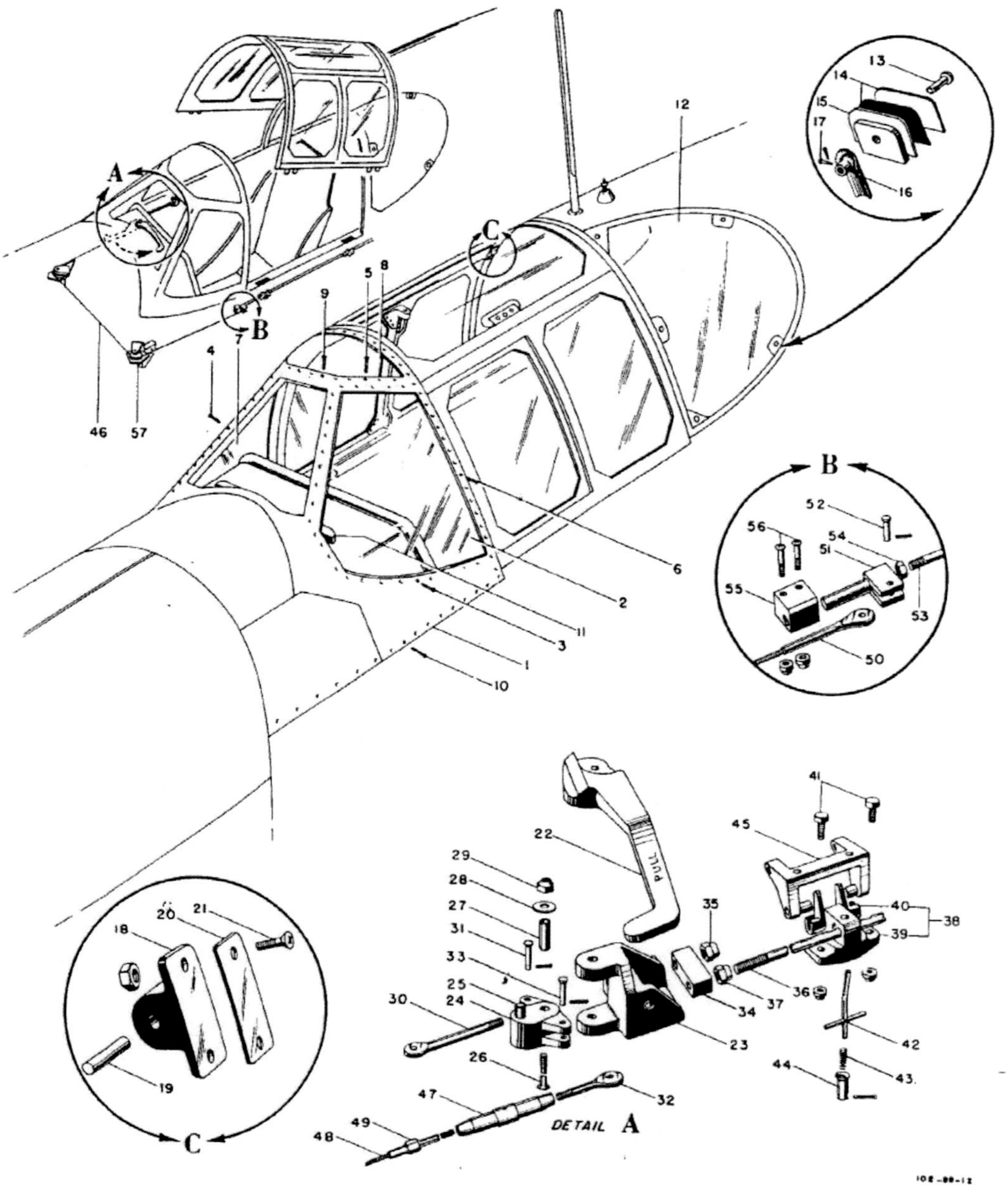

INSTALLATION OF COCKPIT ENCLOSURE

Another wartime photo of the canopy. P-51B-1-NA this time. Note earlier version of the antenna. (US National Archives)

Canopy in closed position with side window moved back. 1st Ll William B. King of 355th FS, 354th FG. (US National Archives)

Below: P-51B-1-NA, starboard side of the canopy. (US National Archives)

Opposite page, bottom: Malcolm hood canopy from above: (R. Malmstrom)

Above: *Malcom hood canopy an a preserved P-51B. Note the ground jack under fuselage fuel filler cap. (R. Boullier)*

Starboard side of the Malcolm hood canopy in closed position. (M. Wasielewski)

Malcolm hood canopy in open position. Note canopy rail details. (Stratus coll.)

This page: *Photos of the Maclcom hood canopy details. (R. Malmstrom)*

Cockpit

Above: Preserved P-51B-10-NA, s/n 42-106638, "Impatient Virgin". Details of the instrument panel.

Below, left: *Carburettor air control on the left cockpit wall.*

Below, right: *Starboard cockpit wall. Note canopy opening mechanism in the top of the photo.*
(All R. Malmstrom)

Above, left: *Port side of the cockpit, bomb control handle is visible.*

Above: *Port wing fuselage gauge is visible in the floor.*

Left: *Propeller control and bomb control handle.*

Below: *Aileron trim control and radiators air control panel.*

(All R. Malmstrom)

P-51B-1-NA Mustang instrument panel.
Model 102A

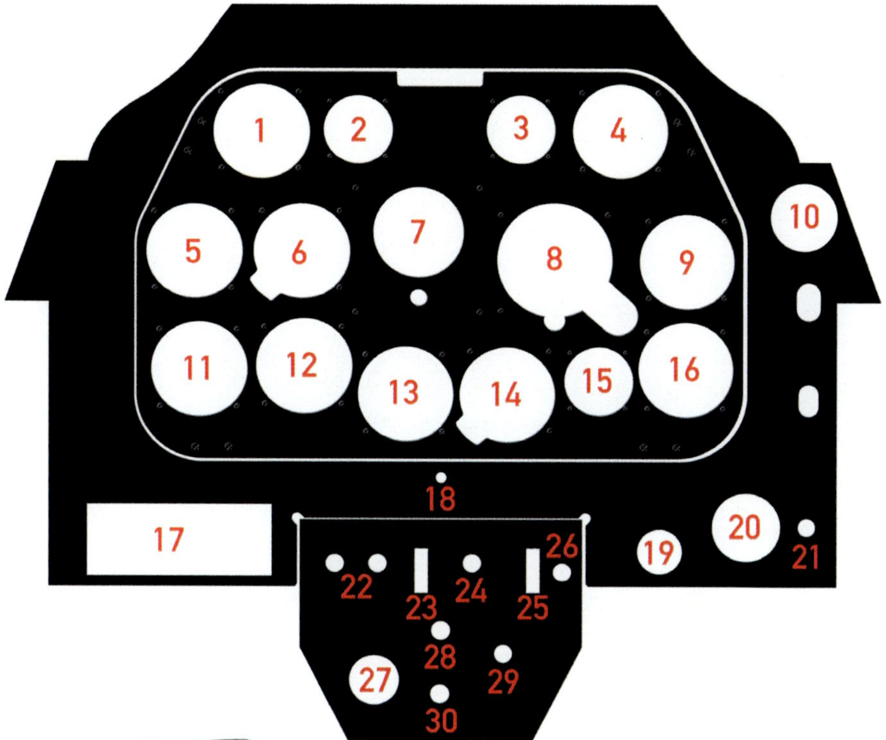

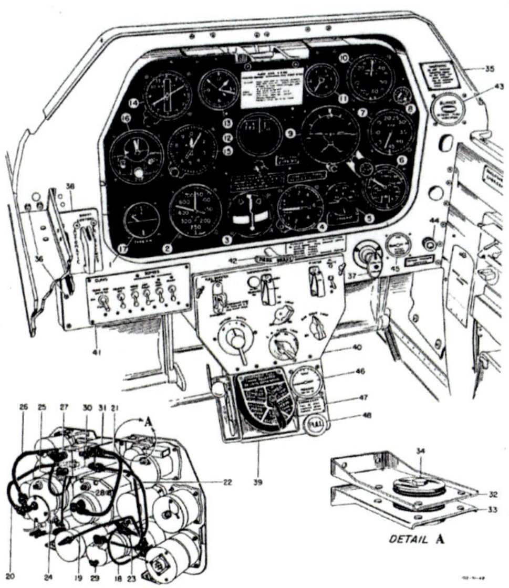

P-51B-1-NA Mustang instruments panel

1. Magnetic compass;
2. Clock;
3. Suction gage;
4. Manifold pressure indicator;
5. Contactor (remote);
6. Altimeter;
7. Directonal giro;
8. Artificial horizon;
9. Tachometer;
10. Oxygen flow blinker;
11. Landing gear position indicator;
12. Airspeed indicator;
13. Turn and bank indicator;
14. Rate of climb indicator (Variometer);
15. Coolant temperature indicator;
16. Oil temperature and oil and fuel pressure gage;
17. Gun and bomb control panel;
18. Parking brakes control handle;
19. Adjusting bank and turn throttling valve;
20. Oxygen pressure gage;
21. Oxygen system warning lamp;
22. Booster pump switches;
23. Supercharger control;
24. Supercharger warning lamp;
25. Starter switch;
26. Oil dilution switch;
27. Ignition switch;
28. Compass lights control;
29. Gun sight light control.
30. Ultra violet lamp control.

Drawings by Dariusz Karnas

P-51B/C Mustang instrument panel LATE VERSION, used on models 103, 104 & 111.

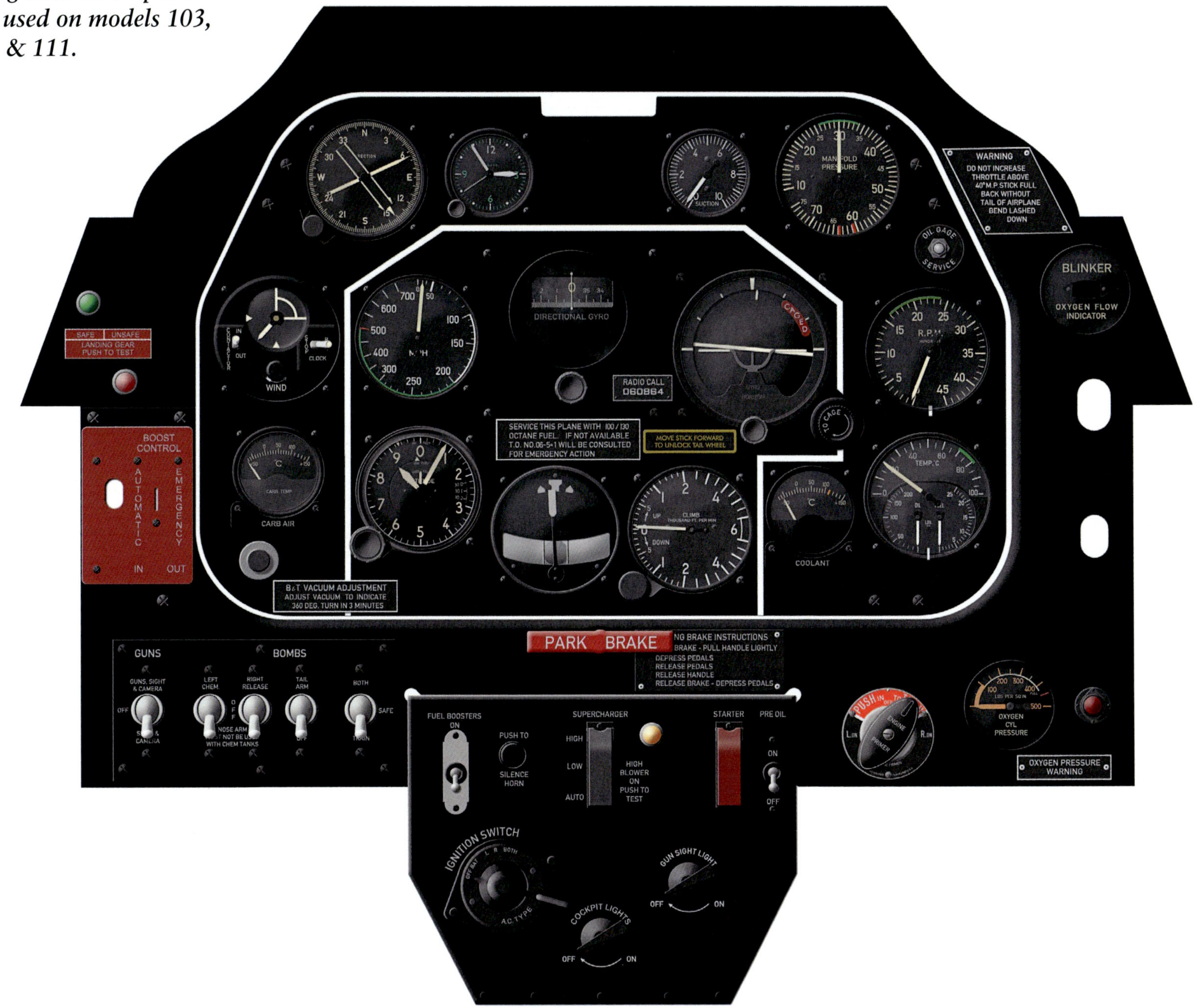

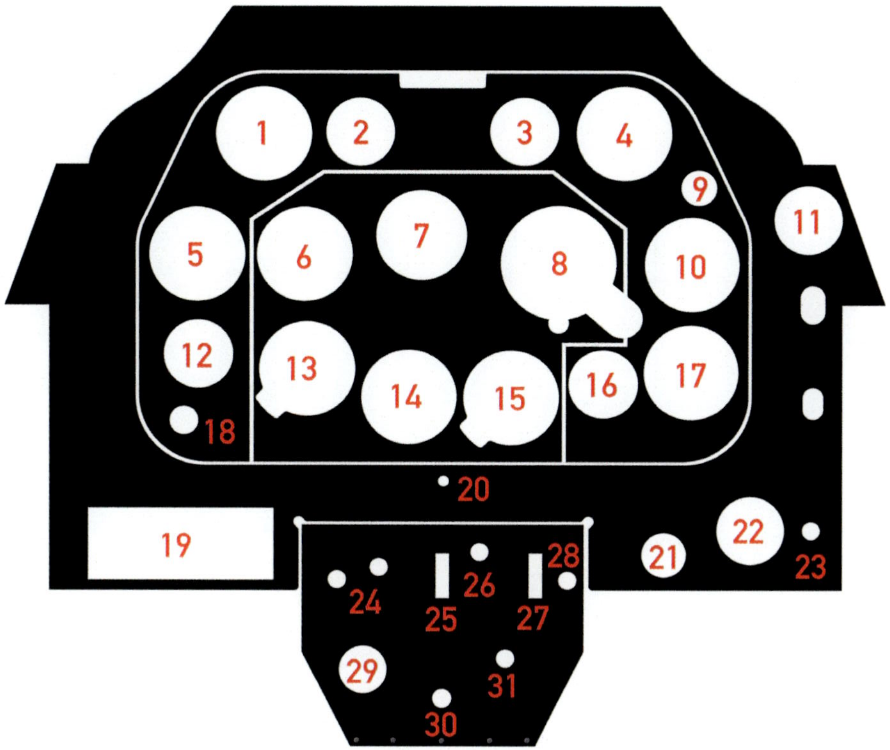

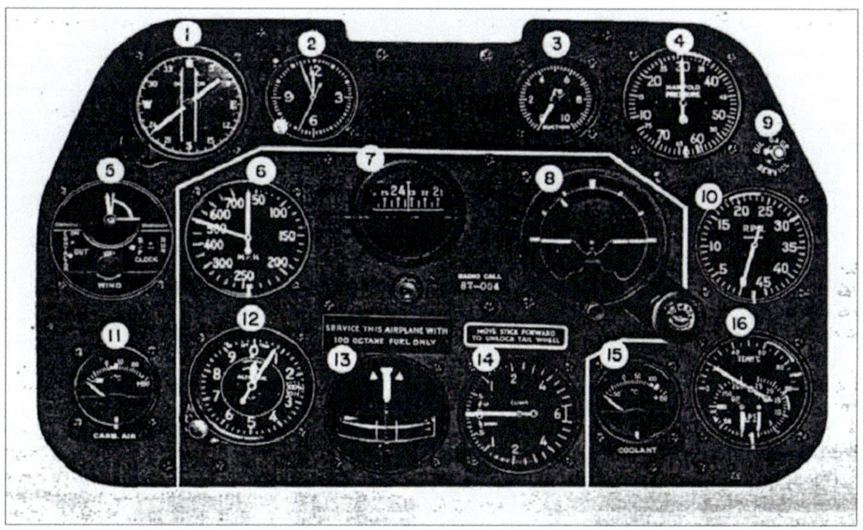

P-51B/C Mustang instrument panel
LATE VERSION, used on models 103, 104 & 111.

1. Remote-reading compass Indicator (ADF), type AN5730-6;
2. Clock, type A-11;
3. Suction gauge, type AN5771-5;
4. Manifold pressure gauge, type D-10;
5. IFF contactor;
6. Airspeed indicator, type F-2;
7. Directonal giro, type AN5735;
8. Artificial horizon, type AN5735;
9. Oil pressure filler valve;
10.Tachometer, type AN5530-1;
11. Oxygen flow blinker;
12. Carburetor air temperature gauge type AN5790-6;
13. Altimeter, type AN5760-2;
14. Turn and bank indicator, type AN5820;
15. Rate of climb indicator (Variometer), type AN5825;
16. Coolant temperature gauge, type AN57900-6;
17. Oil temperature and oil and fuel pressure gauge, Type B-7;
18. Adjusting bank and turn throttling valve;
19. Gun and bomb control panel;
20. Parking brake control handle;
21. Engine primer;
22. Oxygen pressure gauge;
23. Oxygen system warning lamp;
24. Booster pump switches;
25. Supercharger control;
26. Supercharger warning lamp;
27. Starter switch;
28. Oil dilution switch;
29. Ignition switch;
30. Cockpit lights control;
31. Gun sight light control.

Drawings by Dariusz Karnas

Port side of the P-51B-1-NA cockpit. 1. Flare pistol openinig; 2. Cockpit light; 3. Coolant radiator scoop handle; 4. Sliding window lock handle; 5. Oil radiator scoop control; 6. Left fluorescent light; 7. Mixture control; 8. Propeller control; 9. Throttle; 10. Emergency boost control; 11. Flap control handle 12. Ram air control; 13. Rudder trim tab control; 14. Left fuel gauge; 15. Elevator trim tab control; 16. Landing gear control; 17. Aileron trim tab control; 18. Bomb control handle; 19. Armament switches. Photo from Pilot's Manual.

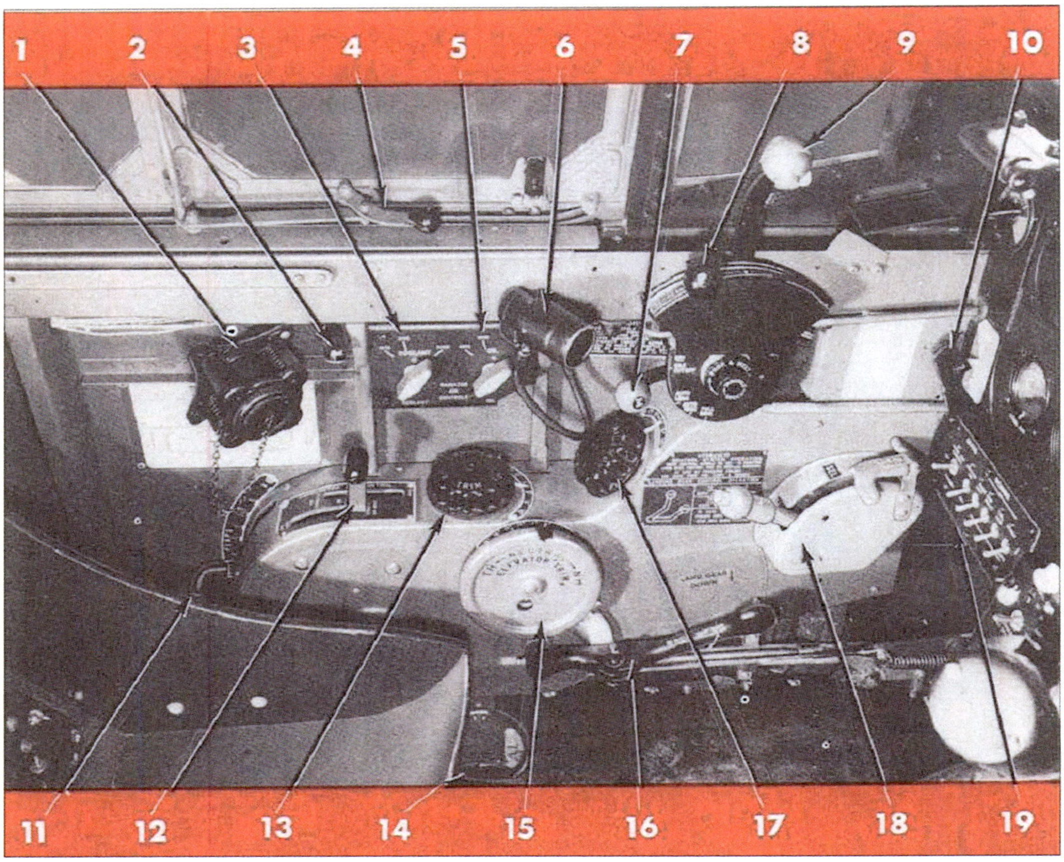

Right: *Drawing from Technical Manual showing cockpit pedestal assembly, P-51B-1-NA.*

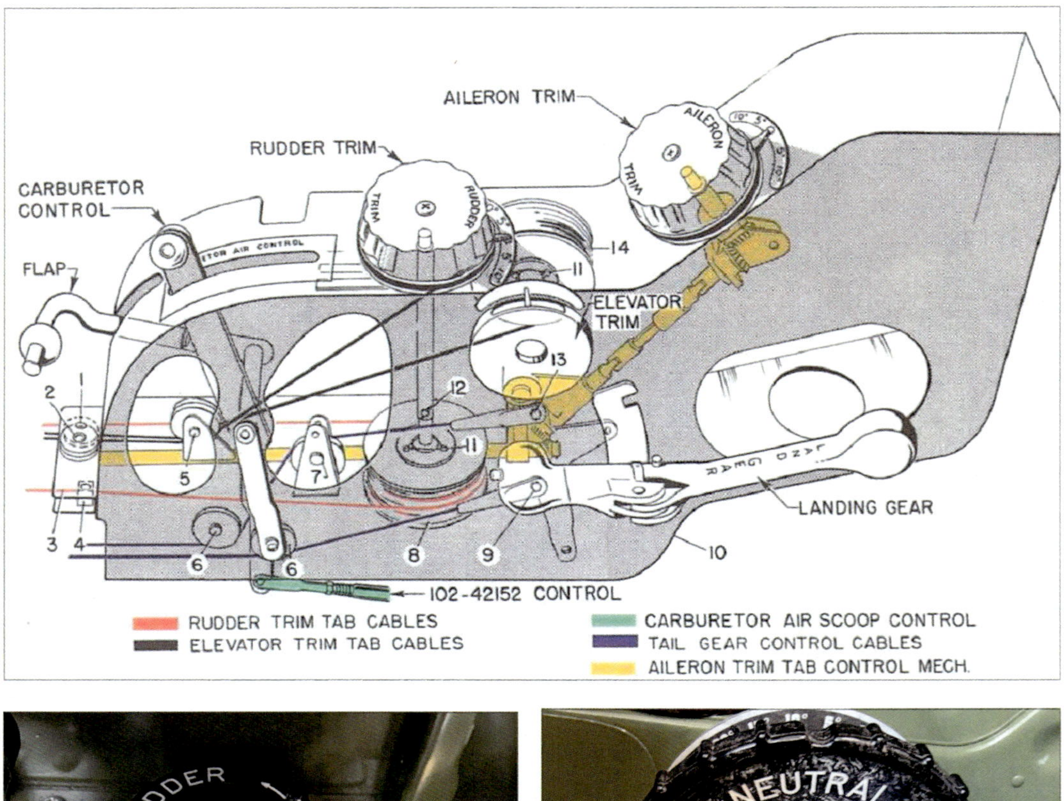

Left photo: *Rudder trim tab.*

Right photo: *Elevator trim tab control. (Both R. Malmstrom)*

Starboard side of the P-51B-1 cockpit.
1. *Emergency canopy release;*
2. *Generator disconnect switch*
3. *Battery disconnect switch;*
4. *Pitot heater switch;*
5. *Landing light switch;*
6. *Engine limitations table;*
7. *Wing and tail positioon switches;*
8. *Flight limitations table;*
9. *VHF control box;*
10. *Hydraulic pressure gaude;*
11. *Right fluorescent light switch;*
12. *Circuit breaker switches;*
13. *Hand hydraulic pump;*
14. *Ammeter;*
15. *Cockpit light;*
16. *Right fuel gauge;*
17. *VHF volume control;*
18. *Detonator buttons;*
19. *Clips for radio plugs;*
20. *Case.*

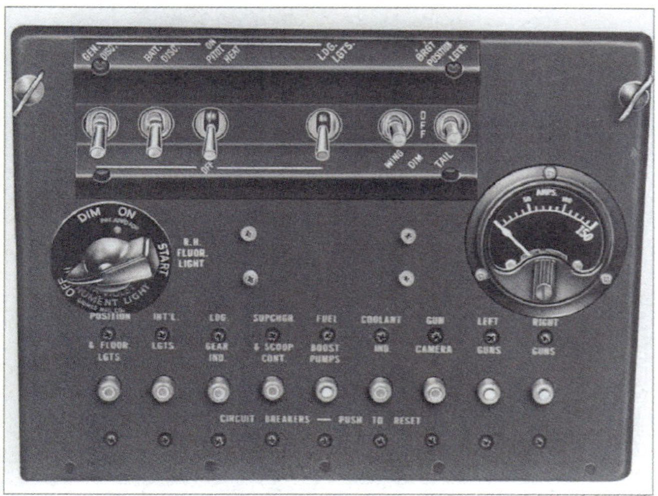

Left: *Circuit breaker switches and ammeter of P-51B-1.*

Below, left: *HF volume control at preserved P-51B-10.*

Below, right: *VHF control box and engine limitation table (left), flight limitation table (right).*
(photos R. Malmstrom)

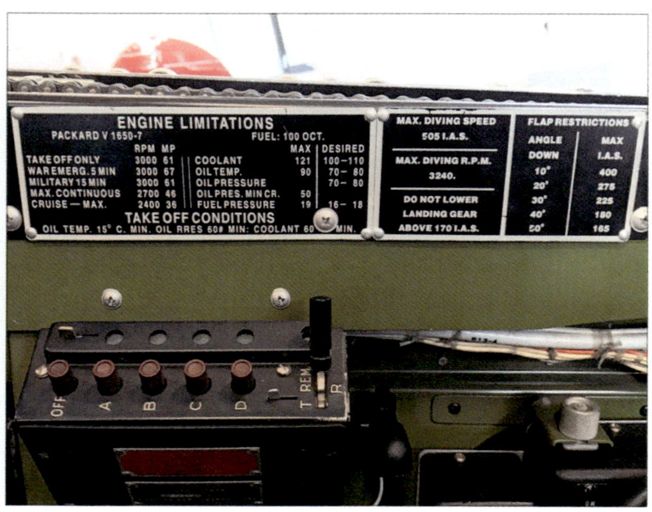

Pistol mount on the left cockpit wall. (Pilot's Manual)

Pistol mount, no pistol installed. Note also carburettor air control plus rudder trim control. (R. Malmstrom)

Starboard wing fuel tank gauge in the floor. (R. Malmstrom)

2nd Lt. Glenn J. Geyer, Suichuan, China – this photo was taken of Lt. Geyer on 18 January 1945, 2-days before being shot down on his seventh combat mission in airplane s/n 43-25185. Details of the cockpit are shown. Note Type N-3 gunsight. (R. Bourlier coll.)

British Mark II gunsight shown on a preserved P-51B-10-NA. Many US pilots mounted British gunsights during WW2. (R. Malmstrom)

Type N-3 gunsight is well visible in the P-51C-10-NT. (US National Archives)

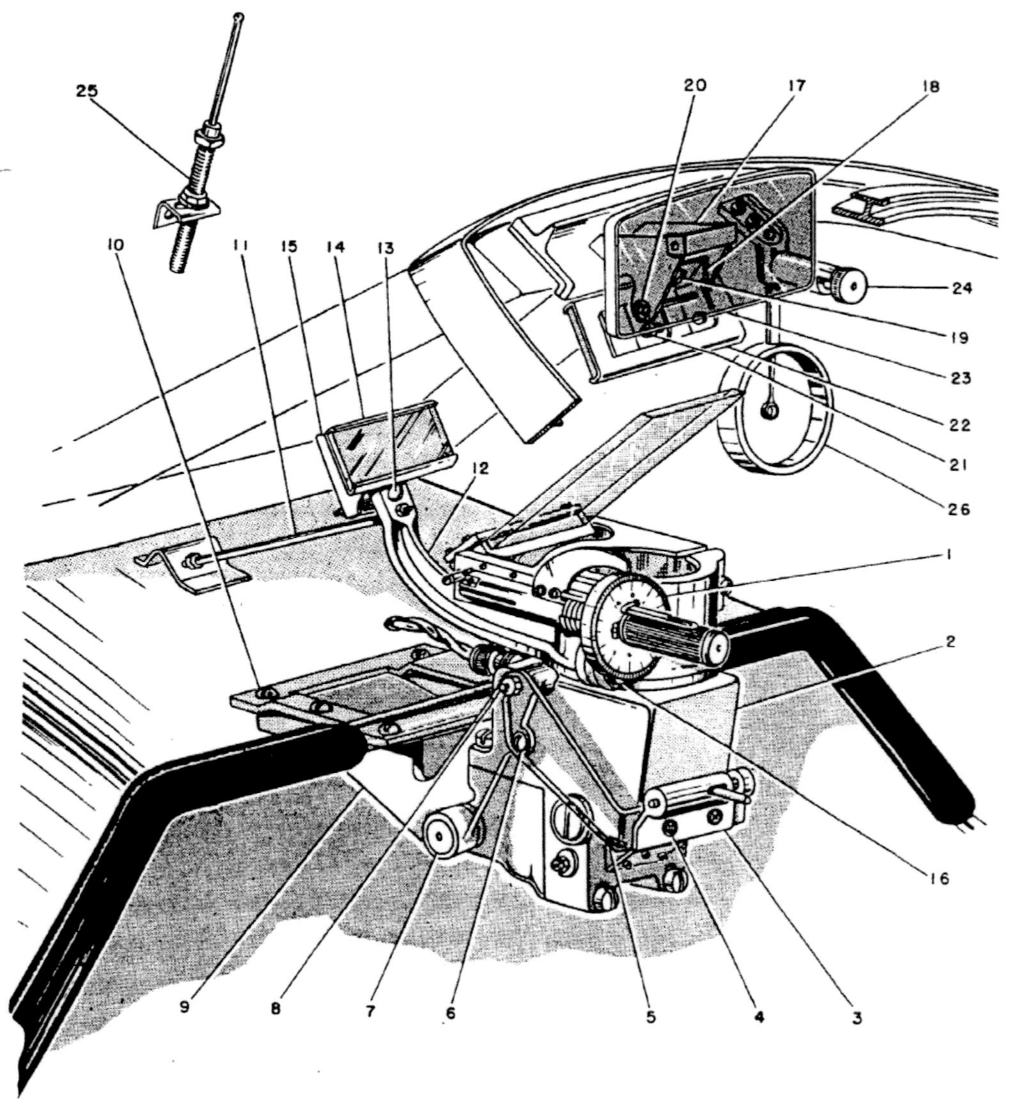

Type N-3 gunsight assembly. (Airplane Parts Catalog)

RESTRICTED
AN 01-60JD-2 Section IV

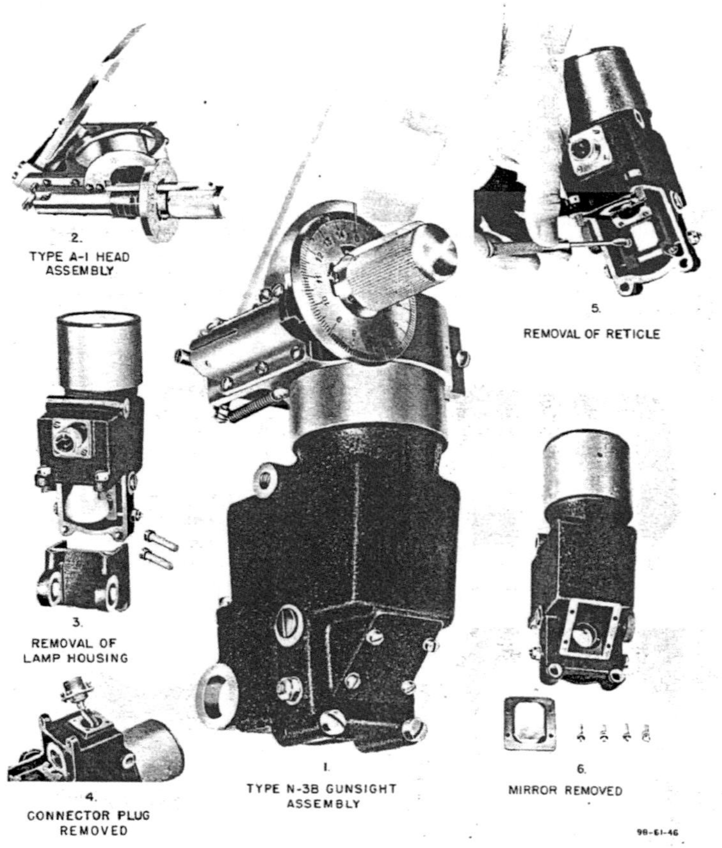

Figure 399—Gun Sight Disassembly—Later Airplanes

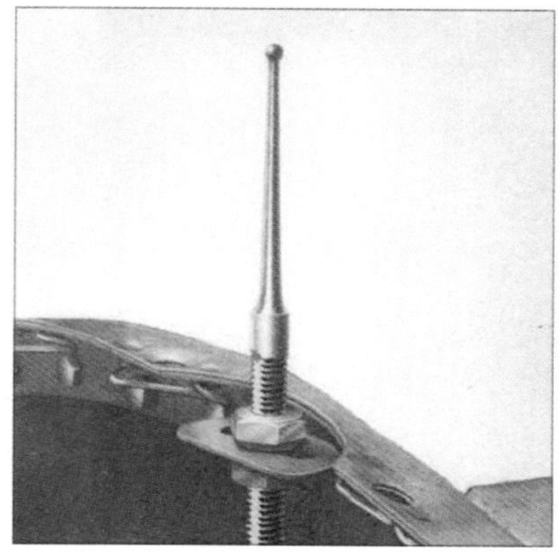

Above: Bead sight installation. (Erection and Maintenance Instructions)

Right: Type N-3 gunsight details. (Erection and Maintenance Instructions)

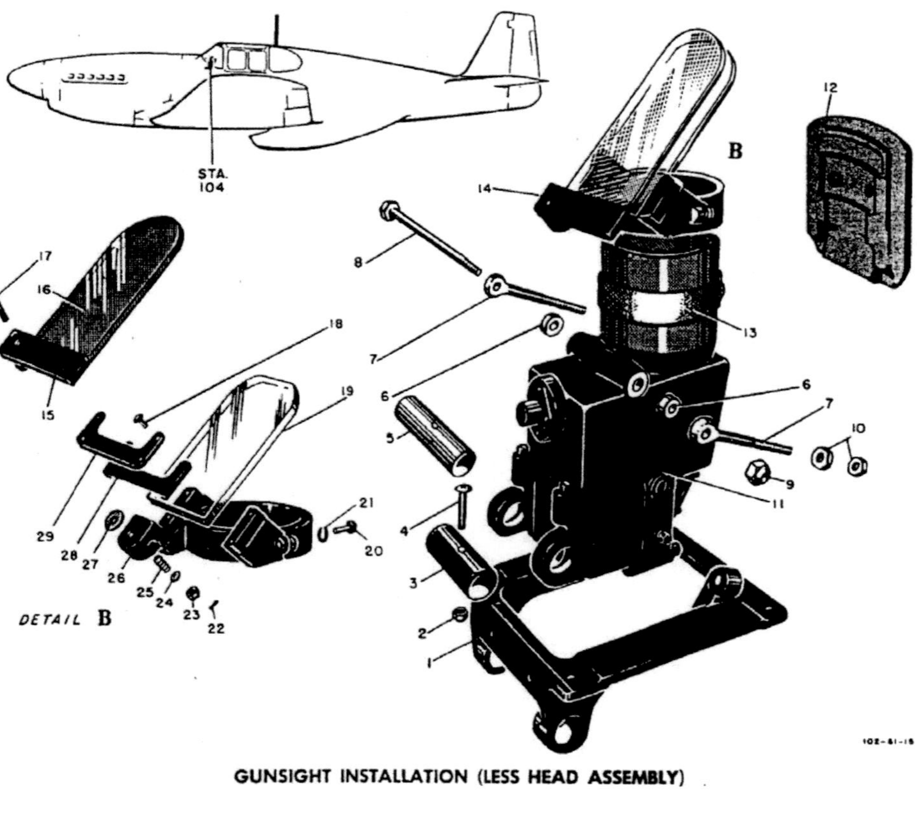

GUNSIGHT INSTALLATION (LESS HEAD ASSEMBLY)

Another version of the gunsight mounted on the Mustang. (Erection and Maintenance Instructions)

Wartime photo of the control stick.
(US National Archives)

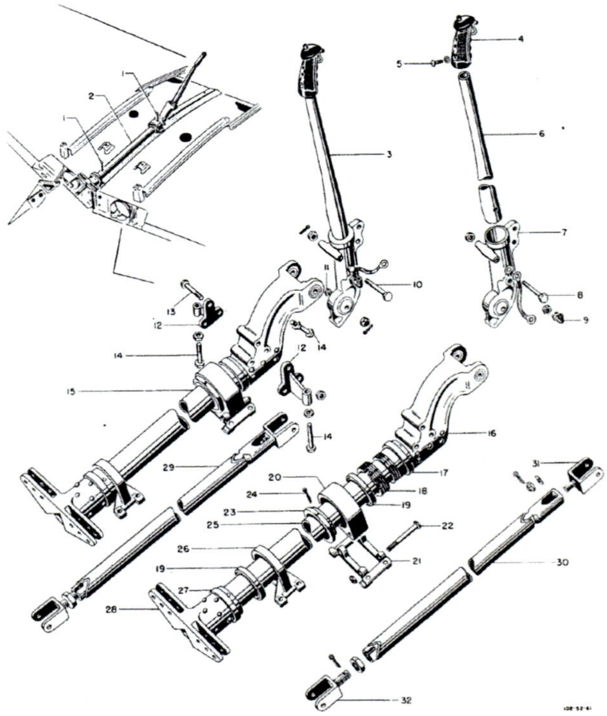

PILOT'S CONTROL STICK

Above: *Control stick assembly.*
(Airplane Parts Catalog)

Left: *Detail photo of the control stick grip in a preserved aircraft.*
(R. Malmstrom)

Below: *Control stick grip details.*
(Pilot's Manual)

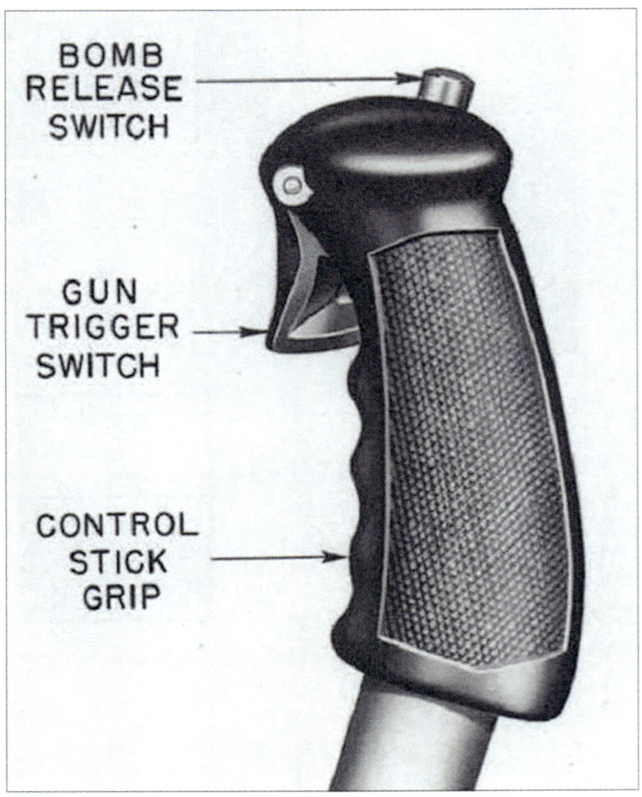

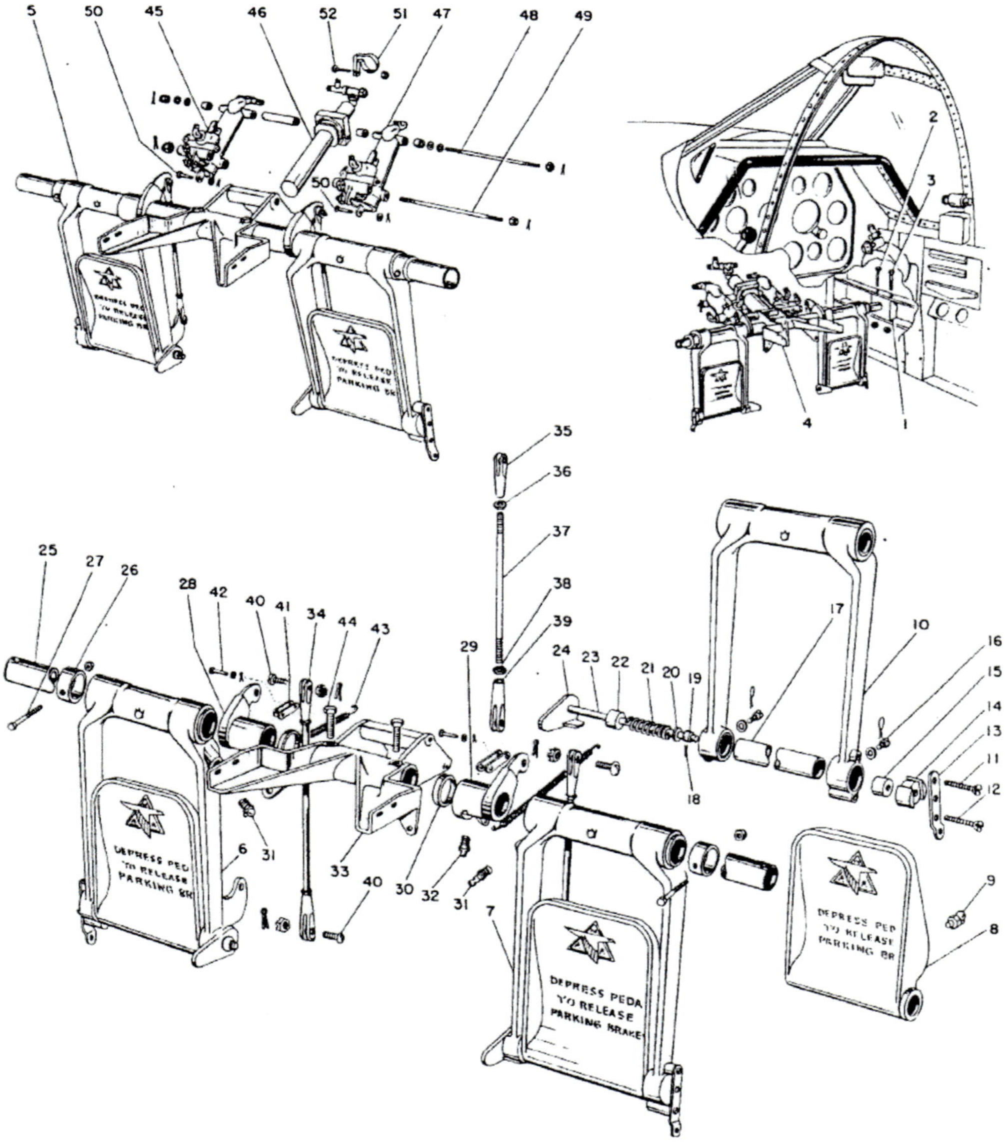

Rudder pedals assembly. (Airplane Parts Catalog)

Rudder pedals and fuel tanks selector panel in preserved aircraft. (R. Malmstrom)

Pilot's seat assembly.
(Airplane Parts Catalog)

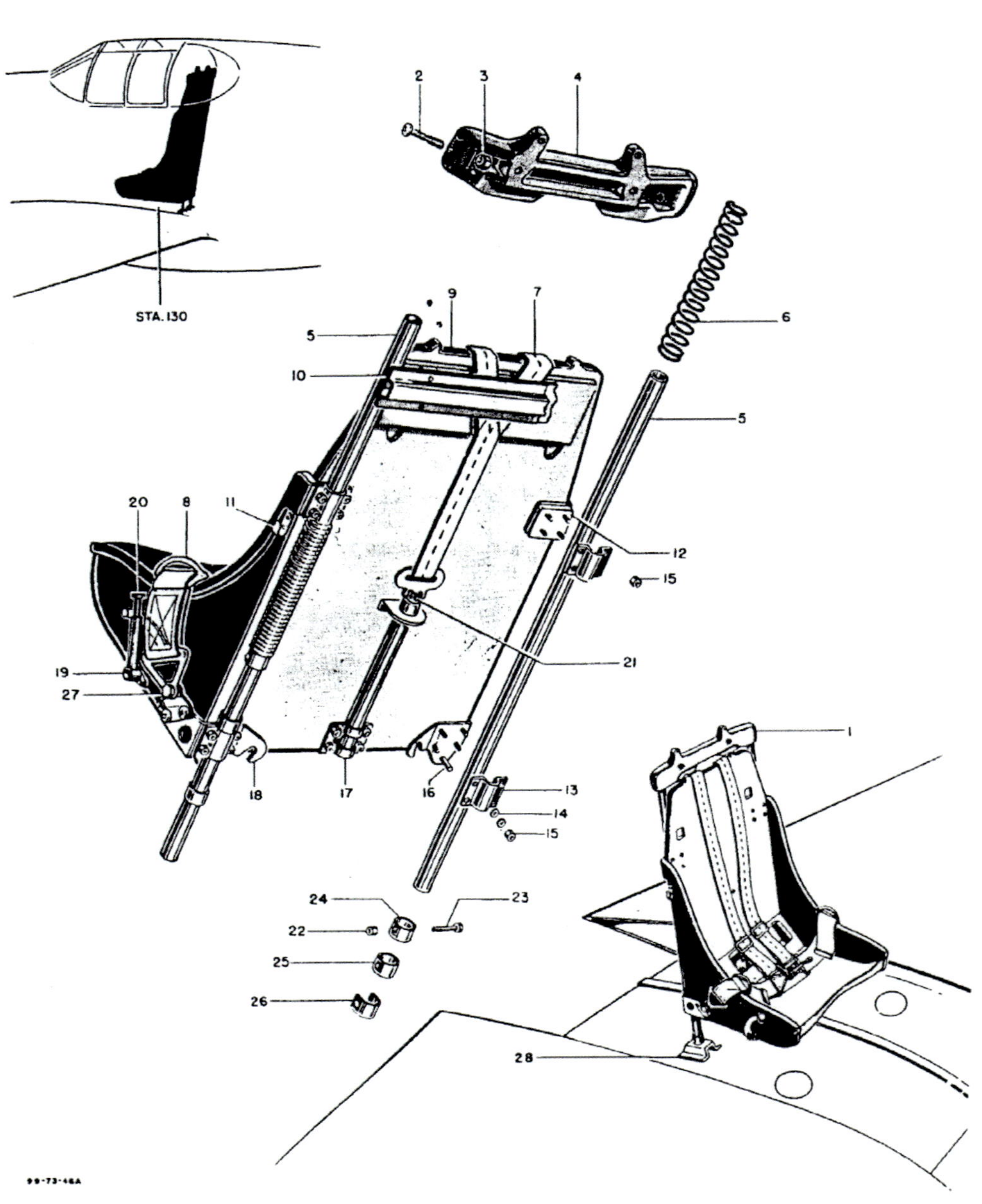

Pilot's seat from above,
preserved aircraft.
(R. Malmstrom)

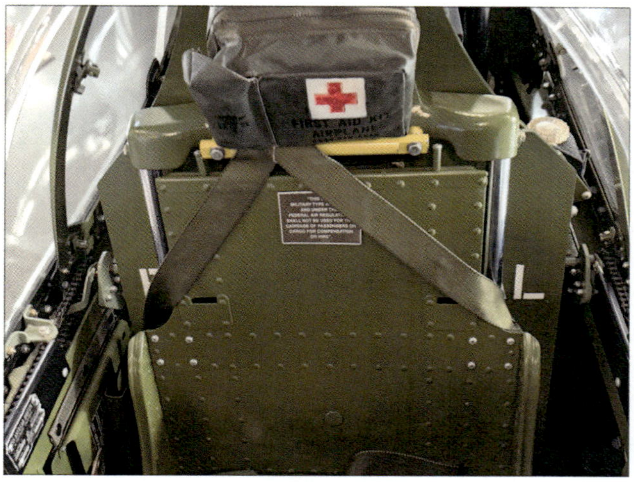

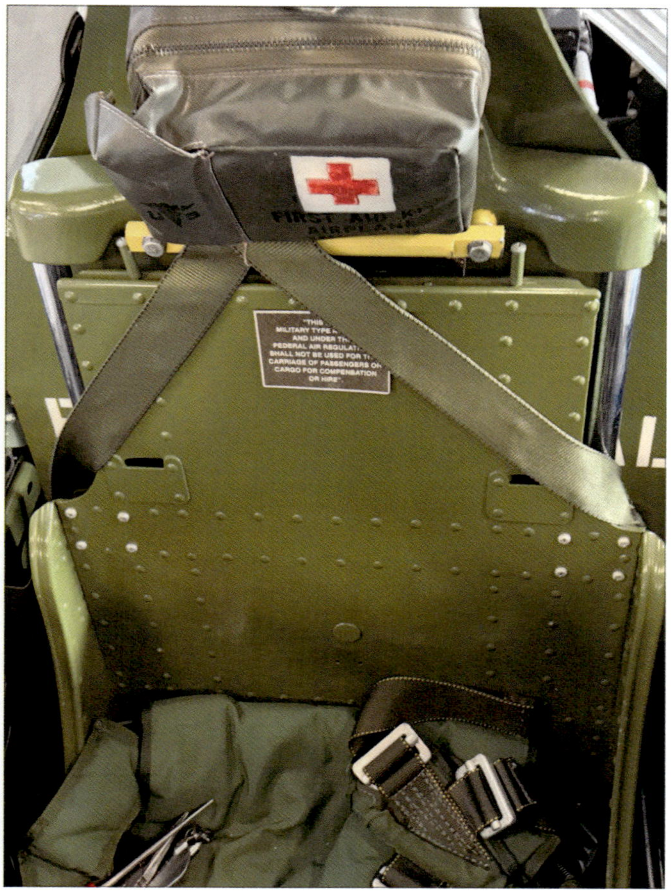

Three photos of the pilot's seat in a preserved P-51B-10-NA. (R. Malmstrom)

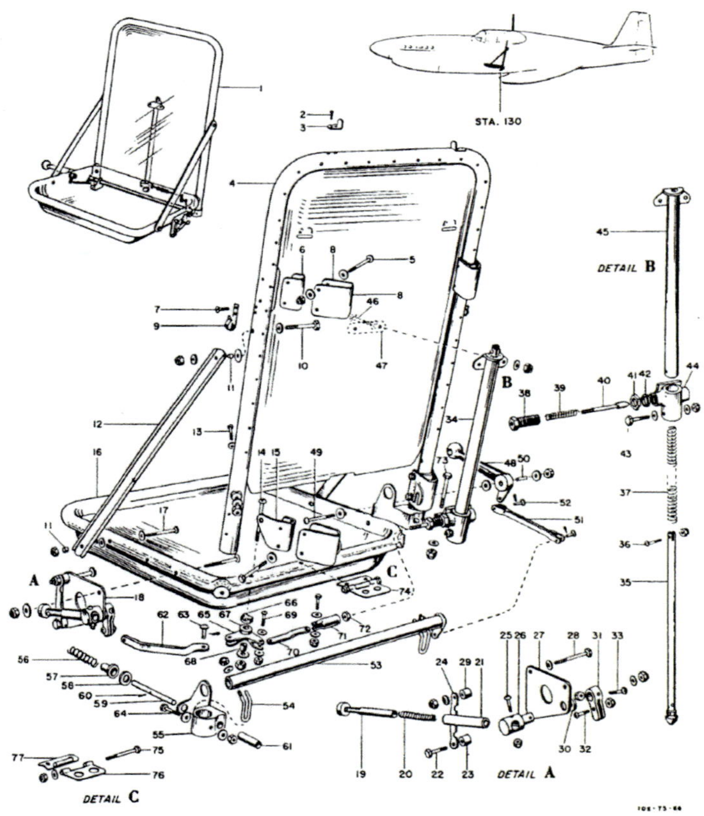

PILOT'S SEAT (WARREN McARTHUR)

Another version of the pilot's seat (Schick-Johnson type) installed on some models. (Airplane Parts Catalog)

Radio sets

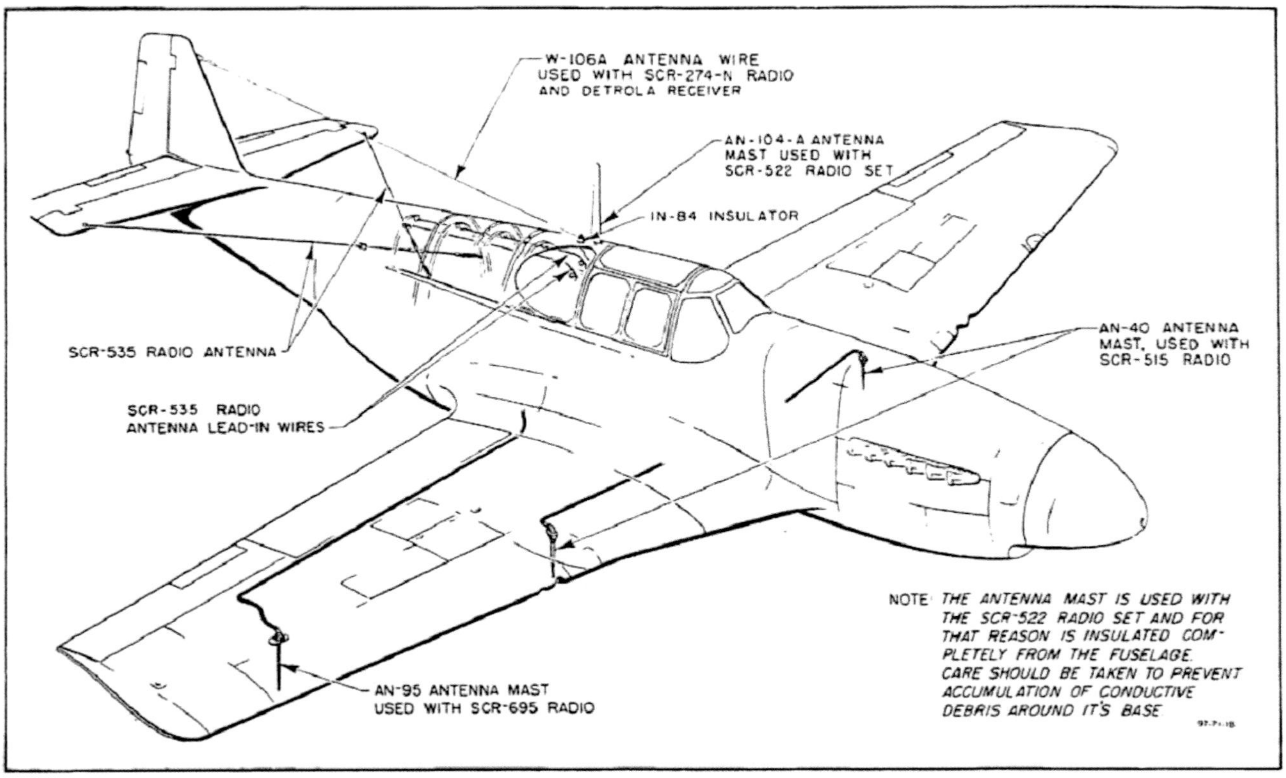

Different versions of the P-51B/C antenna wires shown in the one picture. Note that all antenna versions were never mounted at the same time. (Erection and Maintenance Instructions)

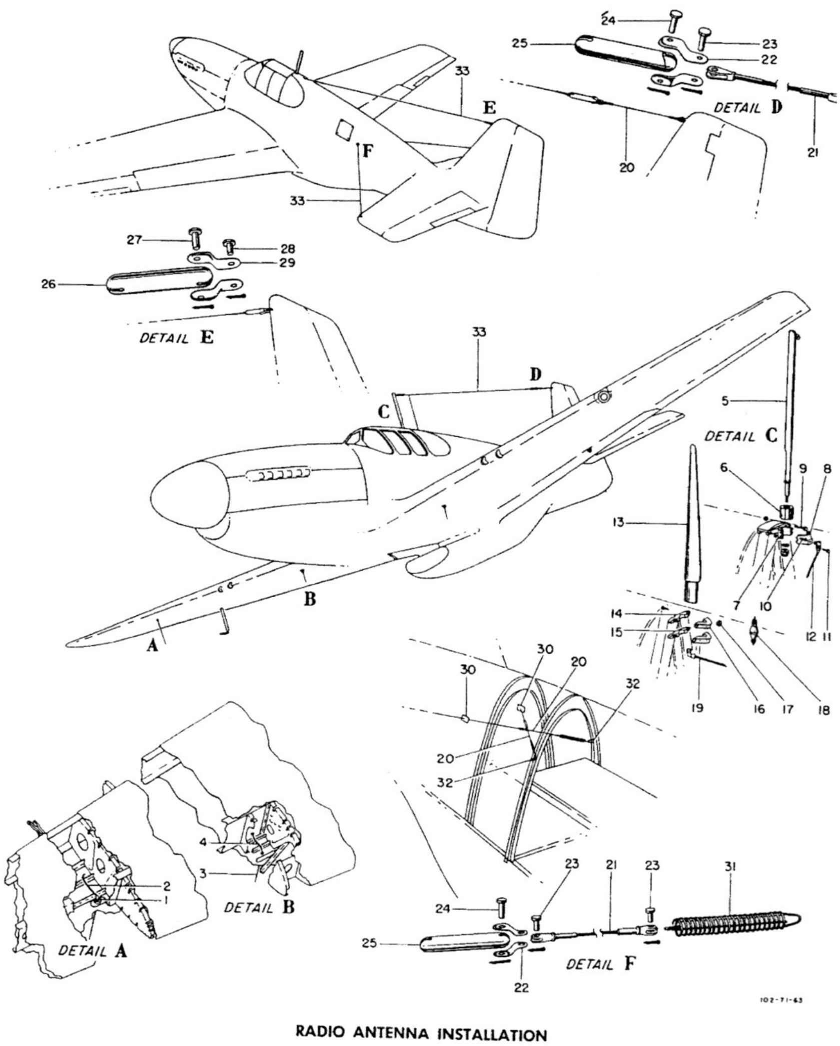

Radio antenna installation. (Erection and Maintenance Instructions)

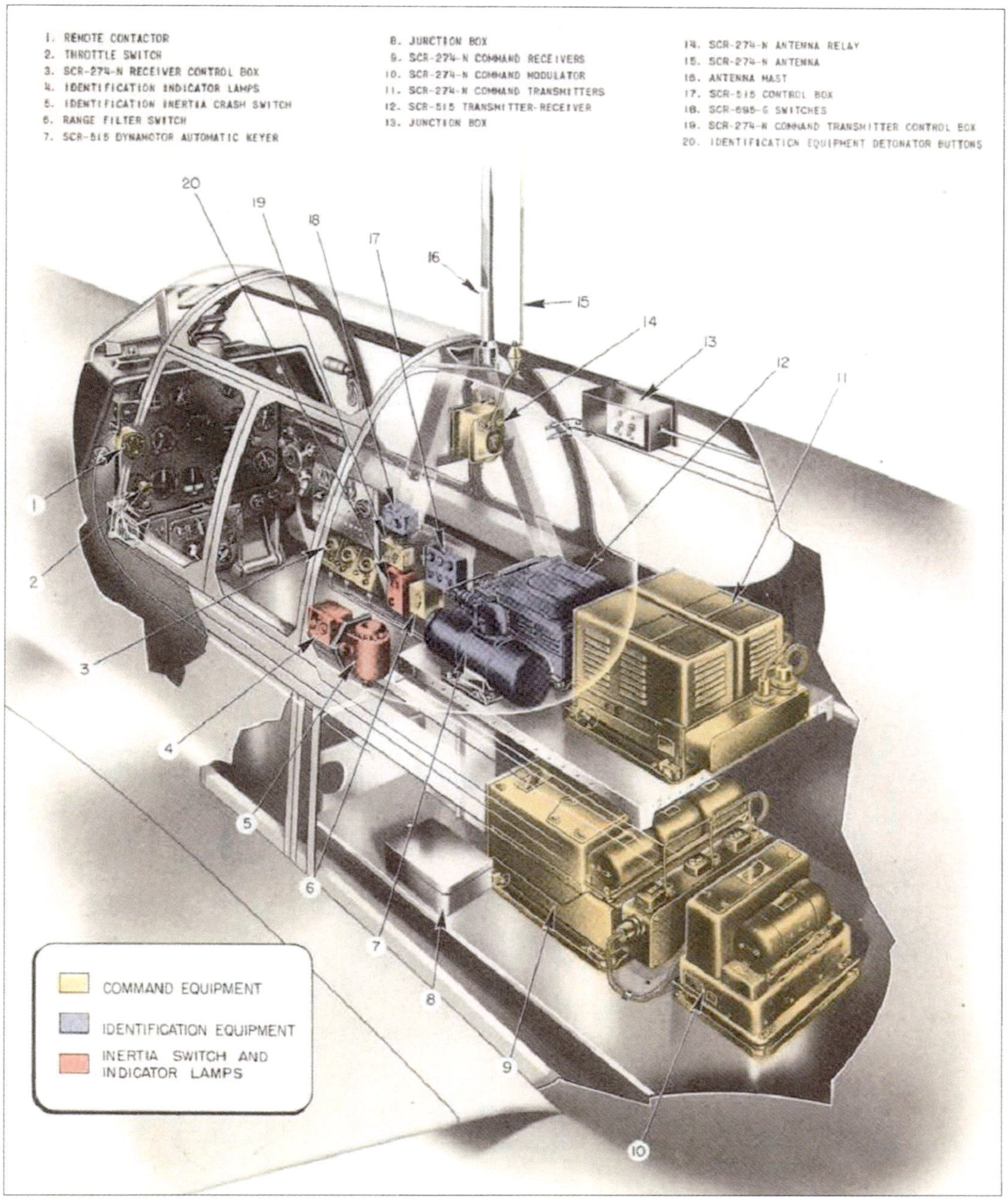

Radio type SCR-274-N equioment, aircraft without fuselage tank. (Maintenance Manual)

Below, left: SCR-274-N transmitter. (Maintenance Manual)

Below, right: SCR-535 arrangement. (Maintenance Manual)

1. RESONANCE INDICATOR MIRROR
2. PLUG-IN CRYSTAL UNIT
3. RESONANCE INDICATOR TUBE
4. RECESSED TRIM ADJUSTMENT SCREW
5. ANTENNA COUPLING (FINE ADJUSTMENT)
6. ANTENNA COUPLING (ROUGH ADJUSTMENT)
7. LOCKNUT
8. FREQUENCY BAND ADJUSTMENT

Figure 331—SCR-274-N Transmitter Adjustment

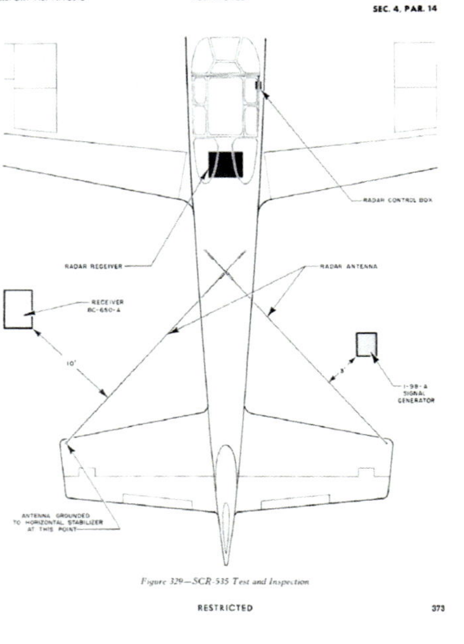

Radio SCR-522 equipment. (Maintenance Manual)

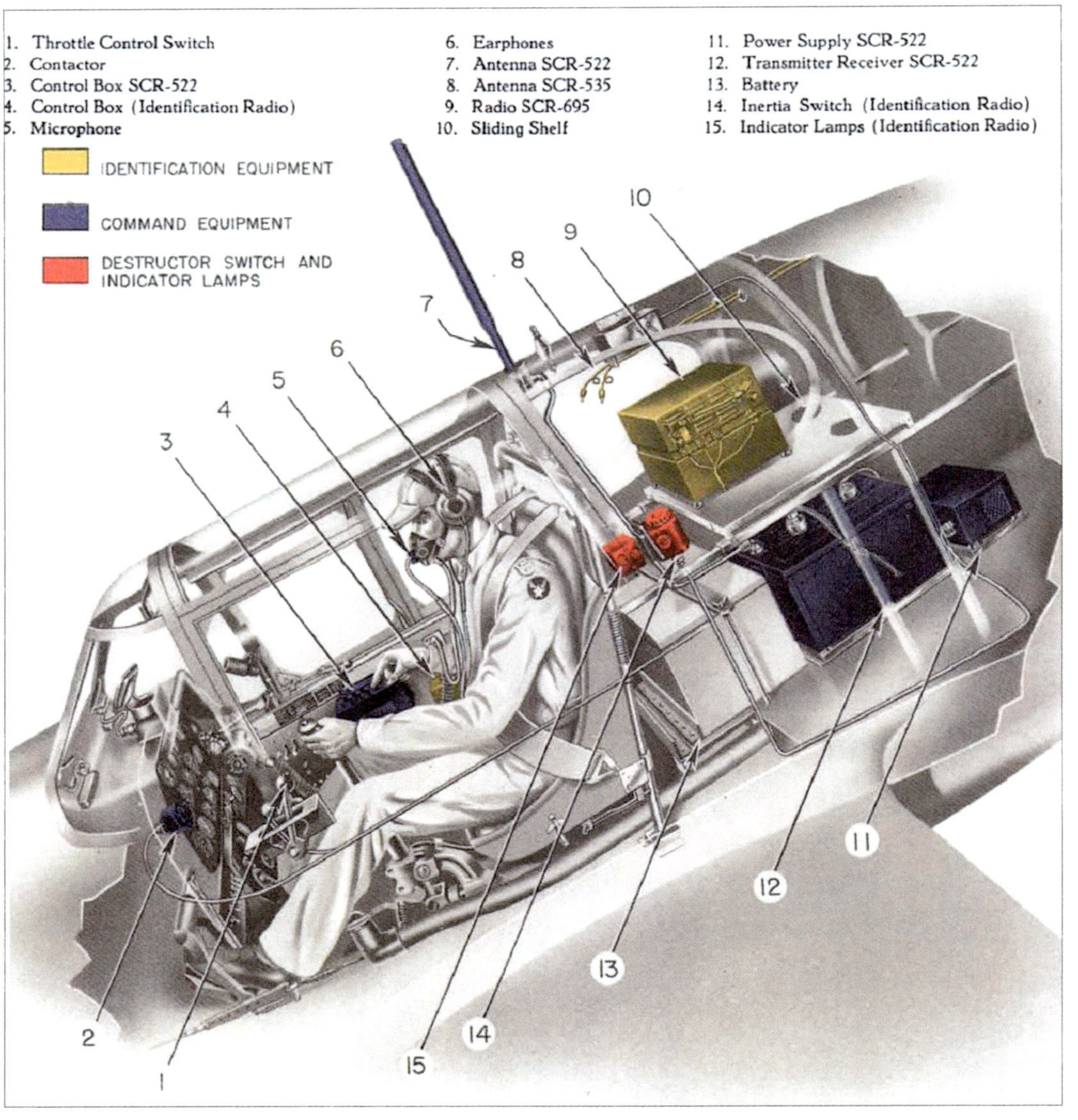

SCR-695 IFF antenna shown in Maintenance Manual.

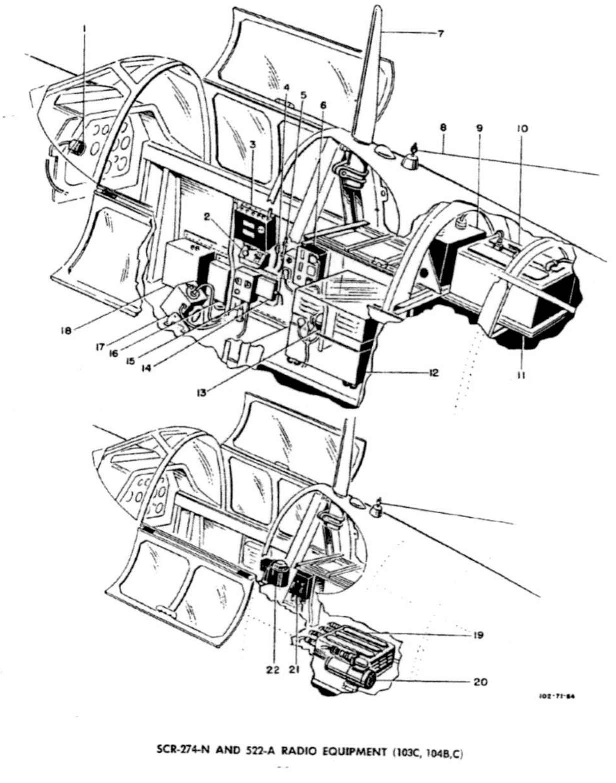

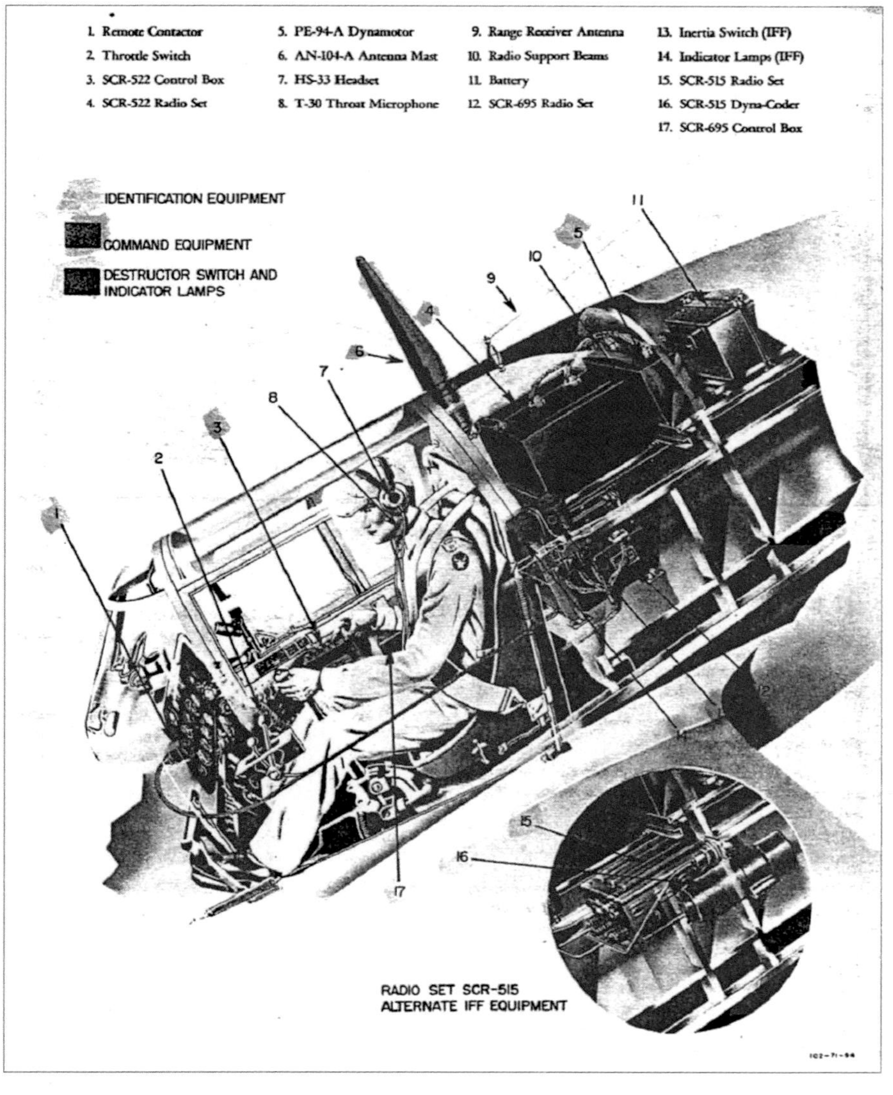

Above, left: *SCR-274-N and SCR-522-A radio equipment, aircraft without fuselage tank.*

Above, right: *SCR-522-A radio equimpment, aircraft with fuselage tank instalaltion.*

Left: *SCR-522-A and SCR-515 radio equimpment, aircraft with fuselage tank removed.*

(all Maintenance Manual)

Machine guns

Machine guns in a P-51B. Mechanics are removing the inner machine gun. (US National Archives)

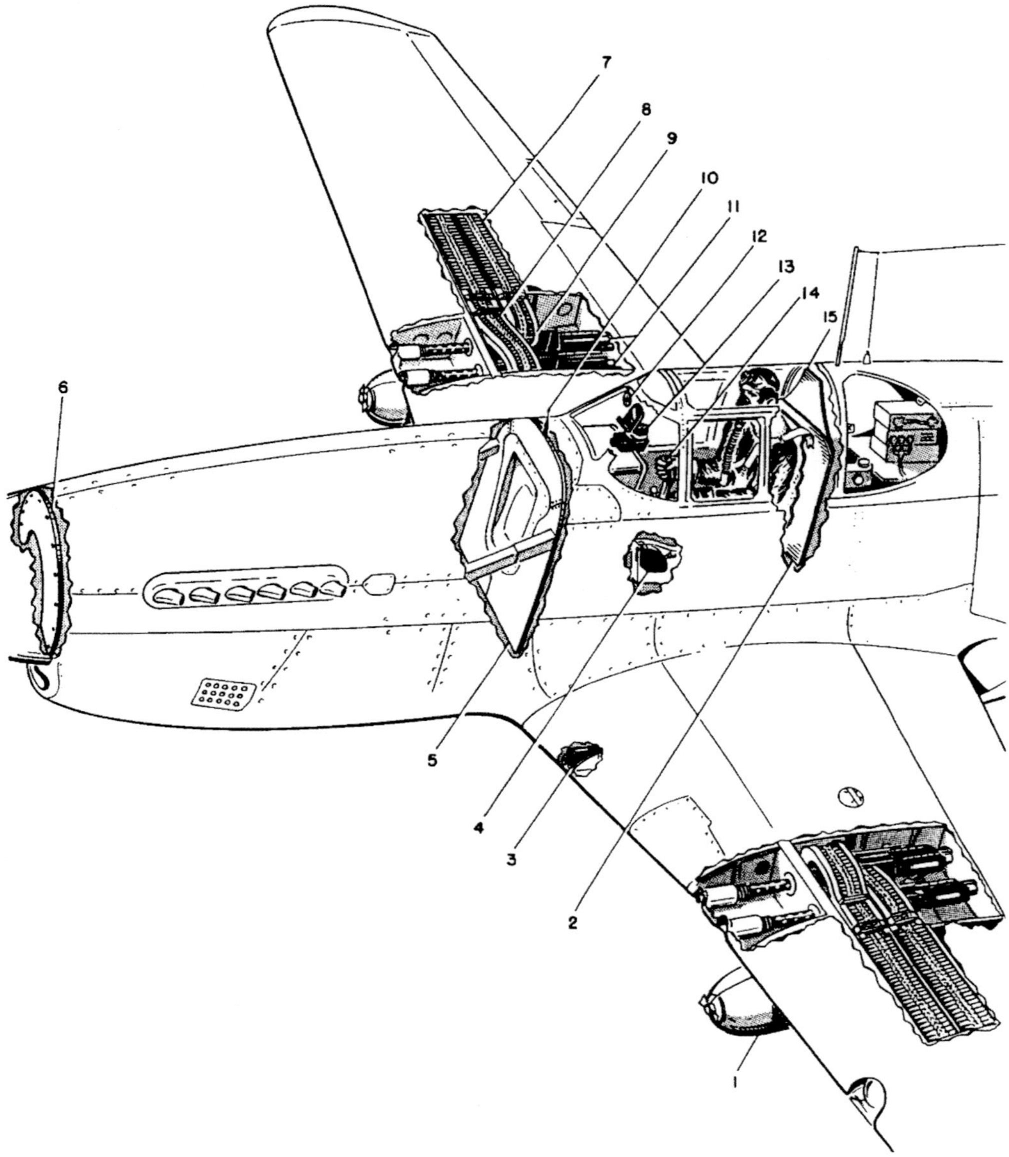

Installation of armament.
1. Bomb rack;
2. Pilot's rear armour;
3. Camera
4. Bomb rack control;
5. Firewall – armour plate;
6. Coolant tank armour, plate;
7. Ammunition box;
8. Chute, inboard;
9. Chutel outboard;
10. Sight, auxiliary bead;
11. Machine gun, type M2 – .50 cal.
12. Sight, auxiliary ring;
13. Gunsight;
14. Switch, trigger, type B-5;
15. Pilot's rear head armour.
(Maintenance Manual)

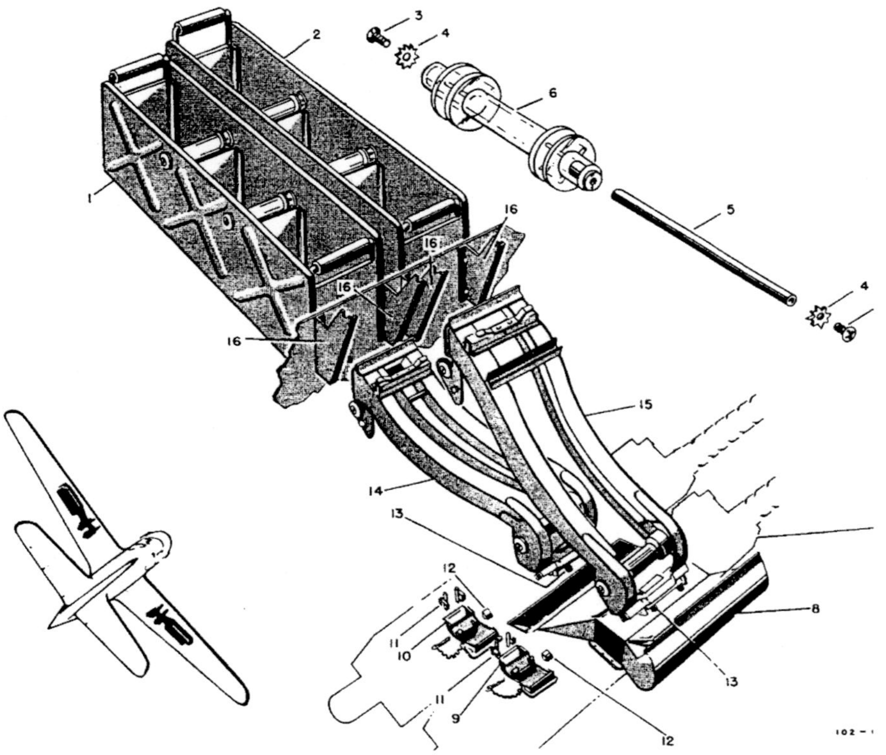

Wing ammunition boxes and chutes. (Airplane Parts Catalog)

Machine gun muzzles in the wing leading edge.

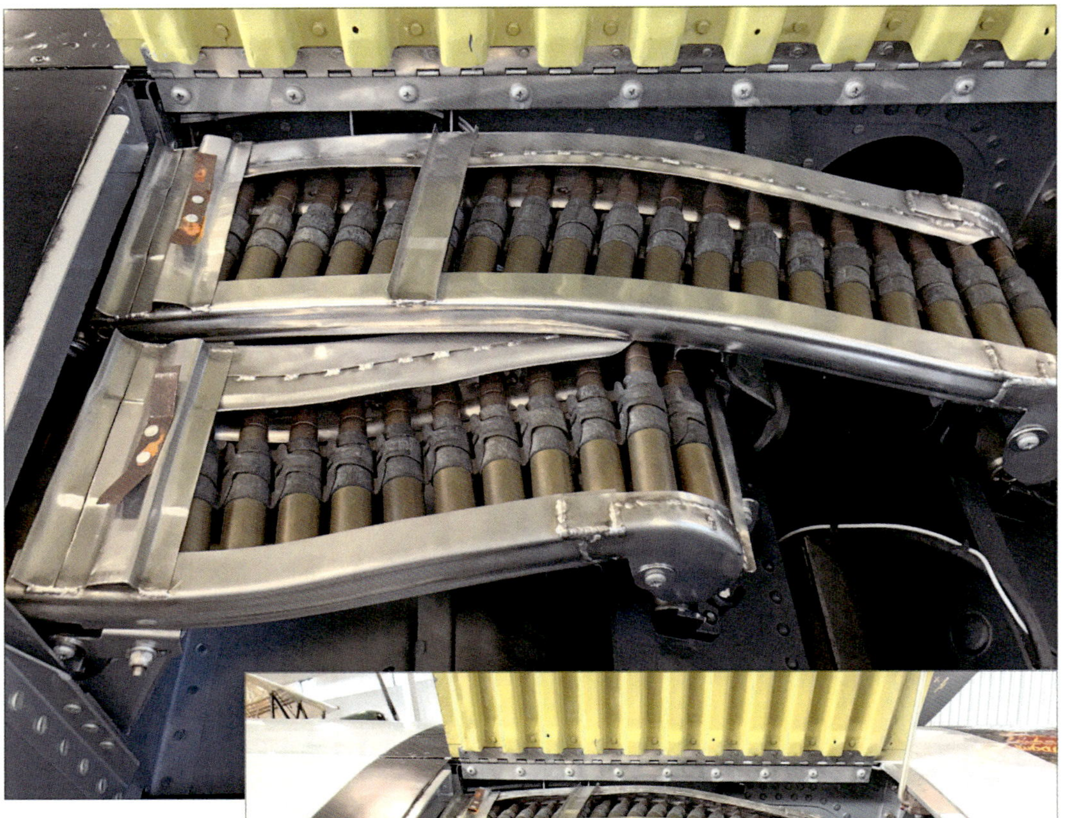

Feed chutes in a preserved aircraft.

Machine guns and feed chutes. (All photos R. Malmstrom)

Starboard wing guns installation, wartime photo. (Maintenance Manual)

Starboard wing guns installation at the wartime photo. P-51C "Stinky II" of the 100th FS, 332nd FG in the background. (US National Archives)

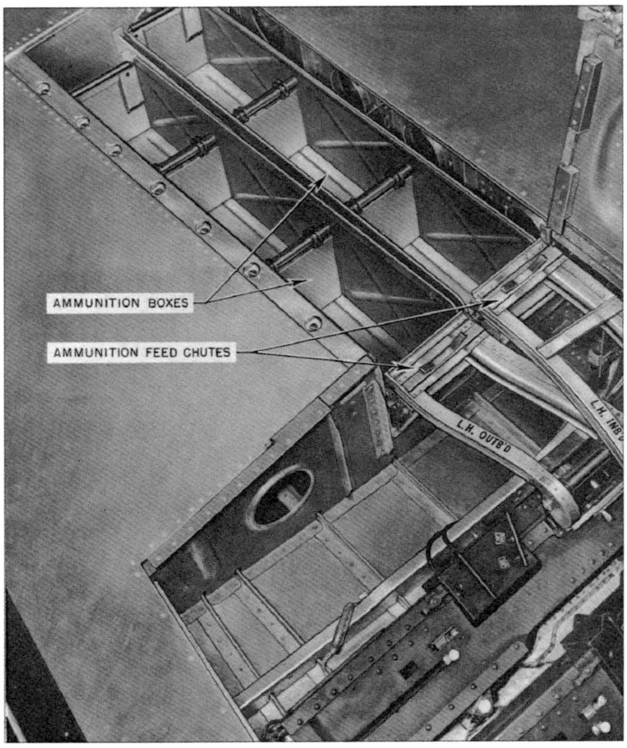

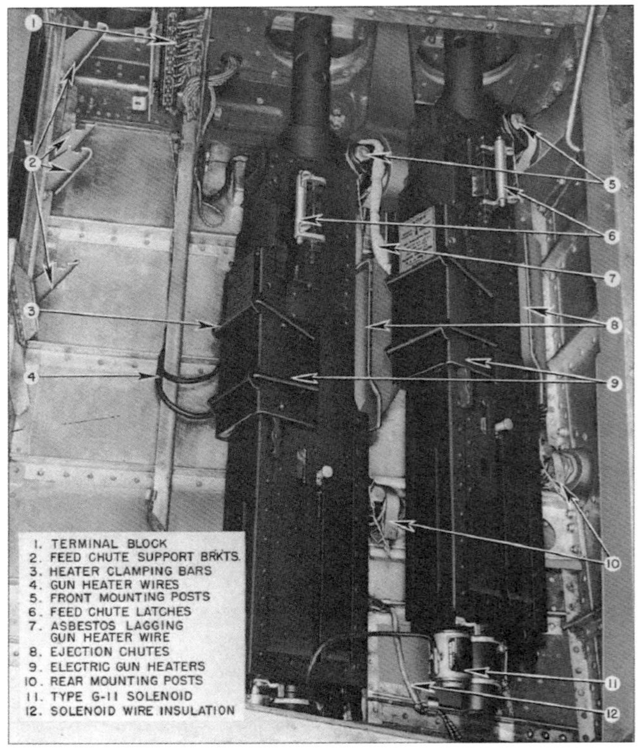

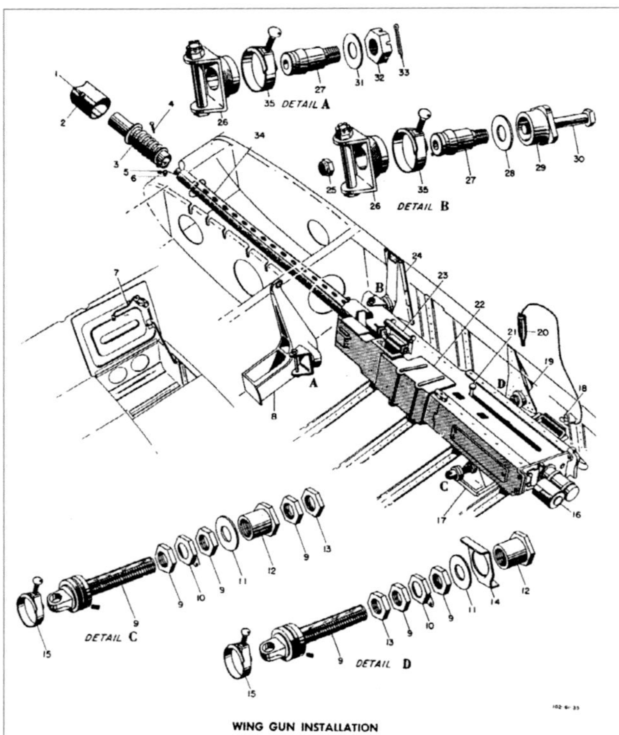

Above, left: *Port wing ammunition compartment. (Maintenance Manual)*

Above, right: *Port wing guns installed. (Maintenance Manual)*

Left: *Wing gun installation. (Airplane Parts Catalog)*

Bottom: *machine guns cleaninig. Note guns compartment door in open position. (US National Archives)*

Above: Machine guns reloading. Note door latches.
Below: Another photo of machine guns cleaning on an early P-51B. (US National Archives)

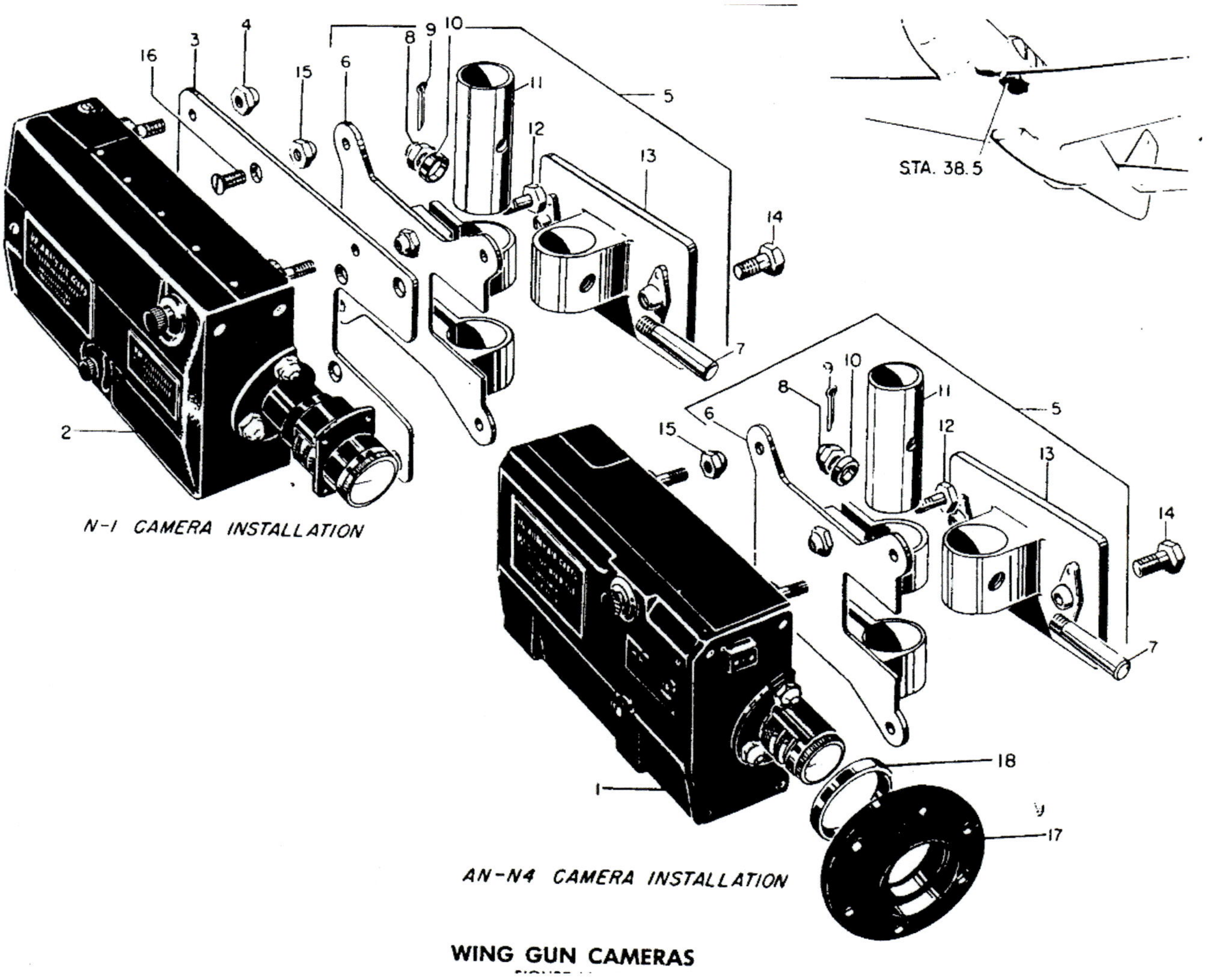

Wing gun cameras, two versions are shown. (Airplane Parts Catalog)

Below: *Wing gun camera is visible in the port wing leading edge. (US National Archives)*

Wing gun camera in the leading edge of a preserved Mustang. (R. Malmstrom)

Stores

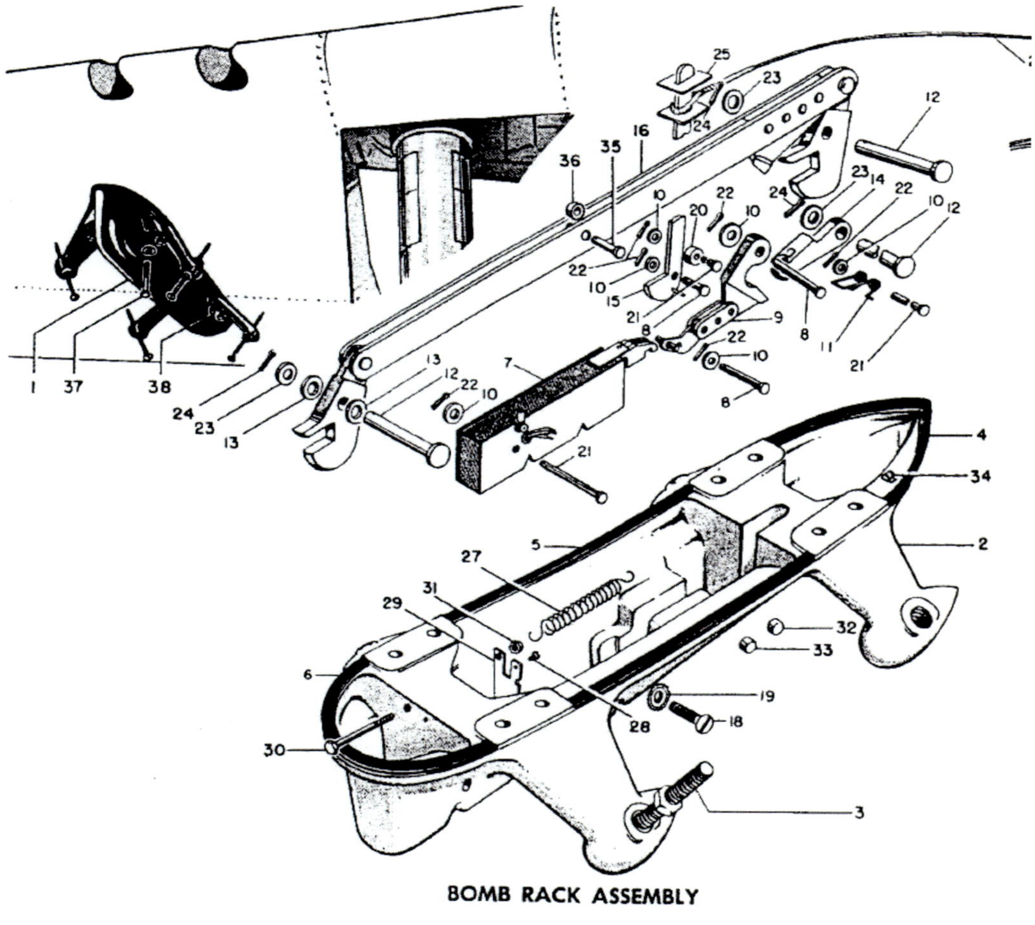

Bomb rack assembly. (Airplane Part Catalog)

Detail shot of the bomb rack, starboard wing. (R. Malmstrom)

Bomb installed on the bomb rack. (Maintenance Manual)

Wartime colour photo of the bomb to be installed on the Mustang's wing rack. (US National Archives)

108 US gallons paper tank under the Mustang's starboard wing. (US National Archives)

75 US gallons metal tank under the port wing. (US National Archives)

Another photo of the Mustang with 75 US gallond drop tank. (US National Archives)

P-51B with Bazooka launchers. Bazooka launchers were mostly used in CBI Theater. (US National Archives)

P-51B-1-NA with bubble canopy

A P-51B-1 (s/n 43-12102) was selected to be modified as the test aircraft for the new bubble canopy. The new shaped canopy gave almost completely unobstructed all-round vision with virtually no distortion from the free-blown glazing. The plexiglas of the hood was mounted on rubber in a metal frame, the sill around the bottom being very deep. The canopy was manually opened and closed by a hand crank operated by the pilot. To accommodate the new canopy, the rear fuselage of the Mustang had to be cut down, but the amount of retooling needed to accomplish this was not extensive. This modified P-51B took off on its first flight at Inglewood on 17 November 1943, with test pilot Bob Chilton at the controls.-

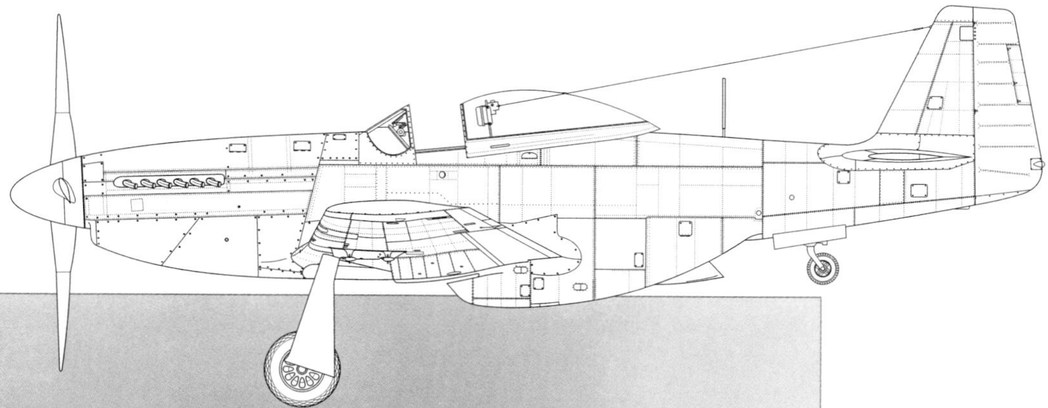

P-51B-1-NA, s/n 43-12102 with bubble canopy. 1/72 scale.

Port side of P-51B-1-NA, s/n 43-12102 with bubble canopy. Aircraft awaiting flights trials. (Mike Jerram via Roger Wallsgrove)

NA-106, P-51B-1 NA, s/n 43-12102 with bubble canopy. The last three digits of the serial were repeated on the nose. (Mike Jerram via Roger Wallsgrove)

Bibliography

Cotter, Jarrod, Hammond, Maurice, *North American P-51 Mustang,* Owners' Workshop Manual, ISBN 978-184425 – 870-3, Haynes Publishing, Yeovil, 2010

Cotter, Jarrod, *Aviation Classics P-51 Mustang,* Issue 2, ISBN 978-1-906167-33-2, Morton Media Group Ltd., Horncastle 2010

Cotter, Jarrod, Hammond, Maurice, *North American P-51 Mustang: 1940 Onwards (all marks),* Owners' Workshop Manual, ISBN 978-0-857338-59-4, Haynes Publishing, UK Sparkford, 2016

Cross, Roy, *P-51 Mustang, Classic Aircraft No.3, Their history and how to model them,* ISBN 0-85059-107-4, PSL London, 1973

Davis, Larry, *P-51 Mustang in Color,* ISBN 0-89747-135-0, Squadron Signal Publications, Carrollton, 1992

Davis, Larry, *P-51 Mustang in Action,* ISBN 0-89747-114-8, Squadron Signal Publications, Carrollton, 1981

Ethell, Jeffrey, *Mustang A Documentory History,* ISBN 0-7106-0070-4, Jane's Publishing Company Ltd, London, 1981

Freeman, Roger, A., *Mustang at war,* ISBN 978-0-71100-500-6, Ian Allan, 1974

Gruenhagen, Robert, W., *Mustang. The Story of the P-51 Fighter,* ISBN 978-066803-912-3, Arco Publishing, New York, 1976

Guerrero, Juan, A., *North American P-51 Mustang,* Editorial San Martin

Hess, William, *P-51 Escolta De Bombardero,* ISBN 84-7140-189-4, San Martin Madrit, 1971

Johnsen, Frederick, A., *North American P-51 Mustang,* ISBN 0-933424-68-X, Specialty Press, North Branch, 1996

Kinzey, Bert, *P-51 Mustang. In Detail & Scale Part 1,* ISBN 1-888974-02-8, Detail & Scale INC., Carrollton

Kolacha, Zbigniew, Żurek, Jacek, B., *North American P-51 Mustang cz. 2, Monografie Lotnicze Nr 56,* ISBN 83-7237-025-7 AJ-Press Gdynia 1999

Lowe Malcolm, V., *North American P-51 Mustang,* ISBN 978-1-86126-830-3, The Crowood Press, Ramsbury, 2009

Lowe, Malcolm, V., *P-51 Mustang: A Comprehensive Guide Part 2 Merlin Powered,* ISBN 97-81-90695-904-3, SAM Publications, Bedford, 2014

Ludwig, Paul, *Development of the P-51 Long-Range Escort Fighter Mustang,* ISBN 1-903223-14-8, Classic Publications, Hersham, 2003

Maloney, Edward, T., *North American P-51 Mustang, Aero Series 15,* ISBN 0816805563, Aero Publishers, 1967

Miller, Kent, D., *The 363rd Fighter Group in World War II,* ISBN 0-7643-1629-X, Schiffer Publishing Ltd., Atglen, 2002

Money, Ann, *The Warlords volume 1,* ISBN 095456051-5, Flight Recorder Publications, Ottringham, 2003

Morgan, Len, *The P-51 Mustang,* Arco Publishing, New York, 1963

O'Leary, Michael, *Production Line to Frontlline No. 1,* ISBN 1-85532-703-1, Osprey Publishing, Oxford, 1998

Skulski, Przemysław, *Mustangi USAAF,* ISBN 83-86153-00-8, ACE Publications, Wrocław, 1993

Wilson, Stewart, *The Spitfire, Mustanf and Kittyhawk in Australian Service,* ISBN 0-9587978-1-1, Aerospace Publications Pty Ltd, Adelaide, 1990

Żurek, Jacek, B., *North American P-51 Mustang cz. 1, Monografie Lotnicze Nr 55,* ISBN 83-7237-024-9, AJ-Press, Gdynia, 1999

Żurek, Jacek, B., Wiśniewski, Piotr, *North American P-51 Mustang cz. 3, Monografie Lotnicze Nr 57,* ISBN 83-7237-129-6, AJ-Press, Gdynia, 2003

Camouflage & Markings Number 2. N. A. Mustang, Ducimus Books Limited, London

Wings Of Fame Volume 1, ISBN 1-874023-68-9, Aerospace Publishing Ltd, London, 1995

Camouflage & Markings Number No. 16 N. A. Mustang U.S.A.A.F., E.T.O. & M.T.O., Ducimus Books Limited, London

Erection and Maintenance Instructions for Army Models P-51B-1, P-51B-5, P-51B-10, P-51B-15, P-51C-1, P-51C-5 and P-51C-10, British model Mustang III airplanes,

Maintenance Manual P-5B&C

Airplane Parts Catalog Army Models P-51B-1, P-51B-5, P-51B-10, P-51B-15, P-51C-1, P-51C-5 and P-51C-10, British model Mustang III,

Pilot's Notes for Mustang III Packard Merlin V-1650-3 Engine

Pilot Training Manual for The Mustang P-51

Magazines

Scale Aircraft Modelling, October 1995

Air International Vol 25 No. 4, October 1983

Air International Vol 25 No. 5, November 1983

Aero Plastic Kits Revue, March 1993

Ciel de Guerre 01, June 2001

Skrzydlata Polska, various issues

IPMS Magazine, various issues

Aero Journal Hors-Serie P51 Mustang, October 2012